withdrawn

CW00828216

THE ULTIMATE CAREER COACH

Everything you need to know to succeed at work

Ken Langdon, John Middleton and Elisabeth Wilson

infinite**ideas**

SALFORD LIBRARIES	
SP05785707	
Bertrams	16/09/2009
650.1082WI	£14.99

Acknowledgements
Infinite Ideas would like to thank
Nicholas Bate, Rob Bevan, Nikki
Cartwright, Jackee Holder, Ken
Langdon, John Middleton, Jon Smith,
Elisabeth Wilson and Tim Wright for the
expertise they contributed to this book.

Copyright © The Infinite Ideas Company Limited, 2009
The right of the contributors to be identified as the authors of this book has
been asserted in accordance with the Copyright, Designs and Patents Act
1988.

First published in 2009 by
Infinite Ideas Limited
36 St Giles
Oxford, OX1 3LD
United Kingdom
www.infideas.com

All rights reserved. Except for the quotation of small passages for the
purposes of criticism or review, no part of this publication may be
reproduced, stored in a retrieval system or transmitted in any form or by any
means, electronic, mechanical, photocopying, recording, scanning or
otherwise, except under the terms of the Copyright, Designs and Patents Act
1988 or under the terms of a licence issued by the Copyright Licensing
Agency Ltd, 90 Tottenham Court Road, London W1T 4LP, UK, without the
permission in writing of the publisher. Requests to the publisher should be
addressed to the Permissions Department, Infinite Ideas Limited, 36 St Giles,
Oxford, OX1 3LD, UK, or faxed to +44 (0)1865 514777.

A CIP catalogue record for this book is available from the British Library

ISBN 978-1-905940-74-5

Brand and product names are trademarks or registered trademarks of their
respective owners.

Text designed and typeset by Baseline Arts Ltd, Oxford
Cover designed by Cylinder
Printed and bound in Britain by TJ International Limited

Brilliant ideas

Introduction: Time to shine!...xi

Quiz: It's not about what you want – it's about what you need...xii

Finding work to make your heart sing xvi

1   BE AMAZING

Unleash your creativity and shine
Quiz: Time to get emotional **4**
1.   Increase your brand value...6
2.   CREATE success...9
3.   Know your strengths 12
4.   A short cut to coping with obstacles..15
5.   Make more mistakes faster 18
6.   Look at things another way 21
7.   Know what you can't do...24
8.   Come back in the morning 27
9.   Don't do lunch..30
10.   Don't reinvent the wheel..33
11.   Take on another role..36
12.   Making swift, smart decisions 39
13.   Revamp your to-do list..42
14.   How to love the job you've got 45
15.   Maximise your self esteem...48
16.   Being the best version of you..51

Unleash your charisma and get what you want

Quiz: Are you a player? **56**

17. How to make everyone love you 58
18. ¿Que? Speak their language 61
19. How to read minds 64
20. Become a people wizard 67
21. Before you act, rehearse 70
22. How to give incentives 73
23. Handling your boss 76
24. Ask, don't tell 79
25. Dress the part 82
26. Just give them the facts 85
27. Listen – really listen 88
28. Be a networker 91
29. Become fluent in body language 94
30. Be polite and be persistent 97
31. Learn the art of negotiation 100

2   ROCKET TO THE TOP

Do better

32. Take a pragmatic approach to work 106
33. Make good suggestions loudly 109
34. Taking problems to your manager 112
35. Be in the right place 115
36. Act on decisions 118
37. Know what to say to whom 120
38. Create your next job 123

6 ways to make your boss love you **126**

39. How to negotiate a pay rise 128
40. It's not about time, it's about decisions 131
41. Get noticed by the right people 134

42. When to work for bastards..137
43. You are totally responsible for you...140
44. Act as if you are the CEO...143
45. Talk less, listen more..146
46. Get a personal development plan...149
47. Impress the senior management...152
48. Get to know the sales force..155
49. Think now and think ahead..158
50. Hone your presentation skills..161
51. Help people think for themselves...164
52. Are you a leader?..167
53. Pick the right management style..170
54. Find out what you are supposed to be doing.......................................173
55. Ready, aim, fire..176
56. Creating a team strategy..179
57. Keep up the good work...182
58. Everybody lives by selling something..185
59. How to succeed at failure..188
60. Make the budget work for you..191

3   UPGRADING YOUR JOB

Quiz: What's holding you back? **198**
Getting your foot in the door
61. Getting back to work..202
62. Top notch CVs..205
63. Look good on your CV…without lying..208
64. Changing employers mid-career..211

Stunning them at the interview
65. Great body language 216
66. How do you balance risk and return?..219
67. How do you work with difficult people? 222

68. So, why do you want this job? 225
69. What would your team change about you? 228
70. Why should we hire you over better qualified candidates?............231
71. Role-plays and assessment centres 234
72. What are your strengths and weaknesses?..................................237
73. Is there anything you want to ask me? 240
74. Panel interviews..243
75. How will you know when you've found the right job? 246
76. What are your salary expectations?...249

4   BE THE BOSS

Quiz: Born entrepreneur or born employee? **256**
77. Read this first 258
78. Raising the funds...261
79. Influencing the bank 264
80. Who are your customers?...267
81. Getting to grips with finances 270
82. Effective budgeting...273
83. Number crunching 276
84. How to be an entrepreneur 279
85. Business banking for beginners..282
86. Business angels and venture capitalists 285
87. Choosing your company's status...288
88. Why you need a solicitor 291
89. Choosing and using accountants...294
90. Getting the right people 297
91. The business plan 300
92. Know the opposition 303
93. Maximising your company potential...306
94. How to make a profit 309
95. Get the best advice..312
96. The rainy-day fund 314

97.   Keeping on top of cashflow 316
98.   Reinvent. Regularly 319
99.   Roots to market 322
100. Create a brilliant experience 325
101. Customers rule..328
102. Creating time for reflection 331
103. What if everything goes wrong?..334

5   SUPERCHARGE YOUR FINANCES

Quiz: Are you scared of money? **340**
104. Ditch the debt 342
105. Manage your credit 345
106. Be realistic about debt 348
107. How to deal with severe debt...351
108. Jump start your salary 354
109. First save, then spend..357
110. Stick to your budget 360
111. Show me the money..363
112. Conduct an annual stocktake of your finances 366
113. Get thrifty 369
114. The pros and cons of consolidation loans 372
115. Staying on top of your finances 375
116. Love your money...378

6   FEELING BETTER, FASTER

Quiz: Are you living on adrenaline? **384**
117. How to get rich on a not so rich salary 386
118. Find an hour a day to play..389
119. Never procrastinate again 392
120. What's your Plan B?...395
121. Restoration day 398

122. Crisis management 401
123. Dealing with interruptions 404
124. Are you getting enough – pleasure, that is 407
125. Aromatherapy masterclass 410
126. Have a holiday at your desk 413
127. Zap those piles of paper 416
128. Have you burned out? 419
129. Make life easy for yourself 422
130. The energy drench 425
131. A one-minute answer to mid-aftenoon slump 428
132. Booking in peace 431
133. Stress is other people 434

7   MAKE YOUR LIFE–WORK BALANCE – WORK!

Quiz: What are your energy levels like? **440**
134. You're the boss of you 442
135. Be selfish 445
136. Cure yourself of the disease to please 448
137. Take the stress out of your love life 451
138. Stop acting on impulse 454
139. Tame your to-do list 457
140. Perfect moments 460
141. Energy black spots transformed 463
142. Leave the office on time 466
143. Speed parenting –better than stressed parenting 469
144. Me, myself and I 472
145. Guilt be gone 475
146. The perfection trap 478
147. Blitz your home in a weekend 481
148. Live the lottery life 484
149. Run away, run away 487

Introduction: Time to shine!

Feeling lost, a bit adrift, not sure that you've found the work that makes your heart sing, or that even pays you a living wage?
Fed up feeling slightly (or even very) skint?
Exhausted by trying to be brilliant on too many fronts when all you want to do is crawl into bed and hide there for a week?

If your working life or financial status is far from satisfactory, then here are 150 ideas that will give your career a massive boost. Whether you're in a 'McJob' or CEO of a company, if you're not totally happy with your work life, then this book will help you prioritise what's important and then go out and get it.

And what do you do....?

A job isn't just a job. Like it or not, work, whether paid or unpaid, is how we tell the world who we are. Through work we garner self-esteem and a sense of what we're worth. We form an identity by which others judge us. We gain status within our community. We are offered the chance to be creative, to lead, to cooperate as part of a team. What we do is the arena from which we can show off who we think we are to the world. And oh yes – we can earn a bit of money, too.

But not all of us need all of these things in equal measure from our job – and all too often, we get sucked into what other people want or expect from us and forget to check in with what we really need *right now* to be satisfied. Could you be in a job that is delivering too much of the wrong things and not enough of the right ones, and what stage are you at in your life? We have different requirements from our work depending where we are in our 'journey'.

The quiz below will help you pinpoint what you need from your work right now to stay happy.

It's not about what you want – it's about what you need

1. If you work hard over the next 10 years, you:

☐ a. Have no idea where you'll be in your career. It's not the sort of job where you can depend on anything.

☐ b. Can expect to be at the top of your profession.

☐ c. Will be doing well – *if* you stick at this job. But you are feeling a bit tied down. Who knows where life will take you?

☐ d. Will probably be working part-time, either because you've downsized or gone back to work after having children. This may mean not achieving all you could have done but that way you'll have a good work–life balance.

2. 'Going to work means putting on a performance.' How does this statement resonate with you?

☐ a. A lot. You enjoy interacting with others, the cut and thrust and banter. You like to dress up and make an impression.

☐ b. It is a performance and you work out what your audience needs and give them exactly what they want to get their respect.

☐ c. Occasionally, but on the whole you don't think too much of the impression you're making – it's nearly always a good one because of the quality of your work.

☐ d. You understand the statement but, increasingly, you can't be bothered. You want to be with people where you can be yourself.

3. You receive a memo: next week your boss is sending you on a team-building course that will mean being away overnight. You think:

☐ a. Great – you're good at this, and you might meet some interesting people

☐ b. OK, but are the movers and shakers going – it had better not be a waste of time. And why is your boss sending you? What's wrong with your team building skills?

☐ c. What a waste of time.

☐ d. Why overnight? It's such a hassle when it eats into your free time and affects other commitments.

4. You are the one who:

☐ a. Is never in the kitchen at parties

☐ b. Has always known where you're going – even if you change your mind sometimes

☐ c. Goes your own way

☐ d. Everyone confides in.

5. You give of your time and skills to charities/ protests orcampaigning/ school events/church or other community based institutions:

☐ a. Not as often as you'd like. You're too busy right now

☐ b. When it is important to you. For instance, at your children's school because it means you know what's going on with the educational side but you don't have the time for anything but the strictly essential right now.

☐ c. When you feel passionately involved, you always have time

☐ d. More than is necessary probably. You want to make a difference and you seem to be the person that everyone asks first.

6. If you could give career advice to your teenage self, you'd tell him or her:

☐ a. Gravitate to the subjects you are good at, but teenage years aren't for trying too hard at school, they are for experimentation.

☐ b. Have a plan and know exactly what grades you need to achieve your goals.

☐ c. Lots of it is a waste of time so don't sweat too much over results. Develop yourself as a person who can succeed at anything when she decides what she wants.

☐ d. It's important to do well but it's not as important as you might think right now. Work at the stuff you don't like – it's good training for later on and try to enjoy yourself a bit, too.

Mostly As

Work may be important to you but is probably of secondary importance at this point in your life to your relationships. What you get from it is a strong sense of yourself, and perhaps a place where you can take risks, because adventure is important to you. If your work is dull or unstimulating, you're likely to be unhappy. Ideas in part one will help you find ways to express yourself at work.

Mostly Bs

Your place in the world is important to you – and the place you like to be is in front. You can't stand wasting your time following other people's rubbish ideas when you have so many better ones yourself. Make sure you are either working your way to the top or working underneath people you respect greatly or work is likely to be one long frustration to you. Part two is bursting with ideas to make your journey to the top faster.

Mostly Cs

Being autonomous is more important to you than you might realise. Being tied down as part of a team could make you frustrated and you may shine more in a role that allows you the chance to develop your own ideas and be more creative. The number one thing for you is to look for a job where you really see your impact on the world. You can't stand to be ineffective. Perhaps you are considering branching out on your own. If so then the ideas in part four are essential reading.

Mostly Ds

Whether or not you have a family, you have to feel needed, and unless your work satisfies that part of you, you are certain to be conflicted in some way between work and what you want to achieve outside of the work place. You need time to yourself but that is one of the things you find it hardest to negotiate. Go straight to part seven and start to work on your work-life balance.

XV

Finding work to make your heart sing

Do you basically love your job but need to move on? Then terrific, turn to **section 3** where you'll get ideas on landing a new job. On the other hand, perhaps you have come to realise that a new job in the same field may only be a change of location, that the same things that make your present job a dead-end will still be with you because somehow you got off on the wrong path. If this is the case in order to find work that will energise, excite and stimulate you, you will have to do some soul-searching and perhaps face some hard decisions. First though, try a simple exercise. Get a pen and paper and play with the answers to the questions below. Remember no decisions yet. You are only going on a fact-finding mission – about yourself.

1. **When** do you lose yourself? Think back to the last time you were so engrossed in what you were doing that you didn't notice time passing. Were you driving, shopping, helping your child with his homework, listening to a friend's troubles, dancing at a wedding, decorating a cake? Write half a dozen down.

2. **What** do you dream about? If you won the lottery and didn't have to work, what would you spend your time doing? (After you get back from the Seychelles, that is.)

3. **Why** are you scared? Ask why you're not fulfilling your dream. At the root of it will almost certainly be fear. Fear of telling your spouse, fear of giving up a profession into which you've invested a lot of time. Remember, you are transferring skills, you're not wiping years off your CV. Don't be too scared, but acknowledge the fear is there and has been holding you back.

4. **Where** are the soulmates? How much time do you spend with those who are on your wavelength, and how could you spend more time with them. Include more of what makes you happy in your life. Pursuing what makes you happy means you'll meet other people who share your interests, and who knows where that will take you?

1

Be amazing

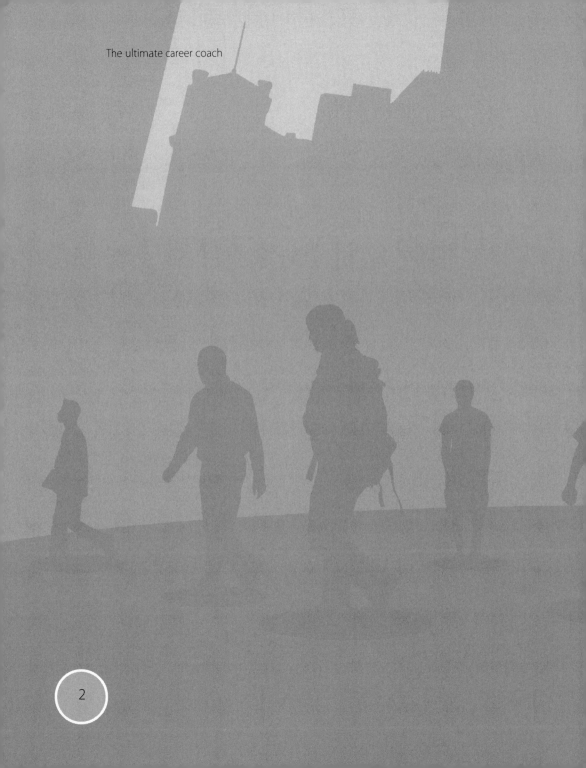

The ultimate career coach

Unleash your creativity and shine

Whatever you want from your working life, in order to succeed you have to be creative, think laterally, stand out from the crowd. In this section we show you how to persuade others to your way of thinking and how to come up with better ideas faster. No matter what sort of career you have in mind for yourself, those are attributes that are going to prove pretty useful.

Time to get emotional

Whether you want to shine at your present job or start a completely new career, growing your emotional intelligence – your EQ – will make reaching your goal easier. Research studies have shown that almost 50% of your success is down to your level of EQ. And it's no coincidence that those with high EQs are also amongst the most creative and popular employees.

1. **Are you aware of your feelings changing throughout the day (as opposed to always being on an even keel)?** Yes ☐ No ☐
2. **Do you find yourself 'naming' your emotions, noticing for example 'I feel sad now'?** Yes ☐ No ☐
3. **Do you usually trace back your feelings to what caused them for example 'I'm sad because…'?** Yes ☐ No ☐
4. **Do you always express your frustration with others in a non-aggressive way?** Yes ☐ No ☐
5. **Do you feel self-confident most of the time?** Yes ☐ No ☐
6. **Would others who know you say you are secure in your sense of yourself?** Yes ☐ No ☐
7. **Do you believe that on the whole you are fulfilling your potential?** Yes ☐ No ☐
8. **Do you feel satisfied with what you've achieved?** Yes ☐ No ☐
9. **Are you motivated and have self –discipline in how you think and act?** Yes ☐ No ☐
10. **Is your emotional well-being on the whole independent of the feelings of those around you?** Yes ☐ No ☐

Score 1 point for every 'yes'.

Score between 8 and 10

This shows a high level of EQ. Those with a high EQ know themselves well, have a high level of insight and self-awareness and this means they have an inner compass to help them decide what they can do to make themselves happy. You probably know what you need to do to be happy, turn to idea 16 for ideas on how to put it into practice.

Score between 3–8

Your EQ is average, but it could be greater. Your EQ determines how well you relate to other people and how capable you are of recognising and achieving your goals – essential for a glittering career. Turn to idea 17 for ways of thinking better of those around you.

Score 3 or under

Getting in touch with your feelings might sound horrendous to you, but it's time for you start taking it seriously. Low EQ is holding you back. Read idea 1 to give you an idea of why it's important to be the best you can be.

1. Increase your brand value

You are a brand and as such your value in the market-place can go up or down. Let's look at ways in which you can build your brand value.

You must have come across them – those selfless, unassuming, committed and dedicated individuals who exist in varying numbers in just about every company. You know the ones: they concentrate on doing the best possible job they can, claiming no credit and paying no real heed to ensuring that their contribution is acknowledged by the company.

At one level, there is something admirable about them, but it is often these highly loyal employees who are the first to be 'let go'. If nobody knows how good you really are, what would your company expect to miss if you weren't around any more?

Look, this is not a career management book. This is about the level of income that you might be capable of generating. And frankly, if you are working in an organisation where you are underappreciated, you are almost certainly underpaid.

So how can you increase the amount you earn?

Enter Tom Peters, co-author of In Search of Excellence and probably the world's best-known management guru. In 1997, Peters wrote an article 'The Brand Called You: You Can't Move Up if You Don't Stand Out'. This brilliant synthesis of economic, marketing and business themes ends with a stark conclusion: 'It's this simple: you are a brand. You are in charge of your brand. There is no single path to success. And there is no one right way to create the brand called You. Except this: start today. Or else.'

Underpinning this concept, says Peters, is his passionate belief that the challenge for any of us who work for a living is to transform ourselves into a brand 'that shouts distinction, commitment and passion'.

> **Here's an idea for you...**
>
> Thinking of yourself as a brand provides an interesting base from which to make decisions about your career. From now on, before accepting any assignment, you should ask yourself this question: will taking on this piece of work add value to my brand, and hence my value in the marketplace? If the answer is 'yes', then take the assignment. If you conclude that the assignment is a poisoned chalice, then do everything you can to get out of it.

In the context of this book, the importance of your career decisions is that they affect what you are worth in the marketplace. If David Beckham had decided to join Yeovil Town Football Club rather than Real Madrid, his brand value would have plummeted. Maximising your income is dependent on maximising your brand value.

If you're not already doing so, it's time to give some serious thought to imagining and developing yourself as a brand. Start by identifying the qualities or characteristics that make you distinctive from your competitors – or your colleagues. What have you done lately, say over the past week, to make yourself stand out?

Defining idea...

'Regardless of age, regardless of position, regardless of the business we happen to be in, all of us need to understand the importance of branding. We are CEOs of our own companies: Me Inc. To be in business today, our most important job is to be head marketer for the brand called You.'

TOM PETERS, *In Search of Excellence*

The key to any personal branding campaign is 'word-of-mouth marketing'. Your network of friends, colleagues, clients and customers is the most important marketing vehicle you've got; what they say about you and your contributions is what the market will ultimately gauge as the value of your brand. So the big trick to building your brand is to find ways to nurture your network of colleagues.

The financial benefits are, hopefully, by now clear. Build your brand in the work marketplace and you put yourself in a great bargaining position for leveraging up your income. But don't just idly contemplate the notion, start today – or else.

2. CREATE success

Use the CREATE model as a path towards your success.

The CREATE model ensures you have a map for coaching yourself and a system that will help you stay on track. The model comprises the following steps:
- Challenge and create
- Reframe and replace your negative thinking
- Engage and energise
- Act and award
- Tools and techniques
- Explore and evaluate

Challenge and create

What challenges are you up against? You'll recognise challenges as those areas of your life that don't function well or where you feel drained or stretched. Once you face your challenges square on it's surprising how much better you'll feel. Whatever the challenge – drink, debt, a relationship, being disorganised – at the very least be willing to tell yourself the truth. Why? Because once you own up to it then you can get on with the business of transforming it. Make a note of your challenges in writing. Without knowing how this will be achieved, take each challenge separately and ask yourself, 'If I had to create a different experience in this area of my life what would it look like?' Make a list of your new positive outcomes for each of your challenges.

Here's an idea for you...

Write a list of outrageous adventures you'd love to have. What would you have a go at? What would you try out? Where would you visit? What would you like to find out more about? Start off with a virtual adventure. Rather than the real thing be open to different ways of experiencing your virtual adventure right on your doorstep, through the internet, television, radio, photos, exhibitions, seminars, cinema, books or magazines.

Reframe and replace your negative thinking

Get into the habit of reframing and replacing your negative thoughts and beliefs. Say you find your inner thoughts telling you, 'Oh, you'll never be any good as a manager.' Interrupt these thoughts by asking yourself this question: 'Is this belief or thought moving me towards positive action or negative action?' If the answer is towards negative action then set about convincing yourself of the opposite. List all the reasons why you'd make a good manager and keep repeating these to yourself regularly and consistently. To reinforce the reasons write them down. Like your old habit, this new habit has to be practised rigorously and regularly.

Engage and energise

Start engaging with life right now, no matter how shitty it is. That means no excuses. If you just learnt that you're going to be made redundant then make a start right away on updating your CV. Don't make the mistake of waiting for your life to be sorted before you start having a good time. Get out there and enjoy yourself. When you start fully engaging with your life right where you are, you'll become energised, and so will your life.

Act and award

One of the most powerful tasks that helped put my life on a better path was learning to take action regardless of how I was feeling. So when I felt depressed I would still push myself to turn on the computer and send one email. The mere action of sending just one email motivated me to send another one. Once you get into the habit of taking action no matter what, build giving yourself awards and acknowledgements into the process. In other words, don't let your actions go unacknowledged. Today, what action don't you feel like taking that you could make a start on right now?

Tools and techniques

Do you have a toolkit of techniques and ideas that work for you? Your toolkit is a valuable resource in your journey to becoming your own best life coach. After several days of not writing in my journal during a particularly stressful time I noticed how disconnected and tetchy I had become. I took ten minutes out of a hectic day and planted myself on my journal pages. Instantly I felt better. Make a list of your life tools, the ones that work and get results, and use them regularly.

Explore and evaluate

Your journey to becoming your own best life coach is a chance to explore and experience life as the adventure that it is. Most of the satisfaction you'll gain will come from the journey itself rather than the destination. On top of this make a conscious effort to evaluate. Ask yourself questions, monitor your progress, record your achievements, make observations of how you navigated around obstacles and setbacks. Make sure you're a partner in your life and not an observer.

3. Know your strengths

Want to get ahead? Then focus on your strengths. A good starting place is to ask yourself: 'What am I naturally good at that other people find hard to do?'

If you were stopped on the street and asked to list as many of your strengths and weaknesses as quickly as possible, which list do you think would be the longest? We all know the answer to that one.

The majority of us would probably struggle with our strengths but be able to reel off a long list for our weaknesses. We're notoriously good on puffing up our weaknesses and dumbing down our strengths.

We're all born with a portfolio of strengths that develop and grow as we do. Some of these strengths emerge naturally and are often qualities and talents we were born with. Charlotte Church's natural strength is obvious – singing. The strengths we are born with often don't feel hard to exercise. We develop other strengths as a product of the environment we were raised in and from experiences we pick up along the way. Consider these your acquired strengths.

But what about the things you're good at doing but don't enjoy? Do these count as strengths? I'm a good cook but I don't advertise this as one of my strengths. Because on a day-to-day basis cooking is not something I really enjoy. I do it because it has to be done. Not quite a natural talent but a strength I learnt growing up. It used to irritate me being called into the kitchen by my mum when I wanted to be outside playing like my brothers. But it meant I developed a skill in cooking.

If someone asked you outright to outline your strengths, could you say them out loud without mumbling and stuttering? Most of us would probably rush through them in embarrassment, just wanting to get the whole thing over and done with. OK you might brace yourself to appear confident in an interview or assessment centre but most of us would rather do a bungee jump than have to proclaim our strengths out loud.

But there is a danger in not acknowledging your strengths. You're more likely to live a life that's based on your weaknesses and find yourself constantly trying to catch up with yourself, rather than taking a more assertive approach and focusing your life on the things you enjoy doing and are good at.

Here's an idea for you...

Ever thought of having more than one type of CV to hand? Have a go at devising a Courage CV. A Courage CV highlights key roles, life challenges, places in your life where you stepped out of your comfort zone, achievements and transformations and things we forget to mention that traditional CVs often leave off. Here's a template for writing your own courage CV. Make a list of ten events from your life that required both large and small acts of courage on your behalf. Whilst this type of CV may not be every organisation's cup of tea, it might be a breath of fresh air in some. Having a range of CVs to hand allows you to highlight your strengths in a range of creative forms. Take a peek at Sofia's own CV on her webpage www.turnupthecourage.com for creative ways of laying out your Courage CV on the page.

13

Next step is to get clear on what your strengths are. But a little pep talk before we continue. In order to get ahead in this game you're going to have to agree not to generalise. That means naming things. So, saying you're good with dogs will not be considered a strength. It will only be validated when you specify exactly what breed of dog you are particularly good at working with. The same goes for the statement 'I'm good at communicating'. Again, this says nothing about the communication skills that you have. Your job is to flesh out the detail that might be obvious to you but not to others. 'I'm good at teaching people how to dance', or 'I help and support people who are trying to work through conflicts in a relationship'. Again get specific. No detail, no strengths. At the same time, don't make the mistake of only looking in the obvious places for your strengths. Look to your losses for strengths that may have emerged from there. You'll notice as you start being specific and detailed that this ensures that the strength is defined as something that you can actually do.

It takes a stranger thirty seconds to sum you up. Practise saying your strengths aloud in thirty-second sound bites in front of the mirror.

4. A short cut to coping with obstacles

For every behaviour or action, there's a payback. When you work out the payback you often drain away a lot of stress from a situation.

OK, this is a brutal one. Don't read on if you're feeling fragile. This is where we take the gloves off.

These are some of the random (cruel) thoughts that have crossed my mind during conversations with friends and acquaintances in the last couple of months:

- If you're over 35 and still trying to please your mother, it's time you stopped, not least because acting like a child isn't going to advance your chances of ever having a half-decent relationship with her.

- If you're a man (or, indeed, woman) who uses work as an escape route to get out of going home, it's pretty obvious to everyone what's going on, including the folks back home. Maybe that's why your family are so darned unpleasant when you bother to show up?

- If you're single, over 40, and unhappy about it, then you made choices even if these didn't feel like choices at the time. Your choice was to run from the

Here's an idea for you...

Write down three situations in the last week that have stressed you out. (Say, missing the train to work, arguing with your sister, staying late at work.) Then work out what the payback was. Make a game out of working out the payback for your actions on a daily basis. It's interesting to observe when you're 'running a racket' (which is life coach speak for kidding yourself).

people who wanted to commit to you in favour of those people who didn't want to commit to you – all of whom, incidentally, you invited into your life.

● If you're a mother in the developed world still breastfeeding a year-old child several times a day, you're doing it for reasons of your own that may have little to do with your child's needs and everything to do with your own. The fact that you're exhausted and your relationship with your baby's father is shaky isn't all that surprising.

● If you're feeling awful because you've had an affair, you deserve to. Not for the mindless sex but for neglecting your primary relationship in the first place. You were too cowardly to address the problems and are too cowardly now, having precipitated a crisis instead in order to force your spouse to make decisions.

● If your child is using explicit swear words to your mother-in-law you probably should feel guilty. Not for giving birth to a delinquent but for being disrespectful to the old bird behind her back even if she is a pain in the neck, even if it is good fun to laugh at her.

Remember I didn't actually say these things. These people were distressed and the last thing a distressed person needs is a know-it-all. My friends wanted sympathy and that's what they got. However, if we were really serious about sorting out our stress levels, we could start by taking our share of the responsibility for creating them.

Take responsibility

When you realise the great truth that you create a lot of your stress by your choices, then you're in a position to work out the payback – your 'reward',

Defining idea...

'I think of a hero as someone who understands the degree of responsibility that comes with his freedom.'
BOB DYLAN

what you're getting from the situation. And I guarantee that there will always be a payback. Sometimes the payback is worth the stress. You choose to look after your ill child. Nothing could be more stressful. The payback is, of course, self-evident.

But others are more tricky and take great honesty. Sacked from your job? But remember, you decided to stay when the company started looking dodgy because the pay was good and it was near your home. Being chased by the taxman? Hmmm, you did wonder why your tax bill seemed low, but weren't concerned enough to double-check your accountant's figures.

So whatever your stress source, look carefully at what choices of yours led to it: excitement, money, security, perpetual childhood, a sense of competence. You might decide that the payback is worth the stress.

But just by recognising that in every single thing you do, every single relationship you have, every single habit you've got, you are getting some sort of payback *or you wouldn't do it* is incredibly liberating. Recognising the payback gives us immense self-awareness. Obstacles melt away because we stop blaming everyone else. Once we're self-aware we tend to change of our own free will. The truth will set you free. Honest.

5. Make more mistakes faster

Working at speed with a high level of error can help you 'fail better'. Which means you'll get to something good quicker.

Creativity is often about speed of throughput. Believe it or not, making a hash of it at high speed may be the key to getting to where you want to go.

This idea is often attributed to Andy Grove of Intel, the processor manufacturing company that helped revolutionise the computer industry in the 1980s and 1990s. When your business is about crashing out millions of bits of finely etched silicon, it's easy to see why you might be prepared to keep the production line rolling even if a few batches get screwed up along the way.

For the sculptor who spends six months working one piece in stone, it may be less easy to write the resulting work off as a failure and start again. Nevertheless, for most of us, Grove's principle is a sound one. You have to keep scribbling and sketching, modelling and planning and thinking, setting things up to knock them down, scrumpling up bits of paper and throwing them in the bin, crashing and rebooting your computer, working continuously with enthusiasm and energy and wit, and above all without any embarrassment about the obvious cock-ups along the way. If you do this intelligently and energetically, other people will almost certainly be affected by your positive spirit and join you on your journey. Those who write you off as foolish and annoying – well, maybe hanging out with them is just another mistake and it's time to move on.

Also remember that mistakes are not always mistakes. Look at them another way and they become happy accidents. According to movie director Robert Altman, 'Chance is another name that we give to our mistakes. And all of the best things in my films are mistakes.' Mistakes, he is saying, are the stuff of life. And for him, they are also the stuff of art. (And according to chaos theory, they are also the stuff of stuff.)

> **Here's an idea for you...**
>
> This week, try and fire off at least a dozen ideas. In many cases, the first eleven ideas will be crap (so try to think of the twelfth one first to save time!). Don't see that as a waste of effort – see it more as a range-finder. Only by working through your early shortcomings will you hope to refine your processes on the fly – and your instincts.

This is the same attitude to life that Oscar Wilde describes when he writes: 'Nowadays most people die of a sort of creeping common sense, and discover when it is too late that the only things one never regrets are one's mistakes.'

Probably the most famous blunderer of them all is Alexander Fleming. Not only did he discover penicillin by accidentally contaminating some Petri dish samples and then not bothering to wash them up for a few days, he also discovered lysozyme when he didn't bother using a handkerchief and his nose accidentally dripped into a dish of bacteria. Are you creative enough not to wipe your nose for a week just to see what accidents might happen?

Defining idea...

'A life spent in making mistakes is not only more honourable but more useful than a life spent doing nothing.'
GEORGE BERNARD SHAW

The true moral of this story might be: if it ain't fixed, break it.

Certainly, one of the best ways to understand how some things work is to break them apart. For your family's sake, it's probably best if you work out how to put them back together again as well, although this isn't critical (unless it's grandma's Zimmer frame). And if it turns out that you've broken something irretrievably, try and find a new use for what you've got left. Look at kids: they rarely throw old broken toys away, but remodel, fuse and repurpose them for use in another game.

And talking of small kids, it's as well to remember that we only ever learn to walk after a lot of falling over. In fact, if you want to get technical about it, walking is falling over. If you don't believe us, get up now and lean forward like you are going to fall – then stick your leg out at the last minute. Almost inevitably, your other leg will kick in and you'll take not one step but two in order to break your fall.

Defining idea...

'If I had my life to live over I'd dare to make more mistakes next time.'
NADINE STAIR, poet

So now you see that even something as basic as walking is really just a controlled way for your body to blunder around the place.

6. Look at things another way

Changing your point of view rearranges your physical relationship with everything around you. And brings a whole new meaning to 'hanging around' at parties.

It can also force conceptual changes – like thinking about a door as a 'portal' instead of just a door. Or thinking of it as 'a jar'. Or even imagining yourself being the door.

You've probably already been told several times to 'consider the bigger picture'. But how do you get yourself into a position to do it?

The next time you want to get a better handle on a situation, try and inspect it from on high: either literally, by standing on a chair or climbing a ladder (best not to do this in meetings too often), or metaphorically by imagining yourself looking from very far away at all the things that are currently up close and personal. This will help you gain some mental and emotional distance from the things and people you work with, and help you think more clearly about the possibilities open to you.

Changing your point of view needn't always be about looking – you can use your other senses too. Instead of concentrating on what things look like, make a note about how they feel (rough, smooth, warm, cold, soft, hard) or smell.

Here's an idea for you...

Another obvious way to change your perspective is to 'rescale'. Imagine big things as small, and vice versa. For example, take a big thing and treat it like a little thing (like a new Lamborghini).

Here's an exercise you can try in the privacy of your own desk. Take a relatively small object, such as a cup, stapler or bulldog clip. Now subject your object to a series of experiments that will force you to look at things in a different way. Keep a notebook handy and write down all the thoughts that occur to you.

First, turn your object upside down (if you picked a full coffee cup, that's your look-out). Think about how its shape has changed, how it might look like something else, how its function may be impaired by being upside down, how it might become useful as something other than what it is.

Draw it roughly with your non-drawing hand so that you have a deliberately naïve and scruffy sketch. What does it look like now?

Now put it outside and look at it through a window, so that it looks abandoned or 'not yours'. Does it look comfortable outside? Does it look like it belongs there? If not, why not? If you can bear it, leave the object outside for a few days and see how it weathers. Does it change colour? Does mould or rust form? If you can't bear it, pluck up courage to abandon it in a public place for 20 minutes anyway and write down how you feel about its potential loss.

Now bring it back indoors. Put it behind you and look at it through a mirror. What you're looking at now is its reverse image. Reach out and try and touch that image. How do you feel, being able to look but not touch? Shine a torch on it and see how light and shadow play upon it, both directly and via the mirror image. What shadow shapes can you create?

> *Defining idea...*
>
> 'Cinema, radio, television, magazines are a school of inattention: people look without seeing, listen in without hearing.'
> ROBERT BRESSON, *French film director*

Now it's time to abuse your object a bit. Put it on a turntable and watch it spin around; put it under water; or suspend it on a wire and swing it. Feel free to play with it like a cat plays with a mouse. Don't be afraid to break it. And when you're done, hide it in a place where you think no one will ever find it (like a dog with a bone).

If you're enjoying this relationship with your object, take it further. Give it a name, or write a caption or slogan to go with it. Wrap it up and give it to someone as a special present. Photograph it as if it were a supermodel. Write a song about it. Wear it. Cook it. Probably best not to eat it.

The important thing is always to challenge yourself about how you perceive the object, how you use and abuse it, and what it could potentially become given your changed perspective.

7. Know what you can't do

Ferret out those failings and look for your limitations if you want to be free to focus on your strengths.

It can be curiously liberating to 'fess up to what you are crap at. There's a real tendency among creative people to control every aspect of their work. But work can suffer as a result.

It seems obvious to say that you shouldn't try to do everything yourself. But if you feel like you're just not getting any support from anywhere else, or that nobody else really understands what you're trying to do or you don't trust anyone to do what you want well enough, it's really tempting to go it alone.

The problem is that it is given to very few of us – if any at all – to be great at everything. If nothing else, there just isn't enough time in your life to be trained up with all the expertise you would need to be great at everything.

We are all, to a greater or less extent, specialists. Perhaps you've never thought about yourself in that way. Perhaps now you should. The easy way to understand what your specialities are is to list them. Is there some aspect of your creativity that you draw upon more than any other? Is there a particular facility you have that makes you and your work stand out from the crowd? Is there some area of expertise that you are always consulted upon by others? Have you won prizes or awards for something special? Have your peers or your audience fed back particular things they like about you or your work?

On a more general level, you should be clear with yourself about both what you're good at – and what you're bad at. So go on, write out in detail all your strengths and weaknesses.

Admitting that you are bad at something isn't as easy as it sounds. OK, you can say 'I'm crap at drawing' and almost feel you mean it. But then if someone else says 'Yeah, you really are crap at drawing', your natural response is probably going to be 'Yeah, well, I'm not that bad'. This is the state of mind that leads you into not asking for help with drawing tasks from someone who is clearly a better draughtsperson than you.

As well as being brutal with yourself about what skills you really do lack, add to the list all the things you actually don't like doing. Chances are that if you don't get any joy out of doing something, you won't be much good at it either. Think of how kids get out of doing the washing up after dinner by pretending to be crap at it (partners too, come to think of it).

> ## Here's an idea for you...
>
> Corporations have lots of tools (personality tests, etc.) to identify basic personality types and assess potential employees in order to build teams. Adopt the same techniques (ironically if you must) to understand more about yourself. Online tests abound for you to play with (check out the sites www.personalitytype.com and www.humanmetrics.com). Use these to add to your strengths and weaknesses list.

Defining idea...

'It's a wrong idea that a master is a finished person. Masters are very faulty; they haven't learned everything and they know it.'
ROBERT HENRI, *artist*

Let's be clear here: we're not talking just about practical things, such as writing or drawing or composing music (or washing up). We also want you to consider more fundamental things that relate to your personality type. Are you a social person? Bad tempered? Analytical? Impulsive? Conventional?

By now your list should be getting long. Don't get depressed. All it really shows you is that maybe you really do need to start collaborating more closely with a whole host of other people if you want your creative ideas to fly. Let them get on with the (in your eyes) dross while you concentrate on doing the important things.

Defining idea...

'We do not know one millionth of one percent about anything.'
THOMAS EDISON

8. Come back in the morning

Know when to put things on the back-burner, and how to let them simmer there rather than just grow cold or go mouldy.

You might very well claim to be a night-time person – an owl rather than a lark – but the fact is everyone works more effectively after a good night's sleep.

Fair enough, if it's getting late but you're motoring and 'in the zone', then stay up and feed off that feeling. Fair enough too if you have a deadline and simply must produce *something* for the next day. At some point, you may have to think tactically about what you can get away with, and burn a bit of night-oil thinking up good reasons why you're not going to deliver under the original terms of engagement. But never, ever bother bashing away at a problem late at night just for the sake of it, when you know in your heart of hearts you're not really solving anything. That really is a waste of time. And nobody will be impressed with your tired haggard expression unless the work itself has clearly been worth the effort.

Here's an idea for you...

If you have an imminent deadline, take your half-finished work to the meeting, admit your problems and ask for help in fixing them. Sometimes this makes everybody feel creative and valued. (Be careful how often you try and get away with this, by the way.) If your deadline is not so urgent, best leave it for several mornings (or months)!

In most cases, admitting defeat and coming back to something in the morning can really help not only to finally complete a piece of work in a good way – but also can ensure that you're in some kind of condition to really deliver at the critical moments.

According to Woody Allen, 'Eighty percent of success is showing up'. If you expend all your energy working fruitlessly through the night, you really aren't going to stand much chance of 'showing up' in the morning – either you'll be in bed fast asleep or you'll turn up at the office with your brain about as functional as a boiled pomegranate.

It really is true that you can see things differently in the morning light, especially if you're well rested and alert. Indeed, changes in light generally can throw a very different slant on your work. If you don't believe us, try working in different types of light, both artificial and natural. Experiment with a range of different light bulbs, perhaps. At different times of the day move to different rooms that have more or fewer windows, or face in a particular direction. Get up really early and sample the light at dawn (but don't stay up to do the same thing). Similarly, try working at dusk. (More accidents at work happen then than at any other time, by the way. You've been warned, so don't blame us.)

Sleep can also bring with it all kinds of strange dreams and thoughts that may come to your aid in the morning. It's amazing, too, how just by letting time pass a problem can go away (shame it doesn't work with toothache). For most creative people it's tempting to think that things only happen because of your presence and your input. But actually things happen without you too. Plants still grow, the world still spins and often what seemed so awful yesterday isn't so bad today. Crucially, you may also find that if you leave something in this way, somebody else will come along with the necessary input to fix things.

Defining idea...

'Why is it I get my best ideas in the morning while I'm shaving?'
ALBERT EINSTEIN

Defining idea...

'One must also accept that one has uncreative moments. The more honestly one can accept that, the quicker these moments will pass. One must have the courage to call a halt, to feel empty and discouraged.'
ETTY HILLESUM

9. Don't do lunch

Drink too much, stay up late, take the morning off, get up at 4 a.m., do all the wrong things and then start being creative.

In the middle of the day you should either be working obsessively or recovering from a night on the tiles.

By avoiding all the usual times for eating and sleeping, you can learn to step outside the normal social timetable. One of Bruce Mau's statements in his inspiring *Incomplete Manifesto for Growth* is: 'Stay up late. Strange things happen when you've gone too far, been up too long, worked too hard, and you're separated from the rest of the world.' Certainly it's important to be persistent when attacking a creative problem and to keep working even when you and everyone else feel like giving up. If you push yourself – don't bother having that break, going to lunch or heading for bed – eventually something will happen.

Working alone at night can have strange effects. The combination of silence, the dark and a sense that the rest of the world is asleep can definitely throw you in on yourself – and give rise to thoughts and feelings that you might not have access to during the day. Charles Dickens was a notorious night-owl, but instead of sitting in his room working on the next great novel, he'd actually get out and about in the wee small hours and walk for miles. Many of the characters who inhabited his fiction are drawn from his encounters with strange folk miles from home in the middle of the night.

Night-walking can allow you to see your local neighbourhood in a very different light. You meet a different type of person at three in the morning, and probably a few animals you wouldn't see during the day. Obviously, there's the fear that you might be mugged or find yourself in a difficult situation with a complete stranger – but that's part of the creative exercise. You can use that fear to take you to places you wouldn't otherwise go. And working your way through a strange and difficult situation is always going to give rise to creative material and memories that you can draw on later.

Speaking personally, if we, the authors (that's Rob and Tim, by the way – nice to meet you) weren't night-walkers, we would have never gone fishing for tuna in the Atlantic, never met the Asian guys in Amsterdam who thought we were undercover cops, never gone home with the French Canadian poetry-loving charity worker (and his bottle of laudanum). Rob would not have fallen in Lake Geneva and Tim would never have had his picture taken with the warthog and jar of marmalade.

> **Here's an idea for you...**
>
> Instead of being at your desk at 9 a.m., bright eyed and bushy tailed, try drinking all day instead, staying up until four in the morning and behaving quite badly (and yes, we are being serious). Obviously there are consequences in adopting this creative strategy. First, you'll have less time for work, because you've wasted it arsing about. You'll also be challenging social norms – your employers may well disapprove of liquid lunches. The good news is that the periods that you do work should have a furious intensity about them. By leaving things to the last minute and generally disrupting your usual working pattern, you'll inevitably start looking at the world in a different way. You'll also have to deal with the hangovers and feeling less than good. But strange things will spring to mind when you're in that tired, fuzzy state.

Defining idea...

'Always make the effort to take things one step beyond.'
MICHAEL IAN KAYE, *designer*

All of these incidents led to new ideas for projects and new ways of thinking about interaction – and also cemented our creative relationship.

Staying up late, drinking too much and then sleeping in is, of course, another great way of missing lunch. It's amazing how many great artists were also piss-artists (Francis Bacon, Dylan Thomas, Kingsley Amis, Richard Burton…). In the case of French intellectual Guy Debord (co-founder of the Situationist International), drinking actually became a key part of his art: 'First like everyone, I appreciated the effect of slight drunkenness. Then very soon I grew to like what lies beyond violent drunkenness, when one has passed that stage: a magnificent and terrible peace, the true taste of the passage of time. Although in the first decades I may have allowed my self have slight indications to appear once or twice a week, it is a fact that I have been continuously drunk for periods of several months; and the rest of the time I still drank a lot.'

10. Don't reinvent the wheel

When pre-fab can mean pretty fabulous.

Not everything you do has to be an original prototype – imagine if every car you ever owned had to be built from scratch.

If the title of this chapter sounds a bit of a cliché, that's because it is. Clichés often start life as useful shorthand for summing up ideas or situations in a succinct way that everyone can understand. So don't be too quick to write them off. Take 'not seeing the wood for the trees'. It's actually a rather snazzy and useful description for what is quite a subtle point.

Quite a lot of the time, we all think in clichés. Our brains and our imaginations operate in pretty much the same way, and our creativity works along very common lines. A lot of the ideas you have will inevitably be generic and not original. But they're none the worse for that. They can still be very useful building blocks to play with.

It's a waste of time always forging completely new and original components for your creative projects. Often, it's how you put your thoughts together that really counts. If you don't believe us, try some flower arranging. Go and buy a couple of dozen bog-standard daffodils or roses. Now spend an hour or so thinking about different ways of arranging them. Start with a plain vase on the table and work your way up from there until you've thought of at least 52 different

> **Here's an idea for you...**
>
> When thinking about making a simple presentation or telling a story for the first time, call upon tried and trusted techniques and formats that have stood the test of time. Use these as the spine of your work – and then add your own twists and distinctive embellishments.

arrangements (there could be a book in that). Do silly arrangements. Do highly technical ones (involving balancing acts, maybe?). Use different containers or coloured water.

Incidentally, flower arranging has become a seriously creative (and lucrative) business in recent years. Recent innovations in the industry (we kid you not) include placing flowers at very precise angles, even placing them in glass vases of fizzy water – upside down!

What we hope you learn from our daft daffodil exercise is that different arrangements of common elements can produce highly original tones and textures.

Another great example of this is twelve-bar blues. The chord sequence is fantastically simple, and easy to play on the piano or guitar. But something happens to this structure when a player who knows about timing and frequency, volume and tone gets hold of it. A great blues artist uses the simple building blocks of the chord sequence to 'play' and explore many different voices and moods.

We've used that term 'building blocks' twice now, and there's a lot be said for noodling around with a few Lego bricks every now and again – even as an adult. In fact, a good team exercise is to give everyone in the office the same limited set of Lego bricks (no more than ten) and see who can come up with the most highly original construction or presentation.

Defining idea...

'Man invented the car but the car – out of pure malevolence no doubt – changed the history of the world by reinventing man.'
HARRY CREWS, *US urban planner*

Writing computer code can be a bit like playing with Lego (indeed, you can now 'program' your Lego constructions with a product called Mindstorms – itself a great creative tool). Programmers often have to make a choice about whether to reuse code from a previous project or write something afresh. Naïve programmers often like to dive in every time and make something new. This is often because one's first programming project is usually very simple and small – and so starting from scratch isn't very taxing, and you feel like you're learning along the way. But when it comes to bigger, multi-part projects, these people are sunk. They're simply overwhelmed by the workload of constantly reinventing the wheel every day for months.

We recommend therefore that you break this bad habit of originality for originality's sake very early on, when you're taking baby steps in the world of creativity. It will stand you in good stead later.

11. Take on another role

Using role-play in your daily life can help you discover things about yourself and other people.

Most of us at some time of our life have wondered what it might be like to be someone else.

It may be a character from history who you identify with or a best friend you admire; whoever it is, it's entirely natural to try and emulate that person. By acting like other people, we are trying to discover a little more about ourselves. It starts at an early age, imitating mum and dad: the obvious way to learn what it might be like to be an adult (or not, as the case may be). Even when we think we've done all our growing up, we still use role-play in order to develop our skills and build up our experience. For example, most business managers don't receive much formal training about how to manage. Instead, they learn from their own bosses. They 'act out the part' of being a business manager until they've gained enough experience to actually become the part.

Human beings love to copy each other. When we talk to someone with a strong regional accent, we sometimes find ourselves talking the same way. Sometimes we'll even subconsciously adopt their mannerisms and verbal tics. Yet despite these natural acts of mimicry, pretending to be someone else is pretty much frowned upon in conventional society. Not being authentically yourself is seen as insincere or devious. Adopting a false identity is the practice of criminals and crazy people – or even worse, actors!

Thus, when we tell you it's good to indulge in a bit of role-play, we're assuming it's something you'll have to do surreptitiously; that is, unless a whole group of you decide to experiment in this way together (like a comedy double act or theatre company might do).

The kind of play-acting we're suggesting isn't wigs and make-up. It's more internalised – a form of creative projection whereby you consider how situations might play out differently if you were actually somebody else. For example, in a particularly stressful meeting, where someone accuses you of some cock-up, you might typically become defensive and touchy (like Tim). But if today you've decided to be a more silent and laid-back person (like Rob), you'll almost certainly end up in a different place by the end of the meeting – both in terms of how you reacted to events and how you moved past them. This exercise, then, is very much about not being your normal self – and thus hopefully becoming clearer about who your normal self is.

Perhaps you have more than one 'normal self', depending on who you're with and what you're doing. If so, try to pick just one to play. Say to yourself: 'Today I'll be the petulant child my mum knows so well.' Or: 'Today I'll be an *ingénue*. Tomorrow I'll be a critic.'

Another way of shaking things up is to experiment with your own prejudices about gender-based behaviour. If you're a man, spend some time thinking what

> **Here's an idea for you...**
>
> Take a trip to the zoo and see what you can learn about body language, facial expressions, mannerisms, social behaviour, eating, goal-based activity, basic desire and playfulness that you can adopt for a while in your own life. Be a stick insect for a day – very still, blending into the background with simple, slow needs. Be a gorilla the next day – park yourself in the centre of every situation, stare, eat noisily and scratch yourself a lot. (Ah, you've done that already!)

Defining idea...

'Play is the exultation of the possible.'
MARTIN BUBER, *philosopher*

you'd be like as a woman, and how you'd behave. If you're a woman, try and think like a man (trust us, men do think occasionally…).

Many people swap genders on the internet and happily chat away with strangers as Glenda when doing the washing-up as Glenn. In most cases, no harm is done and something can be learnt (not all people who take on fake online personas are paedophiles and sex offenders).

In our case, we actually created a completely bogus female character on the Web called Caroline Close, who had her own webcam and would mail you every day if you wanted her to. This was envisaged as a form of interactive drama, but for many people who played it, it also became a form of creative role-play where they could rehearse making friends with a complete stranger online without having to live with the consequences in their real lives. You can still try it at www.onlinecaroline.com.

Putting yourself into other people's shoes can really help when it comes to developing new work. For example, if you were designing a chicken hutch, it would be obvious to make it appeal to the chicken owner who is paying for it. But a really good hutch designer will also spend some time thinking like the other people who may have some influence on the purchase – the partner, the children, the neighbour. And the best hutch designer of all will also think like a chicken – and a fox!

Always try to remain alert to all the possible players in any given situation.

12. Making swift, smart decisions

Learn this vital decision-making formula. You'll free up your mind from niggling worries in seconds, saving your mental energy.

I've had a bit of a dilemma today. I'm staring at an e-mail advertising a two-day self development course that I'd love to attend. There's just one problem. The weekend in question is the one (of admittedly many!) on which we will be celebrating my partner's fortieth birthday. I've promised to take him out for dinner that night and since the course is near my home, I could do both – attend the course during the day and take him for dinner that night. But … but … I've got that sneaking suspicion that by trying to pack too much in, I'm taking too much on. I'll be rushed and late for dinner.

In the past, this is the sort of dilemma I would have spent time on. I would have weighed up the pros and cons, written lists, talked to my partner about it, talked to friends perhaps, spent valuable time dithering when I could have been getting on with my life.

But that was before I learned the magical qualities of what I call 'the power of 10' question.

Here's an idea for you...

The very quickest form of this idea is brilliant for procrastinators. Think of a task that you're putting off. Imagine what the consequences will be in one month (or whatever time span is relevant) if you don't act. If the consequences don't frighten you, go to the pub; if they do, get on with it now. Worrying about it even subconsciously is sapping your energy.

When faced with any dilemma simply stop and ask yourself: what will the consequences be in:

10 minutes?
10 months?
10 years?

When you're faced with a problem wherethere's no win-win situation and someone will end up unhappy, at least in the short term, 'the power of 10' helps you cut through the emotions of the moment and focus on what is really important.

Let's take my present dilemma.

If I decide to go to the self-development course, what will be the repercussions in 10 minutes? None. I'll explain to my partner, he won't really register it – it's down the line and as long as I'm not actually cancelling dinner, he won't care. I'll be happy.

In 10 months? That depends. If there are no mess-ups and I get there on time, probably it will be fine. But if I am late for dinner, in 10 months' time, he'll still be making sarcastic comments.

In 10 years? You know, that's the tricky one. Even if I manage everything, I think he's still going to remember that on the weekend of his fortieth, I wasn't really around. That's the general impression he'll have long after he's forgotten the presents, the party and all the other gestures I'll make to 'big' up his birthday and distract his attention from the fact that I'm not actually there very much. Would I be better off attending the course? I might learn a lot. I might make some lifelong soulmates. But there's no way of knowing if it will be worth it, or not. And there's potentially a lot to lose. So this time, I think I'll have to pass.

Defining idea...

'But all will be well, and every kind of thing will be well.'
JULIAN OF NORWICH.
Medieval mystic

It took me as long to make that decision as it took to type it, and now my mind is free to get on with writing this, and everything else I have to do. I won't waste any more time thinking about it.

This is a variation of an old idea – imagining yourself one year, five years, ten years down the road is commonplace. 'What will it matter in twenty years' time?' we say to each other. But I find 'the power of 10' particularly elegant and easy to use. Try it when you're not sure what route to take and know that either will end up making someone unhappy. The three different timescales help you see through the emotional turmoil of yours or somebody else's short-term unhappiness to what the potential benefits could be when disappointment has passed. It helps you cut through the emotional 'fuss' that occurs when your plans are unpopular with some people, and to see clearly if they're worth the grief.

13. Revamp your to-do list

To-do lists are essential for most of us but they can be a huge drain on energy.

The list that never seems to get any shorter is not so much an aide-memoire as a horrible reminder that we're running fast but getting nowhere.

And what could be more dispiriting than that?

The other side, of course, is that to-do lists are incredibly useful tools for motivating us and making us more productive. Having a clear plan for the day ahead focuses the mind and puts you in control like nothing else. Whether you're a CEO, freelance, stay-at-home parent or student, the well run 'to do' list will give you a sense of full-capacity living.

But for it to work, you have to have a definite system. Try this one. It is based on the advice given to 1930s magnate Charles Schwabb by a young man he challenged to double his productivity. The young man told him to write down the six most crucial tasks for each day in order of importance and work down the list. Then teach his staff to do the same. After a few weeks, the story goes that Schwabb sent a cheque for £25,000 to he young man, which was a huge sum then.

This idea works on the principle that we put off important stuff (or we work to others' agenda so we don't get round to what's important for us) and keep ourselves busy with lesser tasks to distract ourselves. But if we don't do the one important thing, no matter what we achieve, we'll feel dissatisfied at the end of the day. Instead of an abstract list of things to do that you attack randomly, switch the angle from what you *must* do to *when* you are going to do it.

How to revamp your to-do list

In your diary or a separate notebook, draw a line down the left hand side of the page to form a column and mark in the working hours of the day. This can be precise (9.30 to 10.30, 10.30 to 11.30) or loose (morning, afternoon). Now you're set to go.

- At the end of your working day, brew a cuppa, sit for a second, take a deep breath and gather your thoughts. Pat yourself on the back for what you have achieved today. Now. Swing your mind forward into tomorrow.

- Ask yourself what regular scheduled tasks or meetings you have for tomorrow. Block them off on your diary page.

- Remember to add in travelling time, lunch and relaxation.

> *Here's an idea for you...*
>
> Switch off your mobile for as long as you can comfortably get away with, but aim for at least an hour in the morning and an hour in the afternoon. These should be your high productivity times when you aim to really motor through your tasks. The act of switching of your mobile sends an unconscious message to your brain that this is time when your interests are the priority, and it helps to focus your mind on the task at hand.

Defining idea...

'Energy and persistence alter all things.'
BENJAMIN FRANKLIN

● What is your major task? What *must* you do tomorrow? That gets priority and should be done first thing if possible. Set aside a realistic block of time (err on the side of caution). Be precise.

● Put in specific times for phone calls/e-mails. It is more time effective to do these in two or three blocks rather than breaking concentration and doing it ad hoc during the day.

● What's your next most important task? Is there room in your day? If you have time left, you can   schedule in other tasks, but be realistic.

● For each week have a short list of brief one-off tasks (phone calls, paying bills, birthday cards) and if you have a few down minutes, slot them in.

14. How to love the job you've got

Sometimes you can't have the one you want. So you have to love the one you've got.

One in four of us wants to leave our jobs. We can't all do it at once, so here's how to cope until your personal Great Escape.

The bottom line

Hate your job? It's probably for three reasons – you hate the work (it's monotonous or stressful), you hate the environment, including your colleagues, or something else has happened in your life that makes work seem meaningless and you're ready for a lifestyle change. Or it could be that you're in denial. I'm going to come over a bit mystical here, because I firmly believe that sometimes we hate our job because we can't be bothered to address what's really stressing us out in our lives. Our energy is focused elsewhere and until we sort out whatever drama or sadness is soaking up our concentration, we're not likely to find the dream job anytime soon. So the advice here is not about refocusing your CV – there are plenty of other places where you can read up on that. But it will help you relieve stress in the short term and make you feel better about yourself in the long term. And that hopefully will help you raise your energy enough to eventually find another job.

Here's an idea for you...

Boost work morale in a stressful workplace by starting group traditions beyond getting drunk on Friday night and moaning. Go out for a Chinese on pay day or book an awayday at a spa or have a whip-round every birthday and celebrate with champagne and cake.

Love your surroundings...

...Just as much as you can. If your workplace is grim and drear, you are not going to feel good. Clear your desk. Sort out clutter. Personalise your work space with objects of beauty and grace. Pin up photos of beautiful vistas you've visited or would like to visit. (It's a bit less personal than family pix.) But whatever you choose to put on your desk, change the visuals every couple of weeks, otherwise your brain stops registering them.

Love your lunch breaks

A lunch break shouldn't be a scramble for bad food and a desultory walk round a shopping mall. Spend time planning. Every lunch hour should involve movement, fresh air, delicious healthy food and at least one work of art. Works of art are easily available for your perusal (art galleries, department stores) and easily transportable (books, CDs). Always, always take an hour to relax at lunch.

Love your colleagues

Tough one. These could well be the reason you hate your job in the first place. If there are people who specifically annoy you, then find a way to deal with them. Your local bookshop is full of manuals that will teach you how. Allow yourself no more than five minutes a day unloading your woes about work colleagues to a trusted friend or partner – not anyone you work with. This is not goody-goody – it's self-preservation. The more you unload your negativity all over the place, the more you are talking yourself into a hole of unhappiness and stress.

Love yourself

Turn up. Work hard. Do better. Lots of people who are unhappy with their work kid themselves that they are working really hard, when in fact their work is shoddy and second-rate. If you're not up to speed, improve your knowledge base and skills. If your work is lazy, look at everything you produce or every service you offer and ask yourself how you can make it special, imbue it with your uniqueness, breathe creativity and a little bit of love into it. Doing every task diligently and with positivity will vastly increase your self-esteem.

> *Defining idea...*
>
> 'People get disturbed not so much by events but by the view which they take of them.'
> EPICTETUS

Love your dreams

Most of us couldn't have got through school without the ability to drift away on a pleasant reverie of future plans. For five minutes in every hour allow yourself to dream. Read through job pages that aren't related to your present job. You may see a position or course that fires your imagination in a completely new direction.

15. Maximise your self esteem

The ability to draw others towards you effortlessly saves you the sweat of having to go to them. result!

The secret to magnetism is dead simple – love yourself. And remember, high selfesteem isn't a constant; it's a work in progress.

Imagine if life just got easier. If the things you wanted in life seemed to flow towards you effortlessly. That's what the father of life coaching, US guru, Thomas Leonard, called 'irresistible attraction'. Which is a fabulous way of saying 'sky-high self-esteem'.

Without self-esteem you feel helpless, depressed, isolated. Life seems difficult and you don't feel other people care about you enough. Needless to say, it's a major bummer and brings your energy levels crashing down.

Fluctuating self-esteem is a major energy drainer without us realising it. We struggle on, feeling rubbish without really knowing why. Which is a shame, because making a few simple steps to feel better about ourselves can boost our energy immediately and that makes us more attractive to others. Life gets easier and we need to expend less energy to get through the day. Keeping a beady eye on our fluctuating self-esteem levels is a win-win situation energetically speaking.

Answer 'yes' or 'no' to these statements based on how you're feeling *now, today*– not how you felt last week, last year or last millennium.

1. Does life seem unnecessarily complicated?
2. Do all your attempts to make life better seem to get stuck?
3. Do you feel you're at the mercy of your family, job or other people?
4. Are you feeling slightly sick at the thought of all you have to achieve by the end of the week?
5. Do you feel that, if you want something, you can make it happen?
6. Do you feel that you are expressing who you really are through your image, home, work or interests?

Here's an idea for you...

Set aside half an hour and write down every single thing you've been successful at or that you've completedsuccessfully. put anything on the list as long as it's meaningful to you. finding a good dentist could be as much of a success as getting a promotion at work. When you run out of steam, look over the list and write down the qualities you needed to achieve each success – perseverance, courage, quick wit. return to this list until you have at least 100 successes – and then give yourself a really nice reward for being so darn successful.

Answer 'no' to the first four questions and 'yes' to questions 5 and 6, and you can skip this idea – for now. 'Yes' to the first four questions; 'no' to questions 5 or 6, and your self-esteem could use some work. The good news is you can start right now. You'll have higher self-esteem by the time you go to bed tonight.

Make a difference – it makes you gloriously attractive

One characteristic of people with low self-esteem is that, deep down, they don't think it matters if they exist or not. Those with healthy self-esteem know they make a difference to the world. Easiest way of doing it? Pay a genuine compliment and then 'big' it up. Tell the bloke who makes your coffee how good

Defining idea...

> 'The more you touch other people's lives, the more attractive you become.'
>
> THOMAS LEONARD, *coaching guru*

it is, and let his manager overhear. Compliment your assistant on a job well done, then email your boss to let her know about his good work. Paying compliments makes you powerful. You remember the person who gave you a heartfelt compliment for the rest of your life. Don't you want to be that kind of memorable person?

Ditch the martyrdom – it's deeply unattractive

All of us do things we don't want to do, but some of us get caught in a trap of working to other people's agendas too much of the time. And that's majorly exhausting. Think of one chore you really don't want to do: visit your aunt, help at the school fête, paint the bedroom. Now remember – it's optional. Pretty much everything in life is. Cancel it and do something that makes you happy instead. When 'duty' tasks mount up, we feel overwhelmed and out of control. Saying 'no' means you start to question every single time you say 'yes'. Saying 'no' to other people and 'yes' to yourself is very, very energising.

16. Being the best version of you

However much you study the great business leaders — the Richard Bransons or Jack Welches — you can't be them. What you can be, though, is the best version of you. How?

Here's how to get the job that allows you to be the best version of you, through a clear proactive approach.

There is a version of you which is extraordinary, amazing and would make you feel very much 'the best version of you'. A lot of the time you would feel 'in the zone'. You'd be paid for what you do but in many ways that would seem crazy because you would love your work so much!

Does that seem too ridiculous? Well, many of the people you admire in business are good at what they do because they have noticed and exploited what they are good at, rather than choosing a good career, even if that means ignoring formal education. So, how do you get to be the best version of you? One exercise, two stages and three factors. Please read on…

Here's an idea for you...

Be proactive with the job you want; don't wait for the job advertisement which is looking for you. Try and create the role of your dreams where you are, or contact organisations who have such a role. Write, ring and propose. If you are truly passionate about that role it will come across and the role will be yours. Don't expect instant success; keep trying and be willing to take intermediate positions to help you build experience.

One exercise

Take a short break; ten to fifteen minutes would be ideal. Don't 'do' anything during that time. Just walk or rest and let your mind wander; don't read on until your time is up. Then grab some paper and a pen and answer the following questions as quickly as you can. In the working context:

- What do you love?
- What do you hate?
- When do you feel at your best?
- When does time, well, become timeless?
- Is there any work which you love so much that you would do it for free?

Now take another short break and come back and review your answers. You may well find that this gives you some insight into the best version of you.

Two stages

- The 'do it' stage. Do your utmost to pursue that career, that passion. This may simply need you to have a discussion with your boss, or it might be a three-year quest, but it'll be worth it. To keep you inspired and focused and motivated on this quest, start reading the biographies of those you admire. You'll notice this 'on a quest' point as a constant in their lives rather than the reluctant 'I've got to get a job'!

- The 'learn' stage. Continue to amplify what you enjoy and look for opportunities to leave out what you do not, in your current career and in any new career you take up. If you start a business, continue to 'morph' it so that it allows you to play to your strengths rather than suffering your weaker points. One particularly interesting variation on this is the portfolio career, in which you have a collection of mini-careers all running at the same time, maybe a part-time job with an IT company for two days a week or your own low-key, often evening, consultancy. Then you also sell your artwork online.

Three factors

- The 'don't be worried about what others think' factor. There are many 'prescribed' routes for you in your career, life and culture; these will not necessarily allow you to express yourself. Sure, it would be prestigious to be marketing director within a brand-recognised organisation, but is it really you? Would it get you out of bed in the morning with a leap and a bound? Yes? Great! No? Maybe consider something else.

- The 'you'll change' factor. As you grow and develop – and doing the job 'which you are destined to do' should particularly allow this kind of development – you will change your desires over time. You thought you wanted the management route, but you've discovered that it's not really you.

- The 'you'll know' factor. This is the answer to the question 'how will I know whether this is it?' You'll know. Be logical, but be sensitive to your intuition and feeling; they will tell you.

It can, at times, be frightening to be making these kinds of choices and it will not be easy. In particular it might appear that you have chosen a high-risk route, but in fact by basing your career on what you truly are good at, you have made it more sustainable in the long term.

The ultimate career coach

54

Unleash your charisma and get what you want

What's the secret to making people love you? Loving them right back, of course. It's hard to get ahead when we don't think much of those around us, because they tend to sense this and not be as supportive as they could be.

Are you a player?

How do you get what you want? There might be more effective ways of doing it. Test your faith in human nature here by answering the following questions.

1. **Do you always assume that people have ulterior motives?** Yes ☐ No ☐
2. **Do you think that most people can be bought?** Yes ☐ No ☐
3. **Could you see yourself as a politician one day?** Yes ☐ No ☐
4. **Do you believe what you read in the paper?** Yes ☐ No ☐
5. **Do you think when you give to charity, 'they'll probably squander half of it on admin?'** Yes ☐ No ☐
6. **Does the end justify the means?** Yes ☐ No ☐

If you answered yes more often than no then you probably are a bit of a player, someone who uses low cunning to get what you want. If you're still not sure then answer these three questions.

7. **Do you tell your mother white lies?** Yes ☐ No ☐
8. **Have you ever exaggerated or otherwise embellished the truth when trying to sell an idea or product to another person?** Yes ☐ No ☐
9. **If you found a wallet in the street, would you hand it into the police?** Yes ☐ No ☐

Questions 7 and 8 score 1 point for yes, question 9 score 1 point for no. Even 1 point in these questions of honesty and trust show that you manoeuvre through life in a rather Machiavellian way. By building up your charisma you'll find you can negotiate what you want without losing others' trust. And that means you'll succeed much faster. Move from being a player to being a charmer. Learn to trust others and you'll find that your working life gets easier. Start with idea 17

17. How to make everyone love you

Take the moral high ground. You'll like the view.

We are approval-seeking missiles. From birth we seek the praise and validation of others. And this constant need for approval is the source of some of life's great stresses.

We start off wanting a smile from mum for playing nicely or using the potty. And it's a direct line from that to remodelling your house so it's bigger than the neighbours' and stealing your mate's ideas at work to impress the boss. Unfortunately, success-driven behaviours don't always supply (hopefully) what we got from our parents when we were kids – the praise and the absolute certainty that we are fabulously loveable and important.

A sure way to feel important is to feel superior and the way to do it is to find someone we consider inferior to ourselves and then demonstrate very clearly to them why we're so much better. This is the origin of most success-driven behaviours. Which is why many of us spend much of the time feeling like schmucks – mainly because we spend much of the time behaving like schmucks. Seeking external approval, although a low-risk strategy as a child (if you have a loving carer, you nearly always get it), is a high-risk strategy as an adult because it's often based on placing ourselves on some hierarchy of success and (a) there's always someone higher up the ladder than you and (b) there is rarely a captive audience taking the place of your mum and cheering you on. (And that's why we need to grow up and build our own inner reserves of self-esteem, but that's a whole other story.)

When we're still comparing ourselves with other people – what they have, what they do – we feel worth less than them. And that sets up a deep anxiety that is stressful and usually leads to you trying even harder to make other people realise your superiority.

Here's an idea for you...

For the rest of the day, try treating everyone you meet with exactly the same warmth as you would your best friend. Smile when you see them, compliment them on their appearance, let them know how they are adding to your general well-being. When you answer the phone, smile. Let your 'thank yous' ring out loudly. Being kind to everyone from the postman to your partner seems to halve stress levels.

And one day you wake up and no one seems to like you much. Not even your kids. Especially your kids as they are the people on whom you probably act out your surreptitious 'inferiority/attempt-at-superiority' routine more than most. In fact, the success-driven behaviours that we embarked upon to win approval are likely to result in the direct opposite. People think at best you're a bit needy and pathetic and, at worse, you're a grade A pain in the backside.

What would Nelson do?
Here is my favourite trick. The minute I start to feel the stirrings of inferiority – whether it's that my boss is unhappy with me, my partner is fed up with me, friends don't phone any more, that I'm generally worthless, I stop and think 'What would Nelson Mandela do?'

Defining idea...

'We can secure other people's approval, if we do right and try hard; but our own is worth a hundred of it, and no way has been found out of securing that.'
MARK TWAIN

He's my man. But for you it could be Jesus, the Dalai Lama, Oprah Winfrey, Batman. Create the fantasy of them reacting to the situation you're in – and then behave as your hero would.

If somebody appears to think you are worthless, try to work out what is motivating their behaviour. This is not the same as worrying about what they think about you. It's not about you. It's about them. Try to see into their hearts – can you see any worry or stresses that could be motivating them to act mean? Do your best to make them feel better. Remember that all of us are approval-seeking missiles – including the people that are acting out their inferiority/superiority thing on you.

Be a hero in your own life. You will stop feeling the need to act superior to stop you feeling inferior. You will speak to people straightforwardly, refusing to be intimidated by those you feel are 'superior' to you, declining to play the silly game of putting yourself on some weird pecking order determined by who has the biggest house, best job, bigger salary, more degrees, cleverer kids, thinnest thighs.

You will be a person walking confidently through life spreading grace and goodwill. You will love the world and it will love you right back.

18. Que? Speak their language

However brilliant your argument, if nobody understands it you might as well give up and go home. You won't get anybody on board without a compelling case.

When we need to influence somebody to have it our way, we must work hard not only to make our point unarguable but also to ensure the other person can understand easily why it is important.

Have you ever been on a foreign holiday – say in Italy – and observed a tourist aiming to confront a problem – say about a restaurant bill – and they are doing it by shouting … in English! It's not going to work, is it? But sometimes we do the same even when we are all working in English: we simply are not talking 'their language'.

Just as English-to-French or Italian-to-Mandarin is not going to work without a translator on the scene, there's little chance of you successfully influencing if you're ranting about child-care difficulties from a single mother's perspective at a male head teacher who has never experienced anything but a traditional family background. Face it: it's just not going to work.

Here's an idea for you...

Think about the next influencing situation you've got coming up and pre-empt the communication breakdown by planning your ripostes. Take a sheet of paper and draw a line vertically down the middle. This, believe it or not, is going to be your vocabulary book. On the left-hand side, jot down some phrases you know are going to come up in that discussion. On the right-hand side, write down the translation. For example with your teenage daughter: she says 'you don't understand me', your translation 'I understand you only too well'. With the bank manager: he says 'it's not a viable business proposition', your translation 'it sounds pretty good but as you don't have security …'

Ranting at your daughter about what it was like when you were a teenager … it's just not going to go anywhere. And whatever the bank manager says about how he 'understands what it's like to run a small business', he doesn't – not really. He's never had to get his own head around what it's like to run a business. So talking to him from your perspective just isn't going to work.

To influence someone, we must talk their language and use their kind of vocabulary. To the builder, ask 'Will you be done with the scaffolding by next Saturday?' rather than 'Are you going to pass the next milestone on my schedule on time?'. To your daughter say 'I'm sure we could be getting along better', rather than 'I think we have a relationship issue'. We must use relevant examples and language that makes sense.

We must respect other people's intelligence. And – here's a tough one – we must assume that, most of the time, people do what they think is perfectly sensible. Much of the time they are not necessarily trying to 'wind us up'. Our daughter just thinks we did things differently when we were younger and things aren't the same now. The builder feels he's done a good day's work and he can't do much more. And so it goes on.

So, talking 'their' language is about communicating in ways that they can understand, make sense and are relevant. For example, compare these two approaches (a team leader trying to influence shop-floor staff to be more customer-focused):

Defining idea...

'Language is not only an instrument of communication, or even of knowledge, but also an instrument of power. One seeks not only to be understood but also to be believed, obeyed, respected, distinguished.'
PIERRE BOURDIEU, *French sociologist*

1. Look, we've simply got to get the customer service metrics up. They're around 85% at the moment; it is simply not good enough because New World of Work marketing requires a threshold of at least 90%. To be honest some of you are in real danger of being 'let go' if we don't sort this out.

2. Okay, so, everyone got some tea or coffee? Great. Now before the shop opens I want to go right back to some basics about working with our customers. Yes, yes, I know we talk about it a lot but it is the difference that makes all the difference. Can anyone give me some example of great service they have received when out shopping? … That's what I mean …

You see how it works: drop the jargon, drop the ego and talk real.

19. How to read minds

To have it your way, you need to know what the other person is thinking and how they are currently feeling. Then you'll know how they'll respond to you.

Being a mind reader is about relating to others' concerns and understanding why they are resisting. It's time to 'get into their shoes' and understand 'where they are coming from'.

One of the best and fastest ways to influence someone is to be able to understand the way the other person ticks – what they think and feel. We know what's on our own minds, of course: the boyfriend who never tidies up after himself; the teenage daughter coming home well after curfew (and not even apologising); or the bank manager who seems to have changed his mind after agreeing to that cheap business loan.

But what was on *their* minds when they made those 'decisions'? The boyfriend *must* know it annoys us when he drops his towel on the floor, surely? The daughter *must* know we are worried when she is home late, surely? The bank manager *must* know this could harm our business growth, surely?

Sadly, they probably don't! Most people don't think very much about the other person's perspective – but it doesn't matter because you do and you're going to be brilliant at it.

Here's what to do. Stop thinking about you for a moment – you know that part! Think about them, the person you want to influence. Imagine you are a detective in a police show. Imagine posing questions such as: why would it be sensible for them to do that apparently odd behaviour?

More importantly, imagine the answers: 'I drop the towels because they magically get picked up' … 'I come home late because my friends think I'm cool because I can do that' … 'I changed my mind about the loan because you didn't get back to me promptly so I didn't think you were that interested'.

Then ask: if I were them, what would get me to change?

- 'If I realise that the dropped towels are no longer magically getting picked up and they would soon start to stink.'
- 'If I could look cool in other ways.'
- 'If I had a carefully worded e-mail.'

> **Here's an idea for you…**
>
> Sit quietly somewhere. Close your eyes and clear your mind. Now imagine in your mind's eye the person you wish to influence; imagine them talking to you. Then imagine what they are thinking – no, not what *you* are thinking, what *they* are thinking. Imagine what they are feeling. Imagine what they are saying. Notice how your perspective suddenly shifted. Notice how you felt a lot more perceptive and open to their perspective and got some good ideas on how to approach the problem. With practice, you'll soon get really good at this.

Defining idea...

'We can never judge the lives of others, because each person knows only their own pain and renunciation. It's one thing to feel that you are on the right path, but it's another to think that yours is the only path.'
PAULO COELHO, *author*

Defining idea...

'Before you judge a man, walk a mile in his shoes. After that, who cares? He's a mile away and you've got his shoes.'
BILLY CONNOLLY, *comic and actor*

See – it's a great approach to finding leverage for what you want. Granted, like most things, it may need a bit of practice but it's worth the effort. You'll be amazed at how quickly you can begin to 'see' the other point of view, and how quickly you can realise how one 'crazy' perspective can seem perfectly sane to another person.

Plus, of course, it'll help you to be seen as a person who respects the view of others, which will make it even easier to have it your way.

20. Become a people wizard

People are so, so different. Understanding that fact helps you to become a wizard at reading them. That's important when working to get your way.

Unless you're one of truly identical twins, everybody in the world will approach a challenging situation differently to you. To influence them you need to tap into their way of working.

An easy way to get into a mess when influencing is to assume people will see 'our logic'. Of course, you see it as logical to start saving now so you can get on the property ladder. Unfortunately, your boyfriend sees it as logical to splash out and enjoy life now.

People see things differently. It's odd that answers we think will be common to all of us – i.e. an 'obvious' or 'right' way to approach a problem or a 'logical' way to sort it out – don't really exist. You've probably noticed this when, perhaps, discussing a film with a friend: you were insistent that the hero shouldn't have done something but your buddy has disagreed. How on earth did they see it that way?

Here's an idea for you...

Take a sheet of paper and jot down the names of some people you find it very hard to influence: your dad or that builder who is brilliant at his job but will never budge on prices. Against each name, write down what annoys you so much about them – e.g. their stubbornness, procrastination …. Take a long, hard look at the list. Notice anything? Yep, it's normally a summary of our own weak points! Recognise these and you'll suddenly open the flood-gates to easier discussions. Something to think about and something to act on.

Imagine you're trying to sell your car. To influence the potential purchaser, you'll need to notice whether they look at colours and feel the seats or whether they are interested in engine size.

Think about the person you want to influence. Let's assume you know them well – your mum, your boss … How do they influence themselves? How does your mum decide on something? She likes to stop; mull it over for a while. What about your boss? He likes to create a table of pros and cons. And your youngest sister, Rebecca? She'll be on the internet, checking out blogs and chat-rooms to see what 'real people' (as she puts it) think.

Your four-year-old, David, likes it when you sweep him up in your arms and influence with bounce and energy – the last thing he wants is a logical lecture. Funnily enough, though, that's just the way your six-year-old nephew likes to be handled – a nice 'adult' conversation.

All very well, you say, although it is true you hadn't quite thought about it like that before. But what about people you don't know? The used-car salesperson from whom you want two hundred off the price of that second-hand people-carrier. The jobsworth at the swimming pool who refuses to give your son a student-priced ticket. Well, idea 1: ask someone who knows them. Idea 2: try one way to communicate, then try another – write, then talk on the phone, then a face-to-face visit.

Defining idea...

'I did it my way.'
FRANK SINATRA – *a powerful idea for all of us to try living up to*

You can do this more formally if you like. Draw – yes, draw! – the faces of two people you want to influence: say, your mum over some of your career ideas and, say, the car salesperson about a price. Around each face write every way you know of that they are influenced. For instance, with your mum: mull it over, quiet cup of tea, what your dad says. With the used-car salesperson, the garage receptionist hinted that he might be more amenable if you could give him some leads to other business. Finally, turn those thoughts and comments into what you need to do:

Mum. Introduce the idea over a friendly chat and cup of tea. Mention a relevant article from Hello magazine and Dad's views. Leave it with her a few days.

Used-car salesperson. Tell him you could put his card up at the community centre with a flattering comment about how helpful he was in exchange for the extra discount.

21. Before you act, rehearse

Tricky conversations are much easier when we've said it all before. Practise as you are driving to meet your boss; say everything you need to get off your chest.

As they say, practice makes perfect. However, that's not going to be helpful advice when you may only have one chance at the real thing – and you don't want to mess it up.

When you have been in a situation before, you tend to handle it better. Remember your first trip to the bank manager's office after you'd just started your business? Yes: your nervousness showed, but you're much more confident these days. Remember your first date? How about your first driving lesson? You were hardly at your best in those two situations, understandably.

Here's the sort of challenge we're talking about:

- one meeting with the MP to get the speed reduced from 50 to 20 in your local area
- one meeting with the farmer about his cattle wandering into your garden at night

- one chance to get the neighbours to cut down the overhanging branch
- one chance to get an injection of capital for our business expansion

- one chance to convince the HR director of the viability of our job-share proposal.

We have got to get it right, and get it right first time.

So, we will do the next best thing to having done it before: we will do what good actors do – rehearse. A top actor wouldn't go out on stage expecting it to go well without rehearsal. A football team would not expect to play a tough game brilliantly without some practice training. Why should we be different? If our brain and body have been there before, we are much more likely to be successful. We need to rehearse what we're going to say, how we are going to move, how we are going to react. And we can do that at almost any time: so let's start.

As mentioned, we need to rehearse two main things: words and body. It's best to practise them separately at first and then combine them as in a real meeting.

> **Here's an idea for you...**
>
> You need about twenty minutes alone in a room. Think about the influencing situation you will be in. Now stand or sit, and practise saying what you need to say. You'll probably find your mobile phone has a simple record facility, so try recording yourself and see how it sounds. If a long wall mirror is available, that would be brilliant. Stand taller/sit taller and notice how much more confident you feel. Perhaps you should practise the opening hand-shake if it's a commercial situation you face – hold your body as you will hold your body when you have the interview for the director's job.

Defining idea...

'Acting is not about being emotional, but being able to express emotion.'
KATE REID, *actor with the Royal Shakespeare Company*

Firstly, words. With words, think about which word/s you will use. For example, you want a 'market rate' (a nice neutral, non-emotional commercial term) for your salary rather than 'a bl**dy decent salary increase'. Or 'more time to plan' rather than 'fewer tasks thrown at me'. Then think about the tone you use. Use a tone that sounds 'can do' rather than 'complaining'; 'professional' rather than 'little girl' or 'laddish'.

Secondly, body. Start with great maintained eye contact and support that with an 'open' body language (no folded arms); top it up with standing up or sitting up straight as appropriate.

Now, bring the two together. Imagine coming out of the lift. Waiting in the MD's reception area. Getting up gracefully. Shaking hands. Declining, politely, with a smile, a cup of coffee. Sitting comfortably on the slippery leather sofa. Making good eye contact and sharing a few pleasantries before easily moving into some 'serious concerns you have about the way female managers are treated in the company', opening your notebook and quoting a few facts. Stay open when the MD's language and tone become dismissive. Stand up and move to his white-board to explain things in more detail and allow you a stronger body language position. Look him in the eyes in a non-hostile manner but insist on some follow-through action.

22. How to give incentives

Most people will do anything so long as you give them a 'why' that's big enough. And that's what great influencing is about: giving a really big why.

To come up with incentives that ensure you will have it your way, you need to get into other people's heads and understand what motivates them.

Of course your boss doesn't want to give you a salary increase: that increase has got to come from somewhere else. And if you get an increase, the danger is everybody else will want one.

Of course your son doesn't want to stay in revising for his exams. Nobody else is doing it yet and consequently he is going to look very un-cool if he does so.

So, your challenge when influencing is to identify a big enough 'why'. Why your boss should give you that increase; why your son should stay in. Why she should go out with you. Why he should move out again. Why the gas board should give you a refund. Why the family holiday should be Spain and not Devon this year. What we are searching for is an answer to the question, 'What's in it for me?' (WIIFM?) – and that answer needs to be: 'Plenty!'

Here's an idea for you...

Think of the whys that will get the others to go along with you in your current influencing situation. Then practise 'chaining' them – just keeping using another 'and'. For example, the reason the church will allow us to use their fete area is: Many of us attend the church *and* ... We are offering to make a large donation to church funds *and* ... We will repair one of the fences in the field free of charge *and* ... We will write a nice article about how helpful the vicar has been.

That's how to find a great why. We think about what's in it for them, from their perspective: the winning answer to 'WIIFM?'. Here are some examples (and notice how we 'chain' the process).

Why should my boss give me an increase? What's in it for him? He gets to keep me; that means he keeps my experience; that experience is getting more and more valuable; it's getting harder and harder to find such experience on the open market; he's actually saving a lot of money by giving me an increase.

Why should Joe stay in and do exam revision? What's in it for him? He gets to feel more confident with the material; he reduces stress and he increases his chances of success; he may be less cool now but he will be more cool later when he gets that job at the BBC he really wants because of the excellent qualifications he has.

Why should Tom's school allow him to do both music and design, which is a major clash on the timetable? Well, firstly, you will keep him at the school rather than transfer him to somewhere that can cope with this subject mix. But also, you'll ensure that an article appears in the local paper about the school's amazing flexibility.

Why should the builder give you a refund? After all, there's nothing in writing that says you asked him to use the cheaper tiles behind the cupboards. You don't threaten him with a solicitor's letter but say that you will continue to recommend him to all of your contacts in the area. Also, you can give him a nice bit of extra work rebuilding the garden wall, which you'd been thinking of leaving to someone else.

Remember the foundations of a good 'why' are often:

- Money: making more
- Time: having more
- Life: being less stressful
- Relationships: closer, more loving
- Business: quicker, easier
- People: better reputation, higher status.

Search for anything you can offer that focuses on these as a starting point.

And one final point. In general, our answer to 'WIIFM?' should be positive, but sometimes – and with great care – it can be worth highlighting the negatives if the change is not made. If you don't do your revision you'll get poor results, which means you won't get to work at the BBC.

> *Defining idea...*
>
> 'But after observation and analysis, when you find that anything agrees with reason and is conducive to the good and benefit of one and all, then accept it and live up to it.'
> BUDDHA

23. Handling your boss

*You may think the boss holds all the cards —
after all, he can fire you. But that's not the
whole story. You can influence your way to what
you want.*

You want to work part-time. They won't allow that: apparently, it's not company policy. Yes, you can, though. That's what this brilliant idea is about.

Once upon a time, the employer held all the power. Employees couldn't do anything for fear of losing their jobs. In the twenty-first century, that's no longer true. And this isn't to suggest in the cynical sense that so much of the legal system is now stacked against the employer that you can get away with murder. No, the situation has changed in a healthy and positive way for you.

Read this carefully and believe it: there are simply not enough great employees around. Think about it: the last bank you went into – what were the staff like? How about the restaurant where you ate last week, or your daughter's school? What are the people like there? Quite.

There really is a shortage of excellent people for employers to choose from. So that's where we will start. Delay the influencing you need to do to get the change you want and start to shine like a great employee. Here's the deal: if you're a great employee, you cannot be replaced (or at least it is very hard to do so). That means you will be listened to and it means you have a good chance of getting what you want: you have become a fantastic influencer. Clever, huh?

No sane employer gets rid of great employees. Hence, great employees are good influencers. Start your influencing career by deciding to be excellent; deciding to be great.

But perhaps you think, 'Why should I? I am not paid enough to be excellent.' That's partly the point. Or maybe you think you will be excellent when you get the team leader's position. This is the trick most people miss: just be excellent for yourself. Nobody can take it away from you and, when you are, people want you. That's when you get listened to and you have your say.

> ## Here's an idea for you...
>
> We know that great employees get what they want so analyse what makes a great employee. It's someone who has a 'can do' approach (*what can we do to get this policy to work?*), someone who is brilliant at the basics such as time management (*arrives at meetings on time*), someone who is customer service focused (*smiles and empathises when dealing with people*), someone who builds rather than destroys ('*it would have been good to have had more notice, but we didn't, so what can we do instead?*'). You're good at all of those, aren't you? Imagine what would happen if you became great at them. As you now realise, it's only one decision away.

If you're thinking you shouldn't have to raise your standards and you should simply have the right to go part-time, then you're not going to get very far with your ambition. It's the wrong mindset. If instead you decide to begin to enjoy getting better at the work and consequently do a great job, you will be recognised and you will start to get more of what you want: the corner office, then the promotion. And all without consciously influencing. It's a self-fulfilling prophecy.

Defining idea...

'It is one of the strange ironies of this strange life [that] those who work the hardest, who subject themselves to the strictest discipline, who give up certain pleasurable things in order to achieve a goal, are the happiest people.'
BRUTUS HAMILTON, *US athlete*

Once you're an excellent employee, you'll have the boss's ear and that's when you can go for the jugular. Make sure you do it professionally, though. For instance:

- get hard data for the changes you want (e.g. current salary ranges for your job)

- book proper time for proper discussion and make sure you're fully prepared (e.g. to explain how the more flexible hours will help your child-care arrangements but won't alter your effectiveness)

- build a relationship that fosters adult-to-adult conversation (i.e. don't allow yourself to be bullied)

- respect the challenges your boss has, so fight the important battles.

24. Ask, don't tell

Asking questions puts you in control. It gets the other person thinking differently and gives you thinking time — just what you want when you're trying to influence them.

We can't influence people if they don't digest our ideas properly and therein lies a problem. That person will possibly be resistant to our ideas and also too busy to hear us.

… Possibly distracted, too. Possibly tired as well. And possibly they're not sure whether they like us, or even whether they can trust us. So, how on earth do we get them to give us time so they can absorb the wisdom we have to offer? Easy: more *asking* and less *telling*. It works every time.

Although it seems obvious to tell people stuff – '… so here are three reasons why you should buy from us …'/'… so, as I was saying, the current leasing arrangements must change because …'/'… when you start at university, you should …' – they only really digest that information if they trust us and they have a bit of time to reflect. However, when we are trying to influence someone, we may not have developed trust and they may well be short of time.

Here's an idea for you...

Think of the 'tells' you want to get across. Before you deliver them, jot them down on the left-hand side of a sheet of paper: (1) You need to give me a refund! (2) You need to decide between her or me! (3) We must move house! On the right-hand side, turn them into 'asks': (1) What do you think would be an appropriate level of refund considering the problems you have caused me? (2) How do you think I feel, being unsure of where your affections lie? (3) What do you think we can do to get more space now the children need their own rooms? Deliver the 'asks' and you'll be one step ahead before you really get started.

A simple and effective way to overcome this challenge is to ask questions. When we ask a question, it causes someone to pause; it causes them to reflect; and, importantly, the process of asking questions ensures someone feels more respected, which gives the natural opportunity to build trust. Compare these:

- A reasonable rent is 1500 (tell). Did you decide that 1500 is a reasonable rent? (ask).

- It's disgusting the way you leave the flat in such a mess (tell). How do you think I feel when I get no help with tidying? (ask).

- You must do more revision (tell). What do you think makes the difference between an A and an A*? (ask).

The former has lower impact. The latter has higher impact. The former simply reinforces the natural resistance to us being influenced. The latter gets us to 'wake up' and think about the issue in a different way. 'Ask' treats people in a more 'consultative' manner; treats them as adults; treats them with respect; and appears less dictatorial. It's not magic, of course, but it's a brilliant idea to add to your influencing portfolio; it's another approach that increases your chances of success in having it your way.

A further bit of fine-tuning you can do is to remind yourself of something you intuitively know, but you also know is often forgotten in the heat of a big influencing discussion. There are questions that are *open* and there are questions that are *closed*.

Defining idea...

'A definition is the start of an argument, not the end of one.'
NEIL POSTMAN, *US media critic*

Open questions encourage conversation – 'So, how will you raise the deposit, do you think?' 'What are you really looking for in your next financial adviser?'

Closed questions angle for a simple 'yes' or 'no' answer or a one-word response – 'How much money do you have to spend on a new car?' 'Will you resign if you don't get your salary demand?'

Both types of question are powerful when you begin to use them deliberately rather than accidentally. They can get you to the decision you want more quickly.

25. Dress the part

It's not that 'power-dressing' will win you the discussion, but dreary dress-sense could damage your credibility. It's worth working on this.

It won't take big money, or mean changing who you fundamentally are. Just a few easy-to-implement ideas will make sure you look the part.

Of course you should be able to express your individuality and of course it shouldn't matter, but wouldn't you:

- Think again about offering a salary increase to a key 'customer-facing' employee who was wearing a badly stained tie?
- Be unnecessarily distracted by a particularly short skirt when having a discussion about marketing strategy?
- Wonder why he's wearing odd socks with his sharp business suit?
- Think the lashings of perfume and extravagant hair-do was more suitable for a day at the races than a serious discussion about her ability to act as an executive coach?
- Be surprised that a wannabe reporter didn't have a pen to hand?

Yes, thought so. We're not saying it's fair: we're suggesting you should be pragmatic.

It's all about balance. Of course the influencing process can be well supported by what you wear. A smart suit to your business start-up discussion with the bank manager sounds ideal. Dress-down V-neck jumper and chinos on the shop-floor to talk to the warehouse staff about their demands seems perfect. Slacks and loose linen shirt to Friday's brain-storming off-site: excellent, just the right tone. And so on.

But don't take it too far. The essential message is that your appearance should support and not distract from your overall message. Consider the following. None can be absolutes of course, but they are worth considering.

These can help (for a man) and are often given insufficient attention.

- Great hygiene, especially hair (even more especially if it's long).
- Think very carefully about designer stubble. If you're a well-established designer/rock-star/male model, great. Everybody else: get a close shave.
- Suit and tie. If you're not a natural with dress-sense, at least find out which is the best colour for your build: e.g. grey or navy blue. And make sure it's pressed. Then get an interesting tie, but nothing from the joke shop.
- Polished shoes. Shoe care is definitely a common oversight.
- If casual, clean chinos, polo shirt, V-neck jumper and/or blazer can work well.

Here's an idea for you...

Try this, and you might even get away with it as a discussion in the pub. If you wanted to influence certain people and the 'first pass' of influencing would be a photograph of you, what clothes should you be wearing? Start with well-knowns such as Bill Gates, Richard Branson. Add a few of your own. Notice what people argue about ('no – simply because he's Richard Branson, that doesn't mean you could wear jeans') and what they do agree about ('yeah, okay, we'll agree on that – smart suit but no tie for Branson'). It will open your eyes to the huge breadth of appearance issues people notice.

Defining idea...

'Do not trouble yourself much to get new things, whether clothes or friends ... Sell your clothes and keep your thoughts.'
HENRY DAVID THOREAU, *poet and essayist*

These can hinder (for a man):

- T-shirts. Only in the right environments (young/technical/not customer-facing).
- Torn jeans. Never!
- Tired suits. Never!
- Oily ties. Never!

These can help (for a woman):

- Simple: clean lines and non-fussy.
- Zero or minimal jewellery. Ditto for perfume.
- Colours that flatter your hair, shape and complexion. If you don't know, get advice.

These can hinder (for a woman):

- Too short a skirt.
- Too revealing a top.
- Too tight an outfit.
- Too low a trouser band.

Plus try and get some variation on the 'easy' black city suit worn almost everywhere every day in some environments.

Remember that your appearance is not just about your clothes. The following can also reveal a lot about you: your pen, your notebook, your briefcase/bag, your purse/wallet. We've sometimes had these things so long that we have forgotten they are looking a little tired. And the shabby wallet bulging with receipts probably doesn't reflect a mind dedicated to organisation.

26. Just give them the facts

If in doubt, get the facts. If doubt creeps in again, return to the facts. Then you'll succeed. You need to learn what the relevant facts are and how to get them.

Influencing has two ingredients: facts and emotion. Both play a big part in helping you get what you want. Let's get good at the facts part.

What are facts: facts are your evidence. The bigger, better and stronger they are, the more likely you are to have it your way. If you then overlay a good emotional story, too, you are on to a winner.

- If you want a 4% pay increase and you can show that other people in a similar position have received such an increase … well … your influencing will be easier.

- If you want to influence your partner, who has recently had a heart attack, to reduce fat in their diet and you are able to produce four recent, well-documented studies that show categorically how fat reduction in the diet is essential … well … your influencing will be easier.

- If you want to influence your business partner on the sales and marketing benefits of starting a blog, you need data, hard facts.

Here's an idea for you...

When presenting facts as part of your influencing, ensure that your language and tone reinforce the fact that it is a fact you are presenting. Quoting a supporting reference can be effective here. You could say, 'We should be reading to the children every night if we want to help them in the long term, rather than letting them watch the TV until it's time for bed.' But you'll add impact if you can add validation: 'It says in *New Scientist* that children's linguistic skills are improved by reading bedtime stories with them. Don't you think we should do that more with our kids and turn the TV off earlier?'

You get the point. But where do you get the facts from? The good news is that now, with the internet, it's really easy. But that's not even the full story. Here are some great sources for facts.

The internet. Search engines such as Google and MSN Search will rapidly bring up pages and pages of information – sometimes way too much. Try using 'advanced search' facilities to reduce the amount of information produced. Online reference sources are available from specialised sources for your own field/s, as well as general encyclopaedias such as Encyclopaedia Britannica and Wikipedia. Much comment has been made about how a lot of info that's available on the internet is not fully validated, nor assembled by people with proper research backgrounds. That's probably very true. However, the internet does allow rapid cross-referencing so that concern can probably be ignored.

Other people. Whatever the subject on which you need data, there will be other people you know who know what you need. And you can ask them questions: How do you defend your price? What does your landlord charge you? How on earth did you convince your boyfriend to reduce booze expenditure? What made your company start recycling seriously? The key thing here is that during any later influencing process you need to be able to avoid the explicit or implicit accusation that, 'of course the facts would say that – you obtained them'. So, choose a large, random sample of people and keep all of the records.

> *Defining idea...*
>
> 'All we want are the facts, ma'am.'
> DRAGNET

Formal data gathering. Of course, there are occasions where the data you need – e.g. the specific benefits of recycling for your organisation or the impact of product withdrawal for your company – are not available in the public domain and so commissioning a research company might be a good solution. In this case, the important thing is to 'reverse engineer' what you are looking for. For instance, 'We need data to convince the board of directors that environmentally beneficial packaging materials are now essential. They will be concerned about the cost increase, which for the first year is significant. So we need data that show the increased cost will be compensated for by (1) specific extra sales, (2) a better public image within the first twelve months and (3) a gain of market share in the long term. So, what questions do we need to ask?'

27. Listen – really listen

Why isn't your influencing working? What are their objections? Listen carefully and you will understand. Then you'll get a better chance of having it your way.

What exactly is their point of view? Why are they so resistant? Why don't they seem to be able to 'get it'? If you hear what they're saying, you'll figure it out.

Have you ever become thoroughly fed-up with someone in a discussion, especially if it's getting really heated and turned into a full-blown argument? Did you say, 'You're not listening to me?' It's so frustrating, because we know that if only they'd listen properly, we would get that breakthrough essential to what we want to achieve.

But, of course, not only are they not listening to us, *we are not listening to them*. The more passionate we are about the subject we are discussing, the closer we are to the reasons for influence and the more the dangers of not listening.

The influencing process has to be a two-way thing: we tell, they listen; they tell, we listen. We comment on each other's views; we refine our views; we come to an agreement.

So, to be a good influencer, we have to be good listeners. How do we become better listeners?

- Informally you can just try this: write LISTEN in block capitals at the top of every page in your influencing note pad. Acting as a constant reminder, it can work surprisingly well.

- More formally, you can agree to take it in turns to explain your side of the story, with the proviso that neither of you interrupts until the other has finished speaking.

- More formally still, the above process can be followed by the requirement that the listener 'explains back', to the speaker's satisfaction, what he/she has just said. This latter process, it has to be said, seems easy but it's actually very hard. However, it is an amazingly powerful technique. Much conflict resolution and excellent influencing can be carried out by 'listening to understand'.

- Taking breaks is another important strategy. As we discuss, influence and argue, we get tired and, often, stressed. Both states make us poorer listeners.

- Remove distractions such as incoming e-mail prompts, open-plan environments, other people talking at the same time, personal worries.

- Prepare for the discussion so it does not take you long to 'acclimatise' to what is being said. Read any briefing notes carefully ahead of time and plan out your case. Don't forget the personal preparation – take a breather beforehand to clear your head.

> **Here's an idea for you...**
>
> Enhance your listening skills whenever you can. If you're in a face-to-face situation, really observe the other person's face rather than taking loads of notes, or looking at PowerPoint slides or your laptop. On the phone, take key-point notes by making a point of asking for 'explain back' confirmation – 'have I got this right?'. Both of these techniques will make you a better listener.

Defining idea...

'Two ears and one mouth: that's the ratio in which they should be used.'
EPICTETUS, *in essence*

How do you get them to become a better listener?

● By being a better listener yourself – your behaviour will influence them.

● By asking them to listen and 'explain back' at regular intervals.

Try this as a useful skill-development exercise with a friend to help him/her prepare for some important influencing they need to do – or, if you are in business, with a team in which you can get people to pair up.

Either way, choose a topic over which the sides differ (or if it is a team exercise you might give out differing business views: a classic one, of course, is company view versus customer view). In each pairing the speaker has a timed four minutes to explain their view. During that time, the listener cannot interrupt; he or she must just listen. At the end the listener needs to explain it back – to the speaker's satisfaction. Things to look for are:

● *Essential details:* did they mention in what way the product was broken, how long they had been waiting, whose birthday it was?
● *Any subtle points:* what was their real worry?
● *Timing of explanation compared with the original 4 minutes:* what ratio; did they just take two minutes, for example?

The exercise can be made more sophisticated with the use of a tape-recorder for 100% accuracy and/or a third person as an impartial observer. It's great fun and really helps develop everyone's listening skills immensely.

28. Be a networker

Of course you know about teamwork, but what about the extended team? The network? Networking isn't just jargon; it's an essential part of any MBA course.

Here's how to choose, manage and profit from your network.

What is a network?

Your network is a collection of individuals who have in common the fact that you know them all through business (one or two might be social friends, too), you enjoy their company and they have skills and/or contacts which may well be useful to you at some stage. Equally you have something to offer them, and you are all interested in becoming more effective and supporting each other. A great network is based – as you'll see – on abundance thinking, not manipulation.

What's the big deal?

Business is tough enough; why not increase every possible chance you can to be more successful? An easy one is to make more use of the great people you meet on a regular basis, all of the time. Your network – well managed – can get you business, get you jobs, find you staff, warn you about scams, help you with great tips… so how do you make a successful network?

Here's an idea for you...

When you meet people, make an effort to be interested in them; find out what they do. Ask if you can stay in touch and add them to your network. They may become an important player, they may not; at this stage it doesn't matter. What does matter is that it is very easy to meet great potential people for your network but, through lack of attention, lack of effort or too much politeness (or even fear), you lose them. Is it pushy to keep in contact? No, only if you act that way. Do it with politeness and most people will be fine about it.

Stage 1: capture your network

This is one of those enjoyable pencil and paper exercises. Grab those. If you can, finding a sheet from a flipchart pad would be great; if not, take a minute or two to stick four A4 sheets together to make an A3 sheet (that's a large rectangle). Right – here's the enjoyable and intriguing part. Keep the writing small; if you can, be patient and print. Put your name in the centre, then draw radiating lines to the names of people you know. This will probability grow organically, with the people with the closest relationships and whom you know best being most adjacent to your own name. Keep thinking and capturing until you feel you have your network – everybody you know – documented. Now add the name of any person that someone on your network knows and whom you would also like to get to know. Now add the names of anybody you are aware of that you would like to get to know, and add them to your network.

Stage 2: formalise your network

Choose a pre-packed networking tool – there are many – or simply type your contacts into a database, recording their names accurately with all the contact details you have. Add a personal note to all of them; you may remember them at the moment, but maybe not in a year's time. So add a personal note such as 'chatted to him for about an hour at Toronto airport while delayed in snowstorm, works at Starbucks, was worried about his daughter's choice of university'. Finally create a prompt which will encourage you to contact the person concerned and decide the level of frequency of contact. I suggest either once a month, once a quarter or twice a year.

Stage 3: ignite your network

Start working through your contacts. Some, of course, you will currently be working with but with the others look for opportunities to contact them, to help them and to support them. For those with whom you have – as yet – had no direct contact, but where you would like to be able to initiate conversation, write being honest: 'I recently read your book and have been fascinated by your blog and I thought the following might be of interest to you…'

Stage 4: be abundant

The key to getting your network to work is to just help and not look for any immediate return. Think 'New Age' if you wish and call it karma; be scientific and call it Newton III. Either way, what goes about does (sometimes after a very long route, agreed) tend to come back. And that's the fun. Be abundant and send all sorts of things: ideas, clippings, links, details of a book you've read, a contact, a postcard from a fascinating place, details of a job, a request to tender for business – whatever.

29. Become fluent in body language

We all intuitively know that there's more to communication than just the words. Great influencers use eye contact, facial expressions and posture to back up what they say.

This is known also as body language, or more formally non-verbal communication (NVC). How we use it can help or hinder our overall communication.

Have you ever been in a discussion with someone, trying to resolve an issue, working hard at influencing, and they never smile? Makes you feel uncomfortable, doesn't it? Or did they sit there, leaning back with folded arms? Infuriating, isn't it? Or when they talked to you did they use their pen to point at you? Rude, isn't it? You have experienced body language at its worst. It might be deliberate; it might be unconscious. Either way it is not helping the discussion.

On the other hand, occasional smiles at appropriate times can make the whole discussion seem more amicable, even if at the moment there doesn't seem to be much common ground. Turning to face the person and keeping arms and hands open just seems more welcoming, as do slower, gentler gestures.

The bottom-line message is: whatever you say verbally will be reinforced by appropriate body language or weakened by the wrong kind.

Here's what will help:

- *Smiling*. This indicates a willingness to work together.
- *Open gestures* (e.g. open palm). This indicates an openness to ideas.
- *Eye contact*. This says I'm listening; I'm attentive.
- *Turning 'square on' to fully face the person*. This reinforces your willingness to reach an agreement.
- *Slower gestures*. This indicates that something is considered important.

Here's what will probably hinder:

- *No expression, or frowns*. This may indicate: I don't like you and/or the idea/s.
- *Pointing*. This may indicate a 'you and me' feeling rather than 'us'.
- *Avoiding eye contact/always looking at notes or laptop*. This says: I'm not interested in your views.
- *Sitting at an angle when talking*. Says: I'm deliberately keeping 'separate' from your ideas.
- *Punctuated gestures*. Indicates impatience: let's just get this done.

Try this exercise. For each of the following situations, state the worst and best NVC. Don't think about it; do it. Don't read ahead until you have done all of them.

Here's an idea for you...

At your next influencing situation, think as much about your non-verbal communication as you do your verbal and do two things. First, choose NVC that reinforces your message (e.g. open palms to show you are open and listening rather than clenched fists). Second, ensure your NVC is in line with your verbal communication (e.g. your movements are slow – rather than fast and punctuated – to match your slower, considerate voice).

Defining idea...

'I speak two languages: body and English.'
MAE WEST

1. Sitting in the head teacher's office waiting for her to return so you can discuss your daughter's apparent repeated wearing of a too-short skirt.

2. Speaking on the phone with the bank, who have charged you a massive unauthorised overdraft fee.

3. Walking up to the girl in accounts who you get on really well with and asking her if she would like to go out for a meal with you.

How did you do? In situation 1, helpful NVC would be to stand as she returns (not out of respect, out of confidence) and greet her with a firm hand-shake; smile; sit, ideally to the side of the desk, and maintain good eye contact. It would hinder to stay seated with a hunched posture (suggesting you're passive/fearful); or sit with arms folded and point (suggesting aggression). Sitting 'perched' on the desk would make you appear intimidating.

In situation 2, it helps to stand, and walk around if you can. Look up. Feel good and in control. It hinders to sit in a hunched position and remain still. That way, you feel vulnerable. For situation 3, walk slowly and steadily up to the girl. Keep good eye contact and smile. Ask clearly and gaily, then pause and wait for her response. Don't shuffle up to her, avoiding eye contact or staring at the floor. Don't stand to one side of her. Don't speak quickly with a tone that sounds like you expect her to say 'no'.

30. Be polite and be persistent

Whatever happens, if you can maintain a decent relationship with the person you want to influence, that'll give you the best chance of having it your way in the end.

If you're rude to people, they're not likely to give you the time of day. That's why you should be polite and be persistent. It is a winning formula every time.

● It's ridiculous! The salesman said you would get 500 free texts on your phone, but your bill shows you have not had that allowance. Trying to get some sense out of these people is like pulling teeth … and the number of people you have spoken to … *But*, should you have shouted at that last guy who finally answered your call and asked your password again?

● She's only your daughter's drama teacher, after all. Who does she think she is saying your daughter has very little talent for acting? *But*, should you have walked off in a huff?

● And the bank … they spend millions, you presume, convincing you to borrow money. You then do, the economy gets a bit tight and they're over you like a rash … *But*, was it a good idea to be rude to that 'idiot' assistant manager?

Here's an idea for you...

Here's a quest for you for the coming week: strengthen the emotional bank account you have with the main person you are currently influencing. Make deposits in the usual way – do what you promise, be supportive, be on time, be respectful and listen to really understand – but then put a cherry on the cake. Be ever so, ever so nice. Be helpful (this does not mean weak; just helpful). Be charming. Notice how it is totally disarming and very profitable in having it your way.

Yes, doing what you did was understandable, but it's rarely fair to behave like that. After all, those people are just doing their jobs. And behaving like that rarely gets results – it makes them less likely to help you and simply gives you another stressful day.

So, what's to be done when people let us down, move too slowly, or don't enable us to get things the way we want? Well, don't let go of that frustrated energy. Harness it and use it in a different way. Channel it into two devastating forces: politeness and persistence. They are world-beating qualities to harness.

So, what does polite mean? Politeness is:

- Not raising your voice.
- Talking to the other person by name. ('So, Tim, how can I get a refund?')
- Not being sarcastic.
- Thanking the other person for every concession, however small. ('Sally, that's brilliant. Thank you.')
- Not threatening them. (You'll get an unproductive reception when you say, 'If you don't sort this, I will report you to your manager.')
- Being reasonable. ('Well, it's not ideal but I guess I will leave it at that.')

Basically, don't attack them; attack the problem. And if you make progress, make sure you acknowledge that step forward by thanking them. Sending a 'thank you' message will make the purr. Send a note to their manager saying how brilliant they were will be the cherry on the cake.

What does persistent mean? Persistence is:

● Keeping on asking for what is rightfully yours. ('Actually, Vip, as we agreed, I do want that corrected in writing.')
● Looking for that one someone who can help. ('Do you think your team leader could help?')
● Not taking 'no' for an answer. ('I'd like someone who could give me a proper answer to ring me back.')
● Keeping on writing and leaving messages.
● Keeping on trying but also keeping on trying in different ways.

Work with the other person's emotional bank account. Do the same as you would to keep the manager of your financial bank account happy. She likes it if you make regular deposits if you are going to make regular withdrawals (and more deposits than withdrawals!), and that you chat to her very carefully before making any unauthorised withdrawals.

Being rude is one such withdrawal but there are many others that can take you into the red. Avoid:

● Letting someone down
● Talking behind their back, negatively
● Being late and disorganised
● Making assumptions
● Judging before knowing/understanding.

Defining idea...

'True politeness is perfect ease and freedom. It simply consists of treating others just as you love to be treated yourself.'
4th EARL OF CHESTERFIELD

99

31. Learn the art of negotiation

Negotiate for everything! Your career will benefit in two ways. Negotiating to reduce your costs and increase your sales is good for performance, and this experience helps you practice for the most important negotiation of them all — your job and salary.

You better believe it, everything is negotiable. Negotiating is a part of our lives; we do it all the time. In fact we do it so often we probably don't realise that we are doing it.

If you have children you've probably already done some negotiation today. Imagine telling a child that anything at all is non-negotiable. Fat chance. You can learn a lot from watching children negotiate. They have no inhibitions, they are prepared to use the sanctions they have available to them and they are completely devoted to the present with no thought for the future. These are all negotiating skills we lose as we grow up.

Never go into any negotiation to 'see what they are going to say'. Prepare positively. If you're selling, look for reasons why the other person should see that your proposition has value, rather than why you should be allowed to maintain your price. In this context negative preparation is a disease with commission-based sales people. Try it out. Give a salesperson the authority to offer a 10 per cent discount, and every deal done from that day will have the discount deducted; that's their opening offer.

> **Here's an idea for you...**
>
> Ring up an internal department who supplies you with a service and complain about their prices. You are, after all their customer. If they say that the price is company policy, go higher up their organisation. Eventually you will get to someone who can vary prices. It may be tricky to steer such a change through the management accounting systems, but where there's a will there's a way.

Prepare all aspects, not just money

Think widely in negotiation. Look for objectives beyond, for example, price. What else could you get from the other party? Now put those objectives into priorities. You will have some objectives that you must achieve, some that you are going to work hard to achieve and some that would be nice to achieve. Now think of the other person's priorities in the same way. In fact think about all aspects of the person with whom you are about to negotiate. The more you understand them, the more likely you are to find a solution they will deem acceptable.

When you negotiate, you use your own flair as well as your company's rules. Managers like people who are entrepreneurial and who know that sometimes they need to walk over the company's normal business processes. Such entrepreneurs are regarded as good, but run the risk of upsetting others who play by the rules. Strike a balance here if you want to impress everyone.

Defining idea...

'Nothing is illegal if one hundred well-placed businesspeople decide to do it.'

Andrew Young, *US diplomat*

Listening is a key skill at the discussion stage. Look at it this way. If you listen more than you talk in a negotiation it almost certainly means that you know more about the other party than they know about you. This logically leads you to a solution that suits them. You already know the solution that suits you. The opposite of listening in negotiating is interrupting. When you interrupt someone you are telling them to shut up. You are demeaning their arguments and suggesting that they can't say anything useful to take the matter forward. Imagine if you told someone in so many words that nothing they can say is important. That's the message that interrupting gives.

2
Rocket to the top

Do better

Do better at the job you've got. Here are the ideas that will take your career from so-so to spectacular.

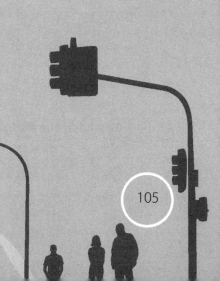

32. Take a pragmatic approach to work

Take a positive, practical but sceptical attitude to your organisation. Don't expect to spend your whole career in one organisation and don't trip over internal politics.

Are you in the right place? People are happier and work better when they can identify with the objectives of the organisation they work for.

It is hard to get up in the morning with energy and enthusiasm if you feel that your work contributes to something you couldn't care less about. Make sure you are working for an organisation that is doing something worthwhile and is likely to be successful. You are much more likely to build a career there.

If right now you're working towards a goal that neither interests you nor inspires you, you've got to make a change. It's up to you. Your career is a key element in your way of life and your general happiness; if you are in the wrong place get out of it.

You have our undivided loyalty until it doesn't suit us
Now let's look at the other side of the coin – the organisation itself. Your organisation is probably chaotic, either all the time, or sometimes, or in places.

This is both a problem and an opportunity for the career minded. This chaos means that whatever it says about looking after you and your career, your company may very well not be able to live up to its promises. Organisations, for example, have to take technological change on board if they are to survive even if it costs careers. In short, the organisation has to look after itself in a businesslike way, so you need to look after yourself in a similarly objective and professional way.

> **Here's an idea for you...**
>
> It is best for your boss to think that other people believe your good ideas are his. You, on the other hand, should ensure people know that your ideas and your boss's good ideas are both yours.

And circumstances change. A promise made to a member of staff in good faith may suddenly become impractical. In this environment the safest view to take of your organisation is that you owe it your loyal support only for as long as your objectives and the organisation's can co-exist. Career planning is now a question of a number of jobs rather than a simple progression up a single organisation. Companies don't offer jobs for life and most successful careerists will change employers from time to time. Keep an open mind and don't get so set in your ways that you get caught out by a reorganisation in which you find yourself 'Co-ordinator of Long-term Planning'. Such a post almost certainly means that you are no longer part of those long-term plans. I'm certainly not encouraging you to be dishonest yourself. But be warned that others are sometimes going to use 'their best intentions' to meet their obligations.

Career players take integrity very seriously. They do not, however, ignore the facts of the new world – the company man is extinct. The key phrase now is 'fluidity of labour'.

Defining idea...

'Success has many fathers, failure is an orphan.' Proverb

Nurture the politician within you

It is not possible for any organisation to exist without some form of internal politics. People often have conflicting agendas and objectives. Face it. Don't make a decision on behalf of an organisation without paying attention to what the implications are for you. If company politics permeate every decision that affects your career, you should face another brutal fact: *in company politics the competition is your colleagues*. After all, this is more than a matter of survival. The Vicar of Bray played his organisation's politics well and survived, but he never made it to bishop. My Dad, watching the politics that my mother got into in a small local church, was heard to murmur, 'The more I see of Christians, the more sorry I feel for the lions.' If the Church cannot avoid internal politics and strife, what chance has a capitalist corporation?

Defining idea...

'Except in poker, bridge and similar play period activities: don't con anybody. Not your spouse, not your children, not your employees, not your customers, not your stockholders, not your boss, not your associates, not your suppliers, not your regulatory authorities, not even your competitors.'
ROBERT TOWNSEND, *Avis CEO*

Finally

So, it's a question of 'us and them', or rather, remembering what we have said about your colleagues, of 'me and them'. Take responsibility for your own career, and work on the basis that no one else will.

33. Make good suggestions loudly

At any point in the chaos that describes your organisation, an opportunity can arise for you to make a sensible suggestion to the powers that be. Career people should grab such opportunities and actively seek them out.

The opportunities are legion. You've found an uncompetitive product feature, an outdated business process or an opportunity for new technology. Now's your chance to make sensible suggestions. Or think about publicity or sponsorship.

If you know the arts or sport preferences of the CEO, for example, you might just stumble across a local opportunity for sponsorship. If you make that happen, you can be sure the chief executive will be there for the event.

High-profile people get noticed, and the higher up the people doing the noticing the better. Form a plan for getting more than your fair share of senior management's attention, and then communicate your ideas clearly in a brief paper.

First make sure that your idea is in an area where the issues are being discussed at least two levels above you. Now put up your paper.

Here's an idea for you...

When did you last meet the most senior person in your building? If you are not based at the company's headquarters the answer to that question has to be at least in the last month. Take responsibility for this – do you know when you will next have an opportunity to meet senior people?

You'll soon realise how vitally important it is that your boss thinks you are top-notch, and that you help to make him or her look brilliant as well. And not only your boss, but also your boss's boss.

Make sure they can bear to read it

So, you have a good idea. Now think about the quality of the communication. Think through, for example, the level of detail your boss wants to read and hear. As you go up the organisation you find people who are capable of going into detail, but less likely to want to. In both written and oral communications, write clear, simple management summaries.

Once you have written your paper, try to shorten it significantly, say by half. Throw out anything except the essentials. Remember you want to have the opportunity to discuss it. If it is too comprehensive you may have given the thing lock, stock and barrel for someone else to dine out on. Release it effectively – in other words in the way that best serves your interests. After all, it was your idea.

A good paper may help in other ways as well. There are lots of conferences out there, and lots of organisers looking for people to read papers. Reading a paper anywhere abroad, for example, looks good on the CV.

Be creative in getting your ideas to the right people

To follow up your paper and for other reasons, there are many ways of communicating with the great and the good in your organisation outside the normal business environment. Volunteer for these. I don't mean volunteer for anything that has a low impact no matter how worthy. There is no point for the careerist in being a member of the St John's ambulance team at the local football ground. But there may be a point in being the fire officer for your floor. Check it out first. Does it get you in front of the Director of Logistics? Is there an opportunity to be a representative on the pension council? That's a high profile place.

Another promising area is promoting the company at sport by wearing the logo. If you are good at sport, senior managers will bask in your limelight. You will also come into contact with the people you are trying to impress if they come to the golf match you have arranged. Ask them to make a speech (and offer to help with some gags perhaps) and present the prizes.

Another good place to get your ideas known is the company newsletter, particularly if it involves interviewing senior people. Only speak at the Christmas party if you are really good at making people laugh. If being witty does not come naturally to you, speak at conferences where being amusing is a significant but secondary requirement.

> *Defining idea...*
>
> 'Think about the 4 C's, Continuous learning, Confidence in yourself, Care and attention to those you love and Communication – wherever you are, well-honed communication skills are highly important.'
> CHAIRMAN, *Scottish Power*

34. Taking problems to your manager

When does a member of a team get their boss involved in a situation? Answer: when there's a problem.

Once you've made it to first- and second-line management the colleague competition has thinned out a bit – that's the good news. The bad news is that the real no-hopers have mostly disappeared and standing out in the smaller crowd is a bit more difficult.

All your competitors have, at some point, impressed senior people with their achievements or just their bonhomie and charisma. You need a career-friendly approach to working with your boss and getting his or her support.

Houston, we have a problem

The best way to understand this idea is to think about second-line managers in the maintenance department of, say, a computer company. They actually only get involved with customers when all is far from well. They spend half their lives talking to customers who are beside themselves with rage and threatening to write to the newspapers.

This 'there's a problem business' happens to all managers and it's pretty demoralising continuously to receive briefings that turn out to be problems. It may come as a surprise to a lot of people but their bosses do not automatically know what to do in all circumstances. It happens at all levels. I have known Chairmen and other senior managers still showing frustration at the way people present them with information in problem form.

> **Here's an idea for you...**
>
> Take the most difficult customer problem you have at the moment. Is it the right time to bring your boss in, or is it too early, or too late? Can you get nearer to the solution before you bring him or her in? Is it worth doing a SWOT analysis to see if you can come up with a solution?

Crisis, what crisis?

There are the three ways of telling your boss that there is a problem:

Take the piece of information (say, a competitor that has brought out a new product or a big customer who has gone bust) to your boss and wait for her to give you instructions.

Analyse your company's position in the light of the information. A very good way of doing this is to use simple SWOT analysis – strengths, weaknesses, opportunities and threats. What are the strengths that your company could use to combat the turn of events? What are the weaknesses that will make an effective response difficult? What opportunities does the new situation offer, and what are threats to performance if nothing is done? This is a much better approach as far as your boss is concerned. It saves her time thinking the analysis through and makes it easier to make a decision. Watch your timing on this. If the problem is that a competitor has brought out a new product you have more time to weigh up the situation than if the customer has gone bust. But don't over-analyse and leave it

Defining idea...

'What we're saying today is that you're either part of the solution or part of the problem.'
ELDRIDGE CLEAVER, *American politician*

too late to tell your boss. Having said that, most people err on the side of going in too quickly where more preparation would have been useful.

Using the SWOT analysis, come to a conclusion. Think through a well-structured line of reasoning that supports your recommendation and present the solution rather than the problem.

Most people take the first approach, some the second but only a few the third. Think about it from the point of view of the manager whose daily lot it is to receive a continuous stream of problems. The people who present the solutions really do stand out in the crowd.

Finally

The help that your 'solutions not problems' approach gives to your boss does have a downside. She may disagree with your solution, or know a better one from experience. But if you never make a mistake you are not trying to add value. It's all part of taking responsibility.

As one manager put it, 'The corporate world is made up of two types of person, those who play the game and those who watch it. You can tell them by what makes them feel good. The watcher goes home fulfilled if they have worked hard and used their skills. They have performed their tasks. The players only feel good if they have accomplished something. They finish things. They don't pass the buck. Funnily enough it is the players who make most mistakes. The watchers can't, because if you are not playing, you can't lose. Mind you, you can't win either.'

35. Be in the right place

Organisations serve their shareholders. Organisations also often include a mixture of businesses. Some are high risk with the potential of high return; others are lower risk and are expected to return lower profitability. Make sure your career's in the right one.

Who's in charge here? A bit of background first. A company exists to serve its shareholders, so it's best to take their requirements into account in planning your career. They are the people who believed in the company enough to put their money in it; but in the end they want a return.

You need to be thoroughly familiar with how shareholders regard companies. This may seem unnecessary at middle levels in the organisation, but your bit of the organisation is, after all, part of the whole.

Shareholders choose investments based on, among other things, the level of risk involved. Someone speculating long term can afford to take on high-risk ventures. A retired person looking for relatively safe income will probably choose low risk. An important point here is that investors are not particularly keen on companies that are difficult to define in risk terms. As we'll see, this can enormously impact your career.

Here's an idea for you...

Look at the risk of any plan or project you are proposing. Does it fit the risk profile of your division or organisation?

Any idea you take to your boss, particularly when you need the company to invest money, must in some way pay attention to both risk and return. If your scheme does not make money and generate cash at some point, it is not aimed at the heart of the company's purpose. OK, I know it's the bleedin' obvious, but you should see some of the fanciful proposals I've seen. Finally, you must predict that the return will come at an acceptable risk.

Thinking about risk and return

Right, which bit of the business do you want to be in? Since you are career-oriented you would probably be best in that part of the business that is leading the field and making the most rapid progress. Ask yourself some key questions: where is growth happening, which division is most tied up with technology, where are the successful teams generating fame and fortune? If you are in that area already, look for opportunities to lead more growth. After all, it is the Derby.

Defining idea...

'Long range planning does not deal with future decisions. It deals with the futurity of present decisions.'
PETER DRUCKER, *management thinker and author*

If you are in the part of the business that's dragging the coal cart you are trying to be noticed in an area that people rarely bother to look at. It keeps delivering mundane profits and it provides good cash flows for the whizz-kids on the racehorses to speculate with; so senior managers are probably leaving well alone. There's another reason, too, for changing tack if you are in the cash cow. Think about the long-term fit of your division within the whole company – if they are looking to thrill the market they may sell your sort of business off or demerge it. In that way they can present a single risk profile to the shareholders rather than a confusing mixture.

Incidentally, if you are financially minded you can gauge the overall risk of your organisation by looking at the price/earnings ratio. If it's above, say, 20 it is an organisation that takes risks. If it is below 12 it probably doesn't much like high-risk projects.

Defining idea...

'It is just as easy to make a profit today as it will be tomorrow. Actions taken which result in reducing short-term profit in the hope of increasing long-term profit are very seldom successful. Such actions are almost always the result of wishful thinking and almost always fail to achieve an overall optimum performance.'
DAVID PACKARD, *computer company founder*

36. Act on decisions

If you have taken a decision and informed your boss of what you and your team are going to do, for your career's sake make absolutely sure it happens.

If you haven't started the action plan, you may as well not have made a decision.

I've a friend who's an elderly painter and decorator. His children have moved on and he now has no dependents. He does not want to retire altogether but he does want to have more time for himself; but he's finding it difficult to cut down the amount of work he does. Unfortunately for him he is brilliant at his job and a very nice chap to boot. This means that his old clients all turn to him when they want work done and he finds it difficult to say no. Plus, his relatives and friends have been used to asking him over, giving him good food and drink and getting him to do some decorating.

Over coffee one day he asked me what I meant when I murmured that a decision is not a decision until there is commitment to the action plan and the first steps are taken. I asked him what he wanted to do in the spare time he was trying to create, and he rather coyly admitted that he had decided to take up golf. He then tried to implement his decision. He resolved to take every Friday off to pursue this new hobby. Four weeks later he told me that he had not been able to do that once. I pressed him to commit to a lesson with the professional on the next Friday morning and another one that afternoon. We agreed that he would pay for the lessons in advance. This broke the deadlock and he started to play. He is now an addict and plays every Friday and quite often on other days as well – but it wasn't a decision until he'd gone into action.

Never disappoint the powers that be

Right, where is this stuff important? Most teams work with some operational targets that they need urgently to achieve. If your team is well organised you'll also have a strategic plan that includes a series of projects aimed at improving the environment in which you operate. If you implement these projects, life will become easier and performance will improve. Being career-minded you will, of course, have told your boss all about the changes the team is going to make – perhaps with a loud drum roll. But in the real world pressure is always on maintaining performance rather than developing new methods. In my experience a boss will ask three times how you are getting on with the new idea. The third time they hear your excuse that unfortunately there just has not been time to get it going, they will forget it and write you down as all mouth and no trousers.

Here's an idea for you...

Pick a team member who has difficulty with the 'do it now' concept. He tends to agree to a decision made by you, himself or the team, and then finds loads of reasons why he can't implement it. Sit him down and tell him the story of the painter. Now get him to take a decision he has been prevaricating over and put the actions into his diary. Phone him just before and just after he should have started to implement the decision.

Defining idea...

'Men of action whose minds are too busy with the day's work to see beyond it. They are essential men, we cannot do without them, and yet we must not allow all our vision to be bound by the limitations of men of action.'
PEARL S. BUCK, *American writer*

119

37. Know what to say to whom

A meteoric careerist can't have too much exposure to top people. Think hard about extending your senior contacts.

You happen to be in the lift with your Chairman, or a senior executive of a major customer. Make sure you know what you would say to them.

Most of us in such a situation are like rabbits caught in the headlights and blow this short window of time with small talk. There is a clue here for the careerist. But it's not just about the Chairman.

You can expand on this by dropping in on anyone. Hewlett Packard used to have a useful slogan, 'managing by wandering around'. It was a neat way of reminding managers that part of their job was to be around and meet people by chance as well as in formal meetings. I extended this to 'selling by wandering around', which meant using the same technique to cruise around customer premises making new, and preferably high-level, contacts. 'Cultivating your career by wandering around?' It's not as snappy but that doesn't mean that it doesn't work.

Plan your absences

Try to be in the office at the same time as your boss. After all, in your absence she might give an interesting and potentially rewarding opportunity to someone else. You need to know her diary so that you can plan your absences at times when she won't notice you're not there.

The clincher for how vital it is to know your boss's diary is that you will know when she is definitely far away. Believe me, there is nothing more embarrassing than being caught nosing around in someone else's files.

Obviously you want high-level exposure to things that go well. You also want cover against being held responsible for something going wrong. Short-sighted people with moderate ambitions keep a detailed record of their activities with a note of the people who supported them on the way. The more ambitious person with her eye on the big picture does it in such a way that the record can prove that others were completely responsible if it goes wrong. Don't forget to have a shredder handy if all goes well, though. It wouldn't do for you to enable someone else to take the glory.

> ### Here's an idea for you...
>
> If, for example, you know your boss's diary you'll know when she is going to be talking to a person you would like to meet. First, prepare. If you did get the opportunity, what would you say? So, you know what you would say; now engineer the opportunity to say it. The best way is simply to breeze in. 'Oh, I'm sorry I didn't realise…' 'That's all right,' says your boss, 'Come in and meet Lord so-and-so.' She will probably add more in terms of a quick description of what you do for the organisation, and that is your moment. 'As a matter of fact, Lord so-and-so, I've been thinking that we ought to have a brief word on…' Brilliant: a new contact – put it in the address book.

Defining idea...

'There is no stronger way of building a career than "working the corridors".'
RICHARD HUMPHREYS, *serial chairman*

'It's not how you play the game, but who you get to take the blame' goes the rhyme. This is the business version of the Olympic spirit. If you're involved with high-level operations it's generally not a good idea to be closely associated with failure. Stay clear of the firing line unless there are massive Brownie points for effort as opposed to achievement.

There is another way of looking at this if the cock-up is really huge. A person in charge of a substantial development project spent £50 million of his company's money on it and was, towards the end, powerless to prevent it having no impact on the business at all. The entire sum was completely wasted. Asked into his boss's office he pre-empted the inevitable by saying that he knew he was there to be fired. 'No way,' said his boss, a very aware woman, 'Now that we have spent £50 million on your learning what doesn't work, we are not about to throw that investment away.' It's a variant of the 'Owe your bank £1,000 it's your problem, owe it a million and it's theirs.'

38. Create your next job

It is a great mistake in career planning to assume that the current management structure is the one in which you have to succeed. Indeed the opposite is the case, when you move on, your old job description should be obsolete; and it's also a good idea to create a new one.

Rock the boat! Many jobs exist because they have always done so, not because they represent the best way of getting things done.

If you go into a job and do things the best way possible, you'll probably find that the original job description bears no relationship to what you are doing. You get results, but when you move on your boss will have to change the structure and job description in line with how you got things done.

Be subtle then savage – you want the job
Don't just abolish your old job. Create your next one. Managers who succeed are the ones who help to prevent the organisation ossifying by suggesting new roles and responsibilities, one role being the next job they want.

Here's an idea for you...

So use your influence and authority to get the best results possible without paying much attention to how things were done in the past. Most people just moan about the fact that 'they've got it all wrong', without attempting themselves to put it right. Again, the people who get to the top are the ones who take responsibility for their own actions. Keep saying to yourself that it is up to you.

Although it's easier to create a new job if the change will help the organisation achieve its objectives more effectively, it's possible to do it for purely selfish purposes. The creation of a new job is a two-part process. First, work out how to change the way of doing business so that the job has to exist. Now sell this idea. Show how the changes will benefit the business itself. If you reveal your hand at this stage there is a good chance that you are mistiming it by going too early. Don't give anyone the opportunity to say that what you are doing is for your own greater glory rather than the advancement of the organisation.

Having sold the change, produce your implementation plan and, of course, include the new positions required. Get everyone to agree the business benefits. Do not at this stage play the shrinking violet; clearly show that you are the person for the role you have chosen and defined. And tell people that you should have the job. Make sure the new job description has all the elements needed for the next step – access to senior management and a high profile when required. The risk and return on this career procedure will be very good if you have got it right. After all, you have moulded a job where the circumstances and your skills will be a perfect fit.

If you are really clever, or really lucky, creating a job can be a low-risk activity. Look for an opportunity where the business benefits would occur anyway, even if you went off on a cycling tour of Bolivia. From your inside knowledge you should be in the best position to understand this. An old Chinese proverb says, 'He who knows where the treasure is, needs no map.' Actually I just made that up, but you get the picture.

Defining idea...

When Henry Lewis was the CEO of Marks & Spencer, he was asked why, out of all the management trainees that he joined with, he had made it right to the top said 'You know, I really have no idea.' After some thought he added, 'But I have noticed that every job I have ever done has been abolished after I left it.'

A President of RCA is reported to have answered the question 'Why, when so many were called were you chosen?' with the opposite of Henry Lewis's remark. He also purported not to know but said, 'I have noticed that no job I ever did existed before I got it.'

6 ways to make your boss love you

- *Talk even when you don't have much to say about work.* Make the effort to communicate. Don't hide. Look for opportunities to chat about light stuff – it will make it easier when you have tough subjects to discuss.

- *Spread the good vibes.* Your boss needs strokes, too. Let them know how they have helped you with your job.

- *Praise where it's due.* When it's all going well, praise everyone who has contributed. This fosters a good team spirit, encourages your colleagues to do well, and by creating a good team, your boss looks good.

- *Never take them a problem without having a solution.* Even better have two solutions and let your boss choose. Being a problem solver rather than a serial whiner is the one way to make yourself stand out from the crowd.

● *Say no.* Occasionally. Bosses are human. Sometimes they respond to pressure by asking for more than can be done. Most of the time, give them what they ask for, but occasionally when it's ridiculous, be strong about what is possible and work with them on what is realistic in the time allotted.

● *Ask what your boss thinks of you.* Giving them the opportunity to give you constructive criticism makes their job easier and makes you seem strong. Find out fro them what you've done well and what you could have done better.

39. How to negotiate a pay rise

Salary is an important component of your brilliant career. It also defines one of the main boundaries of your lifestyle. Negotiate for more when the time is ripe. Make sure you are being paid at least what you are worth and preferably a bit more.

NEVER tell anyone your salary. Whatever you say will do you or them no good. Either it will be less than they thought, which diminishes their respect, or it will be more than they either expect or think you are worth. This leads to jealousy.

Keep the big picture in view. Particularly at the start of your career, keep in mind that the rewards of getting to the top are very substantial. Don't whinge about your early salary. Tell yourself that you are investing for the future. Agree to small or no rises and even no promotions for the first couple of years, then go for the big hike when you have something to argue with.

You might be better off doing an extra few months at 20k a year rather than causing grief by bellyaching. The eventual return could be well worth it.

I was working in a theatre once when an assistant stage manager did a bunk with the £100 she had been given to buy props. 'What a mug,' said a more seasoned ASM, 'If she had waited a bit longer she could have gone off with five times that.' So it is in business. It's only the people with no vision who fiddle their expenses for a couple of pints in the pub, or charge for a first-class train fare and sit in second. This is short sighted in many ways. After all, who do you need to impress who sits in standard class?

> **Here's an idea for you...**
>
> By using recruitment agencies, the internet and the HR department you should be able to work out the top and bottom ends of the sort of salary someone in your position gets. Now work out why you deserve to be in the top 25% of the band. When you have a good case, take it to your boss. If you are already in the top quartile, look for a promotion.

It's a lot about timing

When you are going into a new job make sure that they really want you to join them and preferably have told other contenders that the job is not theirs before negotiating the salary. Asking earlier has two disadvantages. First, you may discover that there is a big gap between their expectations and yours. At that time you are negotiating from a position of weakness, since they have not yet decided if they want you. Second, it makes you look a bit small if the salary is the only reason you're taking the job.

Whatever anyone tells you, you can ask for more money at any time. The key here is timing: ask when your value to the organisation appears very high. Do it when you have just brought off a big deal, or organised the district conference or made a useful suggestion for change. Focus on what you have done and what you will do in the future. Use simple techniques of negotiation like the 'It's only 10 a week rather than 520 a year.'

129

Defining idea...

'The salary of the Chief Executive of the large corporation is not a market reward for achievement. It is frequently in the nature of a warm personal gesture from the person to him or her self.'

J.K. GALBRAITH, *American economist*

The same timing works when you're looking for a promotion. Think, act and look as though you are already in the new job. Seek out, and go after, vacancies. I was managing a small sales team in Scotland when the manager of a large team in a higher job category got a promotion. As soon as I heard the news I telephoned his boss, whom I knew, and asked for the job. I think he was simply saving the time and stress of interviewing when he agreed.

40. It's not about time, it's about decisions

You will never, ever have enough time. That's because you are an interesting and interested person and you live in interesting times.

If you are out of time, you need to get better at making the right choices. Forget time management; get great at choice management instead.

Have you ever said 'I don't have enough time' or 'If only there were more hours in the day'? Have you ever heard any of your clients say 'It's just a lack of time' or 'Well, there's not enough time to consider that'?

What about your business colleagues? Have you come across them saying 'This is really urgent', 'We simply don't have time for that planning, we've got a year-end to close here' or 'That's not important at the moment'?

Of course you have. If there is one topic you can guarantee will occur in any business conversation anywhere in the world, it's the topic of time. Phrases like '100% of the time', complaints about the lack of it, urgency, important… It's *the* business issue and in this busy, busy world it's becoming more of one. Here's the fundamental problem: it doesn't matter how brilliant you are, what fantastic ideas you have, who is sponsoring you – if you don't have time to implement change, if you don't have time to run an off-site meeting, if you don't have time to respond to customers, then your business will die.

131

Here's an idea for you...

Take a sheet of paper. Put the word IMPORTANT across the top. Don't write anything on this paper unless it really is important. Now draw a line down the middle, vertically. Head the left-hand side with URGENT and the right-hand side with NON-URGENT. Fill both sides with the things that you have to do and put them in the appropriate place. Did you rush to put things on 'urgent' and find it difficult to identify stuff for the other side? Perhaps the non-urgent things are actually vital (career, health…)? Cross out 'non-urgent' and put 'investing'.

In the Old World of Work, in the original MBA courses, a topic such as 'time management' could be dealt with in a one-liner. It was usually something along the lines of: '…decide what needs to be done, put them in priority order and work through them'. Open any management or leadership MBA textbook from the 1950s, 60s, or even the 70s or 80s, and that's the suggestion you would have received and it would have worked. Time and decision management was able to rely on:

● A stable and static environment. Whether you were in cars or clothes, music or consultancy, little changed in your world from year to year, even decade to decade. Customers were predictable; competitors were reliable and understood. There was absolutely no need to rush around and a long lunch would do nicely.

● A larger workforce. Remember that word delegation? Laughable now, isn't it? To whom, exactly, do you delegate these days? It's rare to find any real support beyond your laptop.

● Fewer interruptions. Phone calls, of course, but only on a land line; mail, of course, but once a day in the post and occasionally dropping into your in tray.

● Slower interruptions. Factors such as typing, post and distance all ensured that you were the fastest thing around.

Of course in the New World of Work, things are very different:

● There's much more uncertainty: 'Which market are we in? Coffee? Experiences? Music?'

- The workforce is reduced and expensive, or on the other side of the globe.
- Constant interruptions, with email being the killer.
- Rapid interruptions. No longer is there any escape; it is harder and harder to find time to think.

Defining idea...

'The salary of the Chief Executive of the large corporation is not a market reward for achievement. It is frequently in the nature of a warm personal gesture from the person to him or her self.'
J.K. GALBRAITH, *American economist*

So, now that you have reminded yourself of the scale of the problem, what is to be done? Here are some practical suggestions:

- Accept that you will never have enough time. Stop trying to create more time: all you do is steal it from your golf, theatre going or life in general.
- Decide to do a little less, and do what you do decide to execute so well that it has an impact. That's instead of doing lots of things which count for little.
- Decide to ensure that what you do is of value and will count in the long term.
- Prioritise against pay-off, not against what's easy or who is shouting the loudest.
- Be aware that often what seems 'not urgent' now (e.g. planning, team building, long-term strategy) turns out to be vital in the longer term. So do some non-urgent things or, more correctly, 'investing' things now.
- Push back on interruptions so that your greatest asset, your brain, can work again.
- Choose, don't react.

Overall, don't manage time; manage your decisions. Slow down to the speed of your thinking as it's your greatest asset, and do a little less to achieve a whole lot more.

41. Get noticed by the right people

You need to get noticed. Identify who is important to your progress, and get to them. Sometimes that will mean bypassing a human blockage — perhaps your own boss, or some obstructive gatekeeper who is there to keep you away from the decision maker. Here are some tactics to leap such hurdles.

Suppose, for example, that your job is to supply computer and telecommunications solutions to the finance department of your company.

Your customer and decision maker is the Finance Director, but on a day-to-day basis there will be a key person whom you meet regularly and with whom you form plans for future approval by the Finance Director. Such people can usually be divided into three categories – the Good, the Bad and the Ugly.

The Good are terrific to work with. They understand their business and they are happy to tell you all about it, so that you can come up with the best possible plan together. Cultivate such people. Latch on to their coat tails. Buy them lunch. Feign interest when they show you pictures of their family. Help them to enhance their reputations and they will help you enhance yours. They will probably be quite happy for you to talk to the ultimate decision maker should you need to, but they'll do it with you as part of the team.

The Bad are often bad because they are scared. They're scared of their boss, they're scared of making mistakes and they're probably scared of a brilliant careerist like you. They probably don't know enough about their business to really brief you on what it is they want and will probably bar you from seeing the decision maker until you have earned their trust. That is the vital element of dealing with the Bad – you have to gain their trust.

It should be quite easy for a cool careerist like you to do this. Achieve some good, high-profile results that end up on the Finance Director's desk, and make sure Mr Bad gets all the credit. But do this genuinely. If you have to, you can dump on him later by showing that it has been you and your team all along that got the results, but life is easier if you can avoid having to do this.

At the point when he trusts you, Mr Bad should let you meet his boss. There is a problem if he won't. Access to his Director is vital if you are to carry out your role. So, like it or not, you have to get to them.

Remember, 'it is much easier to ask for forgiveness than to ask for permission.' Once you have created a relationship with his boss, Mr Bad will never be in such a strong position again to get in your way.

> **Here's an idea for you...**
>
> Never ask Mr Bad for permission to go and see the decision maker. If he refuses (which he probably will), you're then in an impossible situation. If you go behind his back, then you're heading for a confrontation and the relationship will be ruined for good. No – do it first and beg forgiveness later.

Defining idea...

'It is better to be beautiful than to be good. But...it is better to be good than to be ugly.'
OSCAR WILDE

Now for Mr Ugly. Mr Ugly is mean. He doesn't trust you, he doesn't trust his boss, he doesn't trust anyone. Quite often such people are bullies. You can't really play along with them if they are not allowing you to do the best you can for your customer; so you have to grasp the nettle and probably cause a major stink. Funnily enough, the way to deal with them is to cause them some fear, uncertainty and doubt.

Dealing with Mr Ugly

One of my salespeople had a Mr Ugly to contend with. I had to go in to see him and explain very logically that if my salesperson could not see the boss I would have to go in myself. I then displayed knowledge of what this bloke's competitors were doing and showed him that he was losing ground by not investing enough with us. I kept him just short of blowing his top and his uncertainty made him a bit easier to deal with. Unfortunately, however, he would not keep up with technological change and buy a 2960 B from us.

He would not even talk about it. The time had come to take a big risk. We made an appointment to go and see the Director, his boss, and we specifically asked that the meeting be with him on his own. As we had hoped, the director knew there was something wrong in that part of his business and agreed, albeit with at least a show of reluctance. We were pretty nervous; this was a major knifing job on a fairly senior person in a big customer. The Director's opening was 'Now just before we get to the intriguing question of why you wanted to see me without Rob, I thought I better let you know that he has just recommended that we buy a 2960 B.'

42. When to work for bastards

Some managers are just plain bastards. They are renowned for it and most people try to avoid them. Only work for them if the pay is better, or if it helps your brilliant career.

Some folk just can't do the interpersonal skills bit.

One of these people, a production director, was instructing a friend of mine to bulldoze his project through by making people co-operate. 'I don't care if you make yourself the most unpopular person in the company,' he declared. My friend, who had had enough, explained that that was impossible since the production director already held that position.

I survived one such boss who even gave me a thorough dressing down in front of her mother. Perhaps that demonstrated her problem. I mean if you have to show off in front of your mum when you are in your forties there's something wrong. I got promoted out of her team. I remember meeting my successor in the car park. He was looking crestfallen and I asked why. 'Her car is in the car park,' he said, 'so she's not only mad, but she's in the office.' 'Remind her to take her medication,' I suggested helpfully. To this day I have wondered whether he did remind her, and also whether she actually took medication.

> **Here's an idea for you...**
>
> When you work for someone like this you will frequently find yourself listening to people slagging them off. The easy thing to do is to throw in your lot with them and get it all off your chest. Your brilliant career, however, demands the opposite approach. Suggest that people misunderstand your boss and that he or she is a talented person with, deep down, a heart of gold. Senior managers will appreciate how you defend your boss, your peers will start to suspect that they might be missing something and everyone will respect your loyalty. Managers notice any disloyalty and will remember it if they ever come to thinking about inviting you to work for them.

There are always opportunities where there are problems. If a manager has a reputation for being hard to work for and is generally unpopular, joining him or her may be exactly the right thing to do to. There are a number of possible outcomes:

If he or she is successful, then you can paint yourself as the person who calmed the troubled waters and made success possible.

If he or she is unsuccessful everyone will understand that it was not your fault, and you will be left in charge when they leave.

If the two of you fall apart, you may just be able to get some brownie points for trying.

Keeping the peace

I once worked for a fiery project manager who walked roughshod over anyone he believed was endangering his project. He had a fine line in abuse, and never held back from using it. I developed a good relationship with him and managed to tone down a lot of the vitriol he flung around the company. I also worked hard on my relationship with his boss's secretary, and she and I spoke often about smoothing off the rough edges of his direct approach. Between us we held the fort for about a year, until even we were powerless against a particularly vicious attack on a manager who was supporting an idea that happened to be the brainchild of the managing director. My man left, and I took his job on an interim basis despite my being very junior for it. I also, modestly, accepted the

Defining idea...

'To know all is not to forgive all. It is to despise everyone.'
QUENTIN CRISP

congratulations of his boss for having kept the man's talented contribution going for so long.

43. You are totally responsible for you

It is a great mistake to think that anyone is as interested in your career as you are. Once you are past first-line management, you have to work out where you want to go and how to get there. Use the annual appraisal to get your boss's agreement to what you want to do.

Give your boss an easy time.

Even if you have a very open relationship with your boss the annual appraisal is vital to your career plan. Do the preparation and preferably do it better than your boss. No one is as dedicated to your career as you. No one is as good as you at knowing what skills you need. Help your boss along by working all that out before the appraisal interview.

Get yourself ready and in the right frame of mind by asking yourself these questions:

- What value have you added to your job?
- Where is it that you would like to go?
- What do you need to do to get there?
- Why should your boss support these plans? What's in it for her?

Answering these questions before an appraisal interview will mean that you will make the most productive use of this great opportunity to talk about yourself. Remember, this is your career, not your organisation's. Take ownership of that career and impress your boss with your motivation and determination. If you've got a clear idea of your career strategy you'll be much more impressive than an employee who agrees to whatever is suggested and has no proposals of his or her own. More or less writing your own appraisal should make life easier for your boss as well.

> **Here's an idea for you...**
>
> Lots of managers like to broadcast the fact that they don't really take the appraisal system seriously, that they have done no prep and that the whole thing will be over in twenty minutes. Encourage this thinking, agree that it's a ritual and that only the salary review has any significance. And then go home and do the preparation assiduously.

Sell them on your ideas for your career

While your career is your own, remember also that you are a team player in an organisation with its own aims and strategies. It is an entity in its own right and this must be reflected in the way you express yourself during an appraisal interview. That is why the question 'why should your boss support these plans?' is so important. You need to be able to prove that you are a valuable asset to the organisation and that if it invests in you, you will become even more valuable. Start from the very top. What words can you use that link your activities with the fundamental vision or mission of the organisation you work for? Then come down through the division and eventually to your boss.

Defining idea...

'Always take every opportunity offered to receive training. Give careful thought to your training needs before any appraisal interview.'
GEORGE PAUL, *Chairman, Norwich Union*

Another key thing to remember at appraisal time is that the person interviewing you is not an unidentifiable member of the corporate zoo; she is in fact a person with her own ambitions and career plans. Be sensitive to this. Do not alienate your boss by appearing to be more ambitious, more clued up, more prepared to succeed than her (even if it's true). What you are trying to do is to get your boss to adopt your plan, which you present subtly and sensitively, because she can see how it is going to make her look good. You do not need to ram this down her throat; she can work it out.

A little flattery can go along way. If you're feeling particularly outrageous, you could even suggest that one day you hope to attain the giddy heights of responsibility that your boss has (although this one takes a firm jaw, a straight face and a very sincere stance to get away with it).

You may already have a job purpose statement or job description agreed with your employer. If not, the appraisal is a splendid opportunity to define your own. If you already have a job purpose statement, expand on it to ensure that your future career aspirations are as easy as possible to achieve.

44. Act as if you are the CEO

Don't wait for permission: do it — and 99% of the time you will get away with it. The other 1% of the time you can always apologise!

And when they need a new CEO, guess who will be the natural choice?

Of course, it doesn't need to be the CEO; whatever job or career you are after in the business world, 'act as if'. Act as if you had it. Act as a manager would. Act as a senior consultant would. Then you'll be a natural choice when the formal selection comes along. A quick word of warning here; I'm not talking about stepping beyond your expertise or advising without knowledge. But I am talking about developing the gravitas a director might possess or the listening skills of someone who is at a senior level. And more. Time to get going on structuring your thinking – read on…

Develop the CEO (or sales director or team leader or…) mindset

- Do it, and apologise if necessary rather than not do it at all. Say a client is in danger of being lost if something is not done and done quickly, but nobody is willing to make a decision. All those who officially can do so are out, so you OK the refund. That's CEO thinking.
- No failure, only feedback. Here's an example: you collate some data and ask to make a five-minute pitch to the board on how flexitime would boost, not lower, productivity. More CEO thinking.

Here's an idea for you...

Write a 500-word story called 'A Day in the Life of [the perfect role you seek]'. Here's an example: 'As newly promoted HR Manager I call the team together and announce that there will be no immediate changes, but that I will be talking to each of them separately about what changes they might like to see which would make a more effective team. I would also ask them what is one thing they would like me to do to make their relationship with me easier...' Then review the story and ask yourself 'Even though I am not HR manager [or whatever] yet, what could I do?'

- 'I can.' Think positively. You can get to grips with numbers – yes, you can! Again, that's CEO thinking.

Develop CEO working practices

- Have a personal vision. Where do you want to be in five years' time?
- Have timed plans: a year plan, a quarter plan, a month plan, a week plan, and a day plan. Start 'helicopter view' and 'come into land' – look them up online if you don't know what they are.
- Do what is necessary, such as setting an objective for a meeting.
- Do the things others cannot be bothered to do. Always turning up on time is a good one.
- Do the small things which make the difference, such as thanking people, even for 'just doing their job'.

Create a support team

Who can help you be even better than you are now? Your support team, of course. Ah – you don't have one? Start building a collection of like-minded individuals who help each other. They help you; you help them. Aim for at least a strategic thinker, a pragmatist, a lateral thinker, a financial wizard and a relationships guru.

Dress for success

In addition to following the tips in idea 25 remember that the following can also reveal a lot about you:

- Your pen
- Your notebook
- Your briefcase or bag
- Your mobile phone

If you're worried that all this acting could be a little high risk then remember that what you don't want to do is overstep your official remit. You're using your soft skills, not your technical and advisory skills. Your aim is to subtly add more power to the equation of you = your technical/functional capability x your interpersonal skills. It's the latter that you will be improving, to a significant degree.

You may well be faced with cynicism from your colleagues and you will need to learn how to tackle it early on if you truly want to be successful. Don't judge others, but certainly don't react to their comments. Your success is simply reminding them of what they could be doing – but aren't!

45. Talk less, listen more

It is frightening how little listening goes on. Because of this, your boss's team meetings offer an excellent opportunity for appearing authoritative and getting your own way.

We all do it, we just don't listen.

Defining idea...

'If you know the enemy and know yourself, you need not fear the result of a hundred battles. If you know yourself but not the enemy, for every victory gained you will also suffer a defeat. If you know neither the enemy nor yourself, you will succumb in every battle.'
SUN TZU, *The Art of War*

I did a small piece of research on key management skills. While not statistically valid, the response of some thirty senior business people showed a huge majority put listening at the top of their list of necessary skills. One of them called it 'active listening'.

Here is the art of listening going wrong for an architect. He had the job of advising a couple on how they should use the space and carry out the refurbishment of an old, run-down property they had just bought. Unfortunately there was a hiatus between the architect's survey and his first meeting with the new owners. He used the time to speculate on what they might want to do with the house. What did it lack, in his view, and what would they have to do to put that lack right?

The owners arrived for the first meeting with a list of their requirements for the property. Despite this, the architect went ahead and presented the ideas that he had already sketched. After all, that's human nature. We all want to show our original ideas off since they feel so right to us. The architect was in fact interrupting the customer to make a point. When the customer eventually tabled the list, it was very different from the first thoughts of their adviser. They now had a situation of the customer not wanting to make the adviser feel bad, and the adviser feeling the need to defend his work. Despite all that went after, the relationship never got over this appalling start. Please don't ignore this story because you think that you would never do that. Keep quiet at your next meeting and just watch people, even senior people, not listening at all.

> **Here's an idea for you...**
>
> At your boss's next team meeting don't leap in with your views. Listen until everyone has spoken, assimilate what has been said and eventually summarise the substance. By that time you will know where your interests lie and be able to steer the meeting towards them.

Like all skills you get better at listening if you practice it. Here's an exercise I got from Penny Ferguson. Get yourself and a colleague, or if that's difficult a member of your family, to sit down in comfortable chairs facing each other. Now explain that you are going to listen to them for three minutes without any interruption. Then give them the topic. Ask them to talk for three minutes about things that they appreciate about themselves. Now settle down to do some active listening. Keep your eyes steady on them, although theirs will probably wander as they think about the question. For many people this is quite difficult. Normally we would be in there talking, advising and correcting, but that's not the point.

Here's another statistically invalid finding from my experience. Women in

Defining idea...

'The first component we have to put in place to help our people think very well is for them to know that they are listened to, for them to know that they have somebody's undivided attention. And by undivided attention I mean you focus on them 100 per cent of the time. Your eyes are on them, sending this message, "I am fascinated by what you are thinking about and saying."'
PENNY FERGUSON, *personal leadership guru*

business are instinctively better at this than men. So women, be careful that your listening does not look as though you have no ideas. And men, for pity's sake don't talk so much!

46. Get a personal development plan

One thing they teach on all MBA courses is the importance of a personal development plan. How will you stay employable for the next decade? One heck of a question... And here are some great and exciting answers.

One strong theme – as you are very well aware – on your personal MBA quest is to maximise your employability, to reduce your vulnerability and to safeguard your choice over the career you seek. But in a world which is increasingly one market with a few dominant players, that is becoming tougher and tougher to do. Guess what – you need a plan.

You need a personal development plan, to be specific. Now, if you are currently employed, especially with a large employer, my guess is that you already have one of these. But my guess also is that it is fairly short and focused on making you of more use to your employer (naturally!). It will have plenty of discussion about competencies and the need to do this, that and the other. All well and good. I want to help you get a plan together which is about you and your career – with or without your current employer. Of course, if you are currently between jobs or if you run your own business then you are very unlikely to have a plan, and yet you need one most of all.

149

To help, here are the components of this plan:
- Step 1: Where am I now?

   This defines your current job and role.

   Example: I am product marketing manager at LowerThanYours Jeans

   Tip: Write down a few of the responsibilities for the job; that will help you with the next question.

- Step 2: Where do I want to be in three years?

   It's now time to start doing some serious thinking. You may well need to take a break and come back to this. But this is classic consultancy practice – you need to know where you are going to; what is the change you seek?

   Example: I want to be a marketing director in the leisure industry. I believe the leisure industry will continue to grow and become more important whereas pure retail will stay volatile.

   Tip: Define this as fully as you can.

- Step 3: What exactly is the gap?

   Define this in every way possible. Skills, thinking, geography…

   Example: At the moment I certainly have no idea how a director is meant to operate and my CV would not look at all attractive for the position. I need to up my skills, I need to up my experience. Courses will help but I am planning to run a consultancy alongside my main job to get some sharp-end experience…

   Tip: Write plenty on this.

- Step 4: What do I need to close the gap?

   Example: I'm going to get on my company's leadership course, pay for myself to go on some Institute of Directors' courses and start my own business. Then I'll review this plan in nine months' time.

   Tip: Be specific.

Step 5: What are ten actions I need to take over the coming months to initiate those actions?
Example: 1. See HR to get on the leadership course. 2. Ask to see my manager re more responsibility…
Tip: Create ten definite actions – that will force you to get very specific.

Step 6: What might block me?
Consider anything that might get in the way of your plans.
Example: Time. My manager is currently very distracted about her own career and not much interested in mine.
Tip: Detail each blocker and break them down.

Step 7: How can I overcome or pre-empt those blockers?
Here you need to identify the solution for each individual blocker.
Example: To overcome the time problem, I need to schedule some fixed time on a regular basis to work on my own plans.
Tip: Most blockers tend to come down to time. Recognise that you won't have time, so what you need to do is make time.

Step 8: Plan, review and improve. Make a diary note to improve the plan on a monthly or even weekly basis. Create a 'recurring event' in your electronic

> **Here's an idea for you...**
>
> If you could do your dream job, what would it be? Go off and think about it. No 'ifs and buts'. Get the dream first and make it sensory rich. What would it look like? (Definitely in a major city, maybe San Francisco…) What would it smell like? (Those Singapore markets…) What would you hear? (The buzz and chatter of a great marketing team, the accolade of another award-winning campaign…) Write it up, maybe draw it up. Create something strong in words and perhaps strong visually and put it somewhere where you will see it every day.

47. Impress the senior management

Choosing how to interact with senior managers is key to career development. Here are some thoughts about deference, flattery and managing vanity, all vital ingredients of your relationship with the top folk.

Look after your seniors. Senior managers are all different. When you're about to meet one for the first time make sure you've prepared properly by talking to people in the know.

But you can make some assumptions and one of these is that they will be vain. All human beings are to some extent vain. Top managers are somewhat larger-than-life human beings; therefore top managers tend to have as high a level of vanity as any normal human being, and higher than most.

Tom, a friend of mine, was a manager in the Edinburgh office of a US company. He was about to get a historic visit from the CEO. Tom knew that his counterpart in the Manchester office, Mike, was to have his visit a few days earlier. The plan in each case was that the CEO would fly up from London and spend two days visiting the offices and meeting customers. There would be a customer dinner on the evening of the first day. Tom asked Mike about his preparations. 'Well,' said Mike, 'It's difficult. You know that we are being told to save on expenses at the moment, tightening our belts and so forth, so I thought that we should show that we take that seriously and keep the whole visit fairly low

Here's an idea for you...

Think through your next exposure to a senior manager whom you wish to impress. How can you play to their vanity? How will you feed their pride without appearing nauseating?

key.' 'Really,' said Tom. 'Yes,' continued Mike, 'I thought we would pick him up in a normal first-line manager's company car, that would show thrift, and put him up in the same hotel we use for the graduate trainees when they join. It's pleasant but obviously not overly expensive.' He continued to describe this hair-shirt treatment. At the end of the conversation Tom called in his PA and said 'We are going to give the man a welcome to Edinburgh that makes the plans for the Queen coming up to Holyrood Palace look stingy.'

And so they did. After his visit to Manchester the CEO was not entirely looking forward to the next one. He arrived at the airport to be met by a PA with a clipboard, and was led straight past the luggage carousel to a waiting limo. The PA explained that someone else was picking up his bags.

Tom had carefully chosen where the CEO was to stay, the sort of classy Georgian Hotel that even a well-travelled executive finds unusual. A butler unpacked them and put his things away. Tom had booked a suite so that the CEO could entertain the top customers in private to drinks before they descended to join the hoi polloi for dinner. And so it went on.

Defining idea...

Oh, Vanity of vanities!
How wayward the decrees of fate
are; How very weak the wise are,
How very small the great are!
WILLIAM MAKEPEACE THACKERAY

Subsequently Tom got feedback that the CEO had loved the visit to Edinburgh. In fact he got a warm thank-you note, while Mike just got a note, and another one from his boss saying 'Don't do that again.'

48. Get to know the sales force

Yep, this one is about the sales force. You have to learn to love them, because using a key customer as their torpedo, they can hole anyone's career below the water-line. Here's a way of understanding them that gives you a fighting chance of dealing with them effectively.

What's the problem?

Many organisations fear their salespeople. They seem to be young for the money they can make and often only come to the attention of the rest of the company if something has gone wrong (when, for example, the business is spending time and money trying to deliver a salesperson's promises). Nowadays, it is vital to remove this fear and replace it with a wary respect for the front-line job. That way your career and the sellers will all march in the same direction.

So, how do you set about getting your team to love your salespeople?

Here's an idea for you...

If the sales force is on a straight commission on sales then they won't be fully motivated to get orders at list price. Make sure that any drop in profits caused by their discounting is reflected in their wallets. A 10 per cent discount on the sales price has little impact on the salesperson's income but may have reduced bottom-line profit by more than 33 per cent. If it's easy to administer, a lot of managers use the gross profit of a deal as the basis for sales bonuses, and this works quite well. The other possibility is to discount the sales bonus pro rata to the sales discount, so 90 per cent of list price will yield, say, only 50 per cent of the full sales bonus.

Know the animal you're trying to work with

Make sure, in the first place, that everyone understands that the selling job is divided into 'hunting' or 'farming'. Hunting is about bringing in new customers, farming about increasing the amount of business you do with your existing customers. The skills are different and a major recruitment consideration is how much of each activity the job involves. If you deal with your salespeople in the wrong mode you'll have problems. Particularly if you treat a hunter as though she's a farmer.

For hunters the main requirements are persistence and the ability to take knocks. Their job involves trying to get interviews with strangers who may not only be unaware of their need but antagonistic to an unsolicited approach.

Hunters generally work quickly, have short attention spans and feel very dissatisfied if complications of product or decision-making processes prevent them closing a sale. They are opportunists and in most cases need watching to make sure that they don't promise results your product can't deliver.

Some would say that it is the hunters who give salespeople a bad name. There is some truth in that, but they are also the people who make innovation possible and en masse bear a lot of responsibility for driving the dollar round in a growth economy.

Here's a hunter talking, 'You actually have to start by getting yourself invited into the buyer's office. Then you must convince a probable sceptic that what you are offering has benefits over continuing with the people they are using at present.

> Defining idea...
>
> 'He's a man way out there in the blue, riding on a smile and a shoeshine. And when they start not smiling back – that's an earthquake…A salesman is got to dream. It comes with the territory.'
> ARTHUR MILLER, *Death of a Salesman*

'Then you have to find a project, bid for it and win it. The great feeling is that you made it happen; if you had not made the first move, that company would have remained loyal to its existing suppliers.'

Many people find the prospect of hunting horrendous; but organisations are recognising more and more their dependence on such people.

Farmers develop skills in long-term relationship building and deep knowledge of a customer's business. The benefits to management of professional farmers are predictable orders, competitive intelligence, awareness of market changes and much more.

Finally

Maybe it's impossible to get everyone to love the sales force; but if you can't do that at least make sure they are talking to the right animal. Talk fast, short and assertively to the hunter, analytically with the farmer.

49. Think now and think ahead

Top people need to have two heads. You won't get to the top unless you pay attention to your operational goals, and you won't get to the top unless you think way, way ahead.

You have to think strategically. You need to balance the pressures of today against the longer-term thinking required to build your business and your career. Here's the deal...

1. Without a long-term strategy you run the risk that decisions you are making today will have a negative impact on your results in the future.

2. But we have to stay real; we're also always under pressure to carry out urgent day-to-day tasks. You have to meet today's objectives and overcome short-term problems. You have to respond to your customers, whoever they are. Everyone is involved in such work and in operational, or short-term, planning. In a fast-moving environment it is little wonder that planning for the future tends to take second place.

3. The situation is very stark in start-ups and small
   companies. There is no point in defending an
   action as being right for the long term if it
   makes the business run out of cash. On the
   other hand, making a sale that is outside the
   main route you have planned could be
   catastrophic for the future. Brilliant careerists
   take this philosophy into large company
   planning too.

<blockquote>
Here's an idea for you...

Identify a member of your team who is basically good at producing short-term results. Explain to her that you are going to develop that skill by delegating an increasing amount of today's targets to her. Do it and free up your time to develop a long-term strategy, particularly a long-term career strategy.
</blockquote>

Developing the second head

So we come back to the two heads. The leader of any team needs a 'can do; do it now' attitude. You need to be able to discuss a problem, find a solution and immediately pick up the telephone to start implementing the solution. No one has solved the particular problems you are facing now. You're breaking new ground here so one of your two heads has to look for solutions or activities that less dynamic managers might describe as completely off the wall.

And yet, and yet, no one built a business without an eye on the future shaping what we do now – the second head.

Some people can keep the two heads going at once, reacting, ducking and weaving with the best of them, but also from time to time checking that they are not mortgaging the future or taking short-term measures that endanger the long-term goal. Others form teams of two where one person is clearly the go-getter, and the other the 'just a minute, let's think this through' person.

Defining idea...

In preparing for battle I have always found that plans are useless but planning is indispensable.
DWIGHT D. EISENHOWER

You may well have a leaning towards one of these methods. Don't forget, though, that eventually you need to be the forward thinker. Top people get others to sort out the fires and you're heading for the top. And that's the clue. You can get ahead very fast in the lower echelons by producing clever and rapid short-term results. But you have to grow.

50. Hone your presentation skills

Getting people to agree to your plan of action often requires you to make a presentation. Here's a good tip for making the most important part of the presentation, the opening, effective.

Presentation — the big career boost. At certain points in your career you'll have to make presentations to senior people. If you have a natural talent for doing this, you put yourself way ahead of the competition.

In some customer cultures, indeed, you're pretty much up against it if your presentation skills are poor or if that rabbit in the headlight look lasts right through your presentation. Practice hard, always volunteer to be the person who presents the results of a workshop, or who makes the presentation on some new strategy to the departmental meeting.

I had no idea of how useful presentations were until the following incident. In the dark ages of the 1970s the business world in the UK was burdened with a new tax, Value Added Tax. I was a graduate trainee at the time and my boss, who sometimes found it difficult to think of constructive things for a rookie to do, asked if I could have a look at this VAT business and make a presentation to the

Here's an idea for you...

It is a very good, though simple, idea to announce exactly what you want the group to decide at the start of a presentation. The audience then knows where you are going to take them. Some people avoid this as you do run the risk that someone in the audience will tell you that you won't be able to get there but logically it is better to know this at the start of the presentation than at the end. Who knows, if you know what the audience's objections are, you may be able to use the presentation itself to overcome them.

next area meeting. I got hold of government papers but found the whole concept of the tax hard to understand. I persevered, spoke to a load of people, including government people, who were very helpful. At last I was able to understand how the tax worked in my terms. These were, of course, the terms that my colleagues in the area would also use. A bit of luck had me hear a joke on the radio about VAT inspectors being called 'Vatman and Robin', so I nicked that and used it as a running gag through my presentation. It went well and I knew that it had done me no harm at all. My boss mentioned its success to his boss, who had just sat through an incomprehensible presentation on VAT by a bunch of accountants. I was asked to give the same presentation to the management team at my boss's boss's team meeting – very useful, high-profile stuff, and a lesson in influencing people.

Presentation tips

If you're not a natural at this game, get some training until you can at least survive, although I do know one senior manager who made it to the top and remained a complete liability on his feet. When asked how he did it he replied, 'ducking and weaving, old boy. I avoided presentations like the plague'.

Funnily enough the best tips for making effective presentations are the usual suspects. Set tight objectives and talk exclusively in the terms of the audience. It can be difficult to make the same presentation to the marketing people and research and development at the same time even when what you have to say is interesting to both.

So try to avoid having to talk to audiences whose members come from different professional backgrounds.

Defining idea...

'Presentations are about them, the audience, rather than you, the speaker.'
SENIOR SALES MANAGER

51. Help people think for themselves

To have a successful career, good managers need to build a reputation for breeding good people. They lead confident teams, limit the amount of advice they give and help their people solve their own problems.

Who would you rather work for, a person who keeps staff forever, or one who constantly loses people to better, more interesting positions? Exactly. If you are known to encourage your people to grow and have a reputation as a source of good people, the best people will beat a path to your door.

People come to their bosses in order to find the solution to a problem or some suggestions as to how they should set about exploiting an opportunity – right? Well not entirely, no. Sometimes they come to explore an idea while they make their own minds up. Sometimes they have a solution to the problem themselves and they want to validate it. In these situations hitting them with an avalanche of advice does more harm than good.

After all, how do you know you have found the best solution? And what in the end are you trying to develop – your people's skills or a bunch of folk that do what you tell them? OK, eventually they'll believe that they can do your job better than you can, but that's better than having a bunch of grumblers who feel stuck in a dead-end job.

Don't rush to give advice

Now I admit that I have the advice disease pretty badly. When people come to me to talk something over, I look for suggestions, sometimes before they have finished explaining the background. If the topic is in my comfort zone I jump to an assumption about what they are about to say in no time and start planning my advice. OK, so if advice avalanche is a disease, what is the cure?

Here's an idea for you...

When someone comes to you for help with a problem, try to create a 'thinking partnership' for them rather than an advice clinic. Limit yourself to asking only questions; make no proposals during the session, no matter how long it takes. Look for incisive questions like 'If you could get over that hurdle, what would you do next?' Keep listening as they work out the actions they are going to take.

(I was taught a number of exercises in this area on a course given by Penny Ferguson and with her permission have passed the 'thinking partnership' one on.)

I tried out this technique with an old friend. He has written a number of successful radio plays but has been trying for a while now to write a stage play. From time to time he e-mails me the latest version of his script and asks for comments. Sometimes he asks for specific help on something that is holding him up. My normal method would be to read the script and then phone with fifteen suggestions. He then rejects half of them straight away and asks me to write down a couple of paras about the ones that remain. I do this, send it off and may not hear from him again for a while.

Defining idea...

Action is only as good as the thinking behind it. Thinking is only as good as the way people treat each other. A leader's job is to create an environment in which people can think for themselves and find the courage to put the best ideas into action.

PENNY FERGUSON, *personal leadership guru*

So, the last time this happened I decided to give him a thinking partnership and listen while he worked the problem out. The problem was simple: near the end of act one he had six characters on stage. He needed to reduce this to two for a short piece of dialogue that would set up the beginning of act two. He was having difficulties finding compelling reasons why the other four characters should leave the stage. The key problem was to invent an exit for Maggie and I asked the question, 'If you could get Maggie off the stage what would you do next?' The playwright thought out loud, long and hard; without doubt we had created a thinking environment. After a long time he had worked it out and knew how to lose three of the characters. 'But that still leaves Maggie', he moaned. At this point I cracked. We had been on the phone for about an hour and both my ears hurt. I simply gave out a torrent of ideas, or advice, about how to get Maggie off the bloody stage!

52. Are you a leader?

Let's forget the endless navel-gazing discussions about leadership. Let's get on with it. Let's live by the consequences of our actions. Let's make it happen. That's real leadership!

If there is one skill which cannot be, dare I say will never be, automated, it's the skill of leadership. If you don't have this skill, you're vulnerable.

Nothing happens without effective leadership, so what do you need to know about this subject?

Firstly, you need to be confident in the knowledge that anyone can become a leader. Of course, history has shown time and time again that in any field – be it politics or medicine or music or whatever – there are certain 'naturals' who will rise to the top, whatever might happen. So certainly there is a genetic, or 'nature', element to leadership. But that doesn't stop any of us 'nurturing our nature' or becoming better at leadership. Secondly there are a huge number of models about leadership out there. All have their quirky variants, their own proponents, but there are some factors which are generally agreed upon. Let's look at them, as they can help you become an outstanding leader.

Here's an idea for you...

Write down the names of some great leaders you are aware of in any field – past or present, famous or not, real or fictional. They could come from sport, politics, the military, industry, teaching… Try and get ten names. They might be brand names (such as Richard Branson), they might be just personal to you. I expect you'll have a very varied list. Your mum, Winston Churchill, your old history teacher, Gandhi… now, what do they all have in common? Try and capture it in just three words. What are the three words? Compare your answers with mine opposite.

Mindset: leadership starts with you, part 1

In the New World of Work, leadership is increasingly a mindset rather than a job title. It is something to be taken rather than waited for. It is an approach rather than a job specification. Here's an example. Alf, Vip and Jane are all graduate trainees in a start-up software company. Alf and Vip spend a lot of their day complaining that the training they were promised at their interviews isn't happening. Jane has been out and bought some books, charged them to her expenses, spends part of each day studying – and she will do that until someone stops her. She realises that leadership is not about waiting for permission; it's about getting on with it. You can always apologise later.

Lead yourself: leadership starts with you, part 2

To be a great leader you must be able to lead yourself. Can you? For example, can you:

- Get your report in on time?
- Get up early?
- Go through a whole day without blaming anyone else?
- Be accountable for your actions?
- Plan? And review?
- Manage your time?

● Invest in relationships?
You can? Excellent; you have the basis of outstanding leadership.

Leadership is situational

So leadership starts with mindset. It continues as you develop the ability to lead yourself. Then, as you move your focus to the leadership of others, you must realise that it is situational. Ken Blanchard was probably the first to fully articulate this point, that essentially the leadership of others depends on responding appropriately to the combination of their current competence and their current motivation. For example, if someone is highly motivated and highly competent you can simply leave them to it after the correct briefing; this is known as delegation. If someone is new to the job or role and thus not very competent, yet, but is also highly motivated, then they simply need direction. Good leaders recognise that their default style is not perfect for all situations and constantly adjust it as the occasion demands.

Answer...

Here's my answer to the exercise about three words which describe your personal selection of leaders. I have done this exercise with thousands of people over the years, from schoolchildren to senior businessmen, and in places from London to Singapore. People always agree on three concepts and they often use the same three words as well: vision, energy and communication. Great leaders must be able to articulate the journey and give hope that the journey can be accomplished – that's vision. They must be able to energise people, to raise their standards, and they must also be able to communicate how the vision will be achieved.

53. Pick the right management style

One of the best things you can do for your career is to deliver projects to your boss on time and within budget. Your team will deliver when you lead it effectively. Pick the right management style for the right situation.

There is a spectrum of leadership styles, and you will need to adopt them all at certain points in your working life. Your style will vary from autocratic 'do as I say' to democratic 'consensus-seeking'.

Your predominant style will depend on your organisation, the nature of the project and the characteristics of the team. Try not to make it too dependent on your natural way of leading people. You need to develop more flexibility than that.

You need to show your boss that you do not just hire people who are like yourself, but can manage anyone who you need in your team.

Consider the appropriate times to use these different styles. Obviously when the project hits a crisis and there is no time to consult you'll have to make decisions alone, take the risks yourself and seize control. You will get through the crisis, but at the cost of teamwork. Try to use this style sparingly and remember that such heavy 'push' management tends to get results rapidly but its impact falls off just as quickly. If you want a change in performance to stick, you need to move along the spectrum towards consensus.

Opinion seeking is further along the spectrum. Ask all the stakeholders as well as your team what they think about a wide range of issues. This 'pull' type of management builds confidence and demonstrates that you value the team's views. It is also an opportunity to go high up in the organisation to get the advice of some senior people whose experience you would like to exploit. Stakeholders love it and it spreads the risk a bit if something goes wrong.

> Defining idea...
>
> 'Striking amongst the musicians is their total lack of self-importance. They play a piece and then discuss among themselves as to how it may be improved. They make suggestions for each other directly, not via the director. No actor would tolerate a fellow performer who ventured to comment on what he or she is doing – comment of that sort coming solely from the director, and even then it has to be carefully packaged and seasoned with plenty of love and appreciation.' ALAN BENNETT

Finally you get to the truly democratic style of management. It is essential to use this style on a regular basis. It 'empowers' the team. (Am I the only person who thinks that the buzzword 'empower' is just good, old-fashioned trust dressed up to sound impressive?) Simply encourage team participation and involve them in making decisions. Keep them up to date with your thinking and with issues that are affecting the project. There is no doubt that people blossom under such a regime; they improve and maintain performance and motivation. They also speak well of you to your boss.

Defining idea...

'The function that distinguishes a manager above all others is his educational one. The one contribution he is uniquely expected to make is to give others vision and ability to perform. It is vision and more responsibility that, in the last analysis, define the manager.' PETER DRUCKER, *creator of modern management theory*

Here's an idea for you...

If you can't admit that you can't do something, your people won't either. Encourage them to talk about those parts of your strategy they are less confident of handling. Then you can help them, or rearrange the plan to take that task away from them. I have seen teams thrash out a good strategy, but plainly lack the skills to achieve it. I have even sat with senior managers who were brought in for the final presentation of the plan, and when the team has left the room they have turned to me and said 'Great plan, Ken, but that lot can't do it.' It begs the question, 'Why are you letting them try?'

Develop good team members

In most teams the egos of the individuals can get in the way of sharing suggestions. There are exceptions and they tend to be successful people. Hire them. They encourage openness and constructive criticism of everyone, by everyone. They tend to be laid back, good listeners and understanding of people's problems. They are terrific allies of the team leader and still liked by their colleagues in the team. As team leaders themselves they bring the best out of people. They don't manage everyone in the same way, though. Some of the team they can encourage to be musicians, and some will always be actors.

54. Find out what you are supposed to be doing

Your career depends on your organisation meeting its objectives, and your being widely seen as making a big contribution to those aims. Find out precisely what the organisation is trying to do before you work out your detailed plans.

The word 'strategy' is possibly the most ill-used piece of management speak in the business. Middle managers often complain that their board of directors doesn't have a strategy. This is normally not the case. The board's strategy may be wrong but it does have one. Maybe middle management has not been told about it or maybe they have misunderstood it. It is, in fact, a crucial function of the board to plan and implement a strategy, so you need a reputation as a strategic thinker to get to the top. Memo to self: Start working on that now.

Come down a few levels to team leaders and the accusation that they don't have a strategy can look truer. It is difficult for them to have an up-to-date strategy, particularly in organisations that do not give concrete guidelines on what a strategy is and how and when to review it. Difficulties abound:

● It is difficult for a team leader to build a strategy because it takes time.

Here's an idea for you...

OK, now we have agreed what a strategy is, get yourself a good definition of the strategy of any staff departments that are important to you. The marketing department is a good place to start – after all, they are responsible for agreeing the top-level strategy of what you are going to sell and to whom.

- Short-term pressures stop the team getting on with the job of creating a strategy and even when it does, the strategy is frequently ignored whenever a customer or other significant pressure blows it off course.

- Your best strategy may be impossible because other parts of the business will not change to suit you.

- Building a team strategy needs consensus, so some team members are going to have to compromise – never easy.

But if it's difficult it must be an area where the ambitious manager can build some career points. Put simply, you need to build a strategy with your team, agree it with all your main stakeholders or interested parties, including your customers, and flaunt it. But you've got to know the organisation's strategy before you start.

Keep it strategically simple, stupid

To work out your organisation's strategy it's useful to start with what it's not:

- The annual budgeting round. Don't mistake this for strategy. You come to the budgeting activities when the rest of the strategy is worked out.

- A large book of management-speak containing mission statements of 400 words that attempt to cover all the aspirations of the management team without pausing for breath. Here is one of these at board level...

'Our strategic intent is to strive for leadership in the most attractive global communications segments through speed in anticipating and fulfilling evolving customer needs, quality in products and processes, as well as openness with people and to new ideas and solutions. Based on our resources including technological know-how, market position and continuous building of competencies, we are well positioned to achieve our future goals.'

'Yes, but what are you going to *do*?' you long to scream.

- A document produced by a staff function, carried around only by the same people, who use it solely to demonstrate that what the line departments are doing is against the strategy.

- A matrix of numbers produced once a year and left on the shelf until such time as it is due for review.

Right, keep it simple, what is it? A strategy is a plan of what an organisation is going to sell to which markets and how. The strategic plan allows everyone to know how they should do their jobs, what the boundaries are and how the board will appraise any suggestions for doing new things. It is the strategy's job to bring focus to everyone's work. You must get to know it in terms that are not business school babble.

From now on when someone complains that the board does not have a strategy, confidently ask him or her to explain, 'What exactly do you mean by a strategy?' You will be amazed at the number who can't or who give you a line from a limerick.

55. Ready, aim, fire

Keeping someone in your team who plainly is not going to make it can be very bad for your career. Your business performance suffers by definition and your boss sees you vacillating on an important issue, avoiding doing the right thing because it is uncomfortable.

Try not to create a dedicated enemy. Every manager has to sack someone from time to time. In fact some senior managers regard it is a key management skill. If you have to sack someone, timing is vital; but equally important is how you do it.

Don't forget how small a world the upper reaches of any industry are. You come across people whom you served as a customer, or for whom you worked, frequently enough for you to want to ensure that you only make enemies when there is no alternative. You may also come across people who worked for you in an earlier life, which means, of course, that that you may come across people whom you fired.

Sacking people is not a job that most managers find pleasant. Here are the dos and don'ts:

- Do prepare carefully, not only for the meeting but also for what will happen in personnel terms after it.

- Don't let the firee talk you out of it. If you've made your decision, stick to it. You will never recover with this person if you change your mind.

- Do have a stiff drink before the meeting. You need to look assertive, firm and friendly, not a nervous wreck.

> **Here's an idea for you...**
>
> Sometimes the Human Resources rules cause a hold-up. HR is, of course, quite right to protect the company's position and make sure that you do nothing that would prejudice that. But if the delay is going to cause problems, argue strongly that the company should buy its way out of it. This is often a time to spend the organisation's money lavishly.

- Don't relax too much. Jokes might not go down too well right now.

- Do give a generous if not lavish settlement. This sugars the pill greatly and if you go beyond the company's norms, the person you are firing will know that it is you being generous, not the rules.

- Do go through the process meticulously. It is important that it is you who gives the generous settlement not an industrial tribunal.

It's a jungle out there: try a headhunter

Now's the time to consider the value of headhunters to your career. Headhunters are something else you should spend the organisation's money lavishly on – not difficult given what these guys charge. But they have an encyclopaedic knowledge of your industry and the people and opportunities in it. They have to have; and they are very brazen about contacting people and

177

Defining idea...

'Aim high and achieve this by moving upwards between well-regarded organisations every two years.'
P.R. WILLIAMS, *HR Director, Vodafone Airtouch*

keeping up to date. Perhaps you could help the person you are firing meet with a headhunter you know. That can sugar the pill. At the same time, encourage the headhunters to make suggestions to you at any time, not just when you want people or want a job for someone else. That way you are also encouraging them to do the same in terms of job opportunities for you.

Be very careful of the current fad for 'head-shunting'. This avoids the painful process of sacking someone by getting a headhunter to place a person you are trying to get rid of with another company. In theory, you avoid the expense of severance pay, and remove any threat of being sued for wrongful dismissal. But it would seem that someone who discovers that the ploy has been visited on them can still sue for unfair dismissal, and if the receiving company believes it has been duped, it also might have a case.

56. Creating a team strategy

In order to get to the top you need to be seen as a strategic thinker. To get that reputation you need to do some. Strategic thinking, that is. Here's a short cut to a creating a team strategy.

The aim of this idea is simple. You are going to present a strategy for your team that is going to knock your boss's socks off and make him insist that all your colleagues copy you.

And that's the second benefit – while you're producing a first-class performance, everyone else is tying themselves in knots trying to write a strategic plan. Only you know the short cut.

The first skill involved in creating a strategy is the ability to balance short-term thinking with long-term planning. Put some long-term thinking time into your schedule. You don't have much time; you needed a strategy yesterday. And, who knows, you may need a new one tomorrow.

Once they've decided to create a strategy, most managers think they need a consultant to help them to write it. Other people think they need a facilitator to help the team with the process. From vast, and occasionally bitter, experience I believe it is better if you can to do it on your own. Facilitators have to be perceived to add value to the planning process, so they invent complicated

Here's an idea for you...

It is a really good idea to check this analysis with a few people including, of course, your key customers. Don't be frightened to show them your analysis. If there are bits they don't like or don't agree with, it's better that you know now.

procedures and forms. Actually all you need is some flipcharts, pens and one crucial technique.

Right, you've got your team in the planning room and agreed to do at least half a day on the plan, and another half day in a week's time. Write first on the flipchart your vision for the future. You should have prepared this earlier and checked it over with the key people in your team before the session. This saves hours, and if later it turns out to be not quite right you can change it during the time you are implementing the strategy.

The planning techniques

Use SWOT analysis as the analytical part of the process. Ask the team: in terms of achieving our vision, what are our strengths, weaknesses, opportunities and threats. Don't get hung up on words. Get the ideas down. Remember that you are all going to be living with this plan forever. But it will evolve constantly. you don't have to get it spot on at your first meeting.

And now follows the bit where a lot of teams go wrong. You've got to get from analysis strategic goals and action plan. Give each weakness, opportunity and threat an identifying number. (Ignore the strengths for now.) Write down the following topics: people, skills, facilities, customers and suppliers. Allocate each weakness, opportunity and threat to one of those topics. If some will not fit, choose another key word – it's unusual to need more than six or seven. Now allocate each topic to one or two team members. Send them away to work out the goals the team should set in that area and the actions necessary to achieve this. Tell them that the strengths might give some clues for the action plan. At a second meeting the following week discuss and agree the goals and actions, allocate the actions to a team member – and you have a strategic plan!

> Defining idea...
>
> 'Strategies are intellectually simple; their execution is not.'
> LARRY BOSSIDY, *industrialist*

Throughout the process be prepared to question and challenge accepted norms. The really upwardly mobile careerist will fight tooth and nail before acknowledging that something the company is doing wrong cannot be changed. But watch the politics. It's a tough call, but you have to judge whether your boss's entrenched views can now be challenged by you and your team. In my experience, though, the safety-first acquiescence path is so much easier to contemplate that most people err on that side rather than taking the risk of becoming known as a doubter or, worse, a troublemaker. Courage, *mon brave*, nobody said life was easy.

Prepare to shine. You have a strategy and it is written down. Tell people about it, partly because you are trying to build your career and partly because you want to influence others towards your way of thinking. Make presentations. Sell your methodology to others so that you become the source of the company-wide strategic planning system. And then sit back and watch your colleagues suffer.

57. Keep up the good work

Some of your best career promoters are the members of your team. If they speak with pride of their department and warmly about you senior managers will notice. Replace someone who is running a happy team with great care. You've got to maintain performance and get them on your side.

You can't be a clone of your predecessor. Would you rather take over a team with a positive mental attitude or a bunch of demoralised grumblers? The former could be waiting for you to fail to live up to your glorious predecessor.

This happened to me when I took over a team from Martin, who had got himself a neat promotion after producing very good results and this very happy team.

Martin was a very quick thinker, he was also tactically bold and 100 per cent sure of himself – the perfect mixture for an autocratic manager. The team came to him for everything; no one else took decisions, not even small ones. I knew that I couldn't work like that. It wasn't my style, I didn't think it developed the individuals in the team – besides it looked like bloody hard work and by nature I'm a bit of a skiver.

I thought about it long and hard and discussed the situation with one of my mentors; then I came up with a plan. In the first week I arranged to meet every member of the team individually for a 45-minute slot. During the quiet 15 minutes between appointments I read a newspaper and drank coffee. In that time, of course, the door opened several times and people asked me what to do in particular situations. I developed a catchphrase response, 'I don't know mate, I'm new here.' Eventually they got the idea and I developed a new culture where people came to me with solutions not problems.

Luckily when I took over from Martin I was very careful to keep my boss up to speed. My new team really thrashed around. They looked and felt rudderless. Since I wasn't telling them what to do, they would go to my boss when I wasn't in. She handled it quite well but did give advice in some cases where I would have preferred her not to. She was concerned that what I was doing would

> **Here's an idea for you...**
>
> When you take over a new job, watch out for the people who stay completely loyal to your predecessor and take every opportunity to rubbish you. They can have a huge impact on the team, particularly the junior and younger members, and they are almost certainly pouring poison into your boss's ear as well. This is a time to be ruthless. Get shot of them now. Don't wait for the rotten apple to spread the disease.

Defining idea...

'No man will make a great leader
who wants to do it all himself, or to
get all the credit for doing it.'
ANDREW CARNEGIE, *industrialist*

impact performance, at least in the short term.
Now, funnily enough, it didn't. Not sure why,
although it is probably connected to the fact that
the best people in the team quickly started to just
get on with it and then they started to enjoy it,
and the change had at least started.

58. Everybody lives by selling something

There is no cynical get-out here. You can take all the short cuts in the world but in the end your career depends on your customers doing business with you and expressing their delight with your performance. Keep them at the front of your and your team's thinking.

Keep up to date with what the customer needs.

'Through here pass the most important people in the world – our customers.' This notice is above the door of one of the worst garage workshops through which it has been my dubious pleasure to pass. The thought is right. Everyone has customers on whom they depend for their livelihood. You get to the top echelons of management if you actually deliver on that statement and treat the customer as king. Make them drive every stage of your plan. Try to think ahead of what they will require in the future. There are two kinds of manager in this respect: those who are always trying to catch up because they become aware of

> Defining idea...
>
> 'The best way to predict the future is to create it.'
> PETER DRUCKER, *management thinker*

Here's an idea for you...

Here's an idea for you...

Your seniors will pay more attention to a customer who praises you than to anyone else. So make it happen. When something has gone well, and assuming you have a close relationship with your customer, get them to write a thank-you note to you, copied to the most senior person they know in your organisation, preferably at least your boss's boss. Time this to coincide with another key event, your appraisal maybe, or your big request for more resources. But don't overdo it or your boss will know that it is you setting it up.

changes in their customer's needs after the event, and those who make changes in anticipation of this. When you get yourself ahead of the game, it will be difficult for anything to stop your success. But you've got to deliver it as well as promise it. I'd love to change that sign in the dead of the night to, 'Through here pass the most incompetent people in the world – our managers.'

Get everyone to talk to them

Keep your organisation in touch with reality, by making sure that no one can completely evade customer contact. You can do this individually by insisting your product developer, for example, attends customer progress meetings, or *en masse* by inviting the customer to come and speak at the annual get together. Invite your boss as well. If getting everyone to meet the customer is a new idea, you could be doing your career no harm at all if you introduce this. Engineers, for example, sometimes completely transform the way they think about their work once they have got a real insight into what the customers are trying to do, and how they look at their offerings.

The finance department may seem an unlikely contender for customer contact. But suppose that you ran the financial control department for an organisation based in several locations, none of which is in your building. You wouldn't consider trying to operate without going to see the various sites. You need to get a feel for what they have to deal with. Indeed, if you don't get some of your own people out there as well, you could well be failing to tap into an important source of insights. If your people visit the sites from time to time, they'll probably see how they can make simple changes. You, the manager, may have missed it because of your lack of intimate knowledge of the details.

Defining idea...

'The future belongs to those who prepare for it today.'
MALCOLM X

In the same way it is vital for your finance people, for example, to get direct knowledge of your customers. Get them face to face with customers, and get them amenable to any changes that the customer requests. That way your customers will realise how professional whole team serving them is, and your career will soar on the wings of customer satisfaction.

59. How to succeed at failure

A high-flying career by definition means taking some business risks. If you don't try you can't fail, but you can't succeed either. As you get higher up the organisation protect yourself against making a wrong decision yourself or suffering from a bad decision made by someone else..

One of the quickest ways to get rich is to fail at the top. It works like this: sign a three-year contract and then fail in the first six months. With luck you'll walk away with a million pounds for six months' work.

Klaus Esser, the last chairman of Mannesman, strongly advised his shareholders to reject the hostile bid from Vodafone Airtouch. In the end the shareholders decided to reject his advice. So does Herr Esser disappear into the sunset with a hangdog expression and three months' wages? Not a bit of it. According to *The Times* he received a 'golden goodbye' worth £19 million, of which 'more than half was agreed on the day the German company capitulated'. Mmm.

The Chairman of any public enterprise will inevitably fail eventually. Either he or she will preside over a major cock up (Marks & Spencer), or his or her shareholders will decide that someone else will make a better job of running the company (Mannesman). So what do they do? Easy, they use their own lawyers, at the company's expense, to draw up their contract with failure heavily in mind. They get the security of share options and bonuses round them. They certainly link bonuses to performance measures, but in the small print, and they also make sure that they get paid whether the performance measures are attained or not.

The total leaving package for Klaus Esser, again according to The Times, amounted to 43 times his final annual salary of £470,000. Nice one Klaus.

> **Here's an idea for you...**
>
> It's absolutely true that if you look for unlikely opportunities in your working life they are likely to happen. Whenever you are talking to or listening to senior people try to find an angle where you can help. Listen for a statement like, 'we need to look into this' or words to that effect. Do a bit of research on the topic in question and send it to them with an offer to find out more.

If it's good enough for the top honchos, it's good enough for you

If someone tells you that there is no possible negotiation on your salary and package assume immediately that they are not telling the truth. After all, business is about negotiation. If someone tells you that you're grade 4 with two years' experience at that level, and that, therefore you are worth exactly the same as every other grade 4 with the same experience, either you are a data entry clerk, or you put the tops on baked beans tins in a factory, or they're lying.

So, negotiate in exactly the same way as they do at the top. Examine incentive schemes and make sure that you will get paid whether the targets are hit or not. Make sure the exit terms are generous if it all goes wrong. You are choosing to work for your organisation, so the least you can do is get the best return you can.

Defining idea...

'With full-span lives having become
the norm, people may need to learn
how to be aged as they once had to
learn to be adult.'
RONALD BLYTHE, *writer*

The truth about share grants and options

Let's face some hard facts about share options. We know that the value of a share is what the next person will pay for it. We know that what the last person paid for it is a reasonable estimate, if nothing changes, of what the next person will pay for it and therefore of its value. It's OK to go for share options when the shares are listed and there is an easy trade in them. Don't value them too highly in your salary negotiation; but you can value them.

But this is just not the case for a non-listed company. They have never changed hands except when the founders generously offer them to people they want to attract into the business. There is no next person to buy them, and there is no indication of value from the last person to buy them. You can therefore value them very accurately; they are worth nothing at all. Remember that in the negotiation.

If all the business plans I have seen had come to pass there would be millions of companies listed on the stock exchange. But usually the exit strategy does not work and the shares are never listed. Venture capitalists can make it happen because they back so many runners – and even they have far more failures than successes.

60. Make the budget work for you

No doubt you'll often have heard people moaning about management removing some small perk that they have got used to.

There are two ways of looking at this. First of all there is the budget point. Most managers' budgets consist mainly of the costs associated with employing people. This bill includes salaries, insurance payments, etc., and can be as much as 90 per cent of a manager's budget. It is rarely less than 80 per cent. That is why in looking for economies you have to deal at the margins with some pretty small beer.

The 2 per cent rule
Here's the second way of looking at it if you are in a profit-making organisation. Take your profit and loss account, projected or historic, and adjust all the main subtotals by just 2 per cent. Here is an example:

	No. of units	Price per unit	Total
Sales	100	10	1,000
Variable costs	100	6	600
Fixed costs			300
Profit			100

The customer, you are informed by the salesperson, has a cheaper offer from a competitor. He thinks that if you could knock just 2 per cent off the price per unit,

Here's an idea for you...

You can always improve your profit in the short term by stopping maintenance. If you're running a pub don't repair the chairs, stick the broken ones in the cellar. If you've got company cars put an embargo on servicing. This produces a one-off financial benefit that, because of the rule of 2 per cent can affect your profit and loss hugely. Be careful though. Make sure you're not there when the backlog of bills has to be faced – but with your new-found reputation for improving profitability it should be easy for you to soar onwards and upwards.

the purchaser can take a case for buying from you to his board. That discount plus reducing the order to only 98 units will make the customer's budget work.

The production department have had the agreement of management to a slight increase in the price of the unit; it's only 2 per cent, but in the circumstances you cannot pass this on to the customer.

Administration has been saying for some time that there would be a slight increase in their costs due to increased charges from the IT department. It's only 2 per cent.

You know that these four changes to the proposition are all against the interests of your profit and loss account, but the numbers seem small, the customer has a lot of clout, and the salesperson is going to miss his target if he doesn't get this order. You agree to the changes.

Look at the actual damage this decision makes to the profit and loss account:

	No. of units	Price per unit	Total
Sales	98	9.8	960.4
Variable costs	98	6.12	599.76
Fixed costs			306
Profit			54.64

Each 2 per cent adjustment, all to your disadvantage, has combined to knock nearly 46 per cent off your profit.

Interestingly enough if you make the figures go the other way, you get a similarly dramatic impact:

	No. of units	Price per unit	Total
Sales	102	10.2	1,040.4
Variable costs	102	5.88	599.76
Fixed costs			294
Profit			146.64

Right, how can you use this phenomenon career-wise?

Look at your projected profit and loss account for the next six months. Adjust all the subtotals by 2 per cent positively and look at the impact in absolute numbers. Resolve that the new number is your target for the period. Now get the team together in a conference room on-site. Explain what your new aim is and illustrate how the rule of 2 per cent works. Next tell them that there are times when it is right to spend the company's money lavishly but the next six months is not one of them.

Break your team into groups and get them to come up with ideas for expanding sales and reducing costs. Set these as the new targets and go for the big increase in profits.

3
Upgrading your job

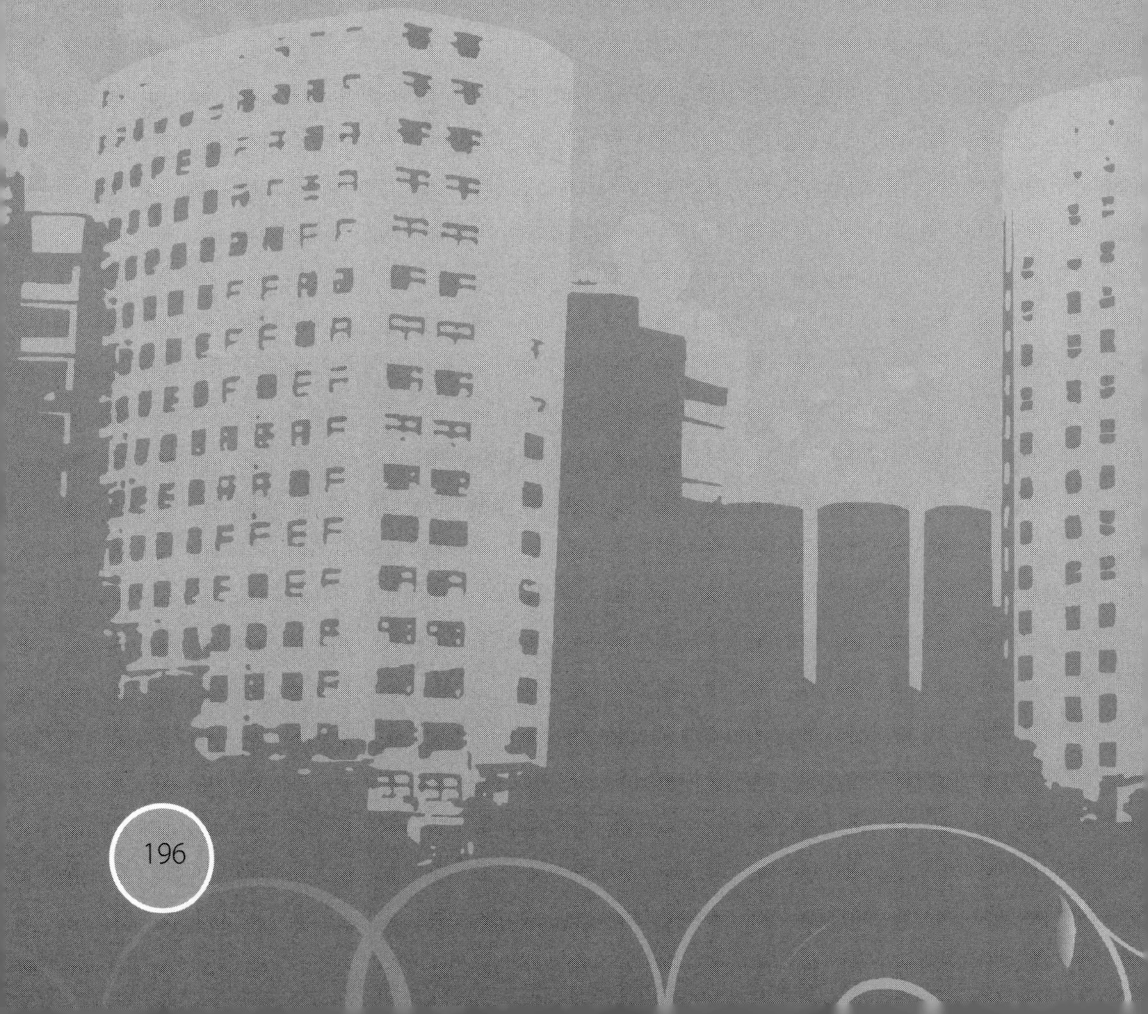

You've taken this job as far as you can go. Now it's time to get a new one. Here we have the inside information on the interview answers guaranteed to land you your next job.

What's holding you back?

Sometimes the only thing stopping you getting ahead is yourself...

1. You've been for several job interviews, but you keep getting pipped at the post. Are you:
- ☐ a. Cynical? It's just luck or who you know. There's no other reason to explain why you didn't get those jobs.
- ☐ b. Learning? Eventually your time will come.

2. Your hair is cut:
- ☐ a. Every six weeks.
- ☐ b. Every six months.
- ☐ c. When you can't see.

3. You have had problems with other colleagues:
- ☐ a. Once or twice
- ☐ b. Half a dozen times.
- ☐ c. Fairly often – it's that kind of organisation.

4. Where is your last phone bill?
- ☐ a. Paid and filed.
- ☐ b. Either in your bag or on the shelf in the hallway.
- ☐ c. No idea.

5. On the whole, your bosses have:
- ☐ a. Annoyed you

☐ b. Taught you loads
☐ c. Loved you.

6. You have been with the same company for some time and now others are being promoted over your head. You will:
☐ a. Work harder for recognition.
☐ b. Start looking elsewhere for a job
☐ c. Complain the treatment isn't fair.

Score
1 (a) 0; (b) 2
2 (a) 2; (b) 1; (c) 0
3 (a) 2; (b) 1; (c) 0
4 (a) 2; (b) 1; (c) 0
5 (a) 0; (b) 1; (c) 2
6 (a) 2; (b) 1; (c) 0

10–12
You'll have a new job soon, possibly by the time you finish reading this page. Your attitude is superb and others recognise you as an asset to an organisation. Read *idea 76* just to make sure you negotiate the salary you deserve.

7–10
You do a lot to help yourself including, probably, asking for feedback when you don't get a job. Make sure you get this across with *idea 68*.

6 or under
Could do better. These questions might seem a bit irrelevant but sometimes we don't get on purely because we're not organised enough. It's also a lot to do with how you are perceived by others. Start with *idea 61* and read all this section.

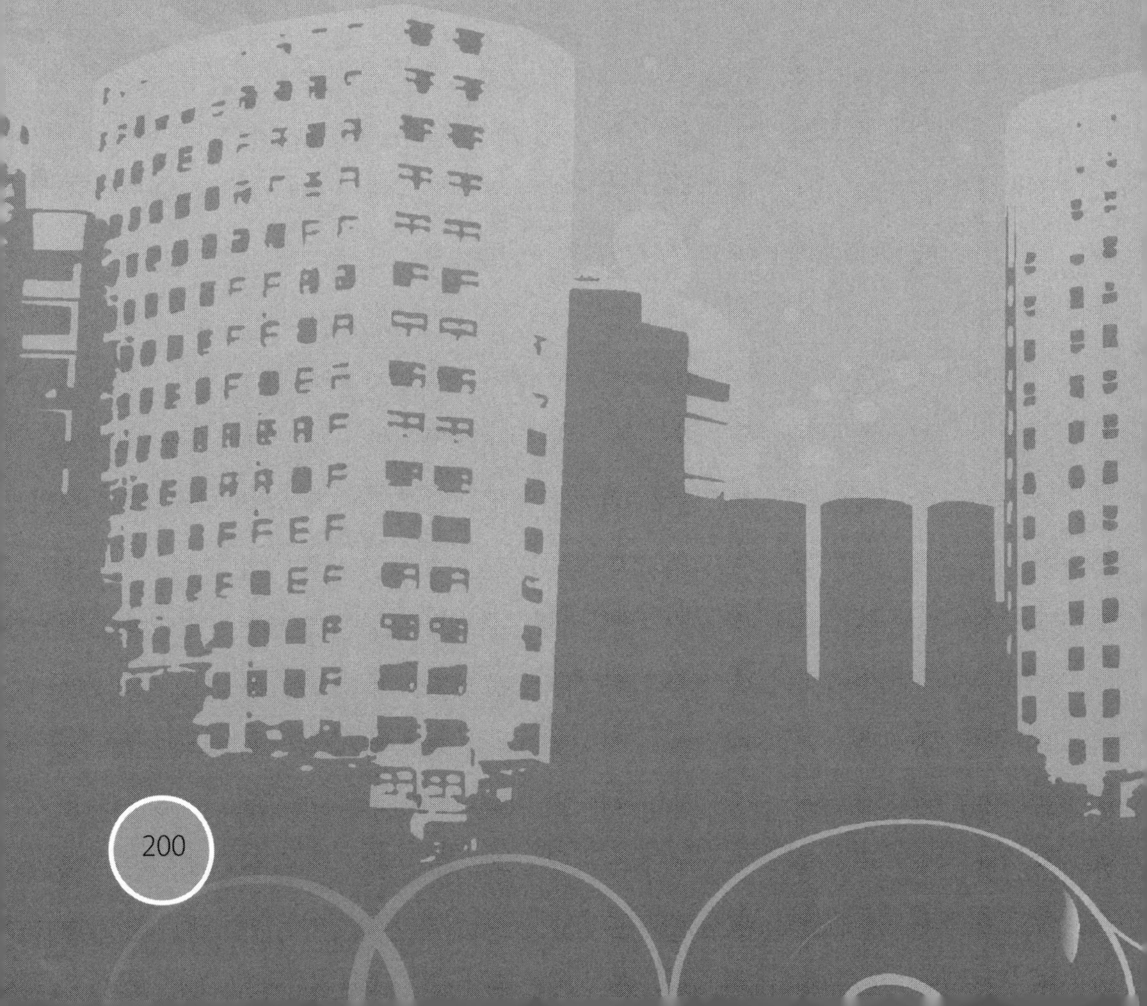

Getting your foot in the door

61. Getting back to work

Only one thing gets you down, and hence stressed, more than work. Not working.

For periods when you're 'resting', or times when you're not earning, you need this idea.

Paradoxically, one of the most stressed periods of any life is when you don't have to worry about the nine-to-five because for whatever reason you're no longer in paid employment.

People in low-paid, menial jobs are far more stressed than thrusting Type A folk. They have little control over their working life and there's nothing more stressful than lack of control. Those made redundant or who are 'between jobs', women who have had children and opted to stay at home – anyone basically who doesn't get paid (note, I didn't say who doesn't work) is vulnerable to the stress of the 'no work' phenomenon.

What's the answer?

Take control
If you're looking for a job, don't fritter away time worrying while making half-hearted or piecemeal attempts to find one. You need a strategy. You need

short-term and long-term goals. You need to break these goals down into tasks and you need to schedule these tasks in your diary. You know this. It's just that when you're anxious it's a lot easier to spend hours fine-tuning your CV and waiting for the phone to ring than to be proactive.

> **Here's an idea for you...**
>
> Aim for excellence. You may be an adequate cook. Use your time 'off' to become a brilliant one. You may love reading. Become an exemplary reader. List all those classic novels, you've been meaning to read but never got round to.

Call every contact you know. Look into part-time or casual work that will at least give you some money until you get a job. At the end of the day having lists of tasks completed will give you a sense of achievement and help you feel in control. Enlist a friend if necessary. The hardest thing in the world is to call ten contacts and sell yourself to them, but asking a friend to call you at the end of the day to check that you've done it is a powerful motivator.

If you're a mother at home with children, structure is vital. Set yourself personal goals – just like you did at work. These goals should not just be about the children. Getting your jollies from 'achieving' with the kids instead of 'achieving' in the workplace is fine when they're really small, but your sense of displacement and low self-esteem may be greater when they grow up a bit even if you have no regrets about the time you've lavished on them.

Build confidence

Here's a difficult tip but one that really works. Ask five people that know you well to answer the questions overleaf honestly.

Defining idea...

'You take my life when you do take the means whereby I live.'
WILLIAM SHAKESPEARE,
The Merchant of Venice

- What is the first thing you think of when you think of me (immediately bin anyone who says 'unemployed')?
- What do you think is the most interesting thing about me?
- What do you think has been my greatest accomplishment?
- What do you value most about me?
- What do you perceive to be my greatest strengths?

OK. A bit embarrassing. But just say you've been asked to answer these questions on a job application and you're (becomingly modestly) stuck for ideas. What you'll be amazed at is the different perceptions people have of you. It also helps you realise that qualities you take for granted aren't qualities that everyone shares. You're unique.

Get happy

When you're short of money, isolated and bored, it's unlikely that you're getting the regular doses of endorphins that we need to stay happy campers. Understimulation leads to fatigue and depression. It's essential to manufacture highs and you have to do it daily. Make a 'joy list' of things that will give you a sense of achievement and happiness that don't cost a lot. By slotting them regularly into your day, you'll fire off endorphins and fool your body that you are still a high-flyer with endless cash to fritter away on life's inanities. You could decide to start every day with an alfresco breakfast, spend an afternoon watching a movie or have a glass of wine under the stars. Every day must have one pure pleasure.

62. Top notch CVs

Your CV is a selling document and the product it is selling is you. You want someone who is trying to fill a new post to reach for your CV and like what they see.

The 'inside salesperson' is salesperson's jargon for someone who supports the salesperson and advances their case internally when the salesperson isn't there. A CV can do the same thing for a person seeking a job or promotion.

Present it well

Nowadays it is very easy for the CV's presentation to be first class, so anything else is an inside suicide note. Make sure it is also in pristine condition, every time.

An actor of the old school with a booming voice that made every phrase sound as if it were by Shakespeare was frequently out of work and always short of money. He used to go around the local shops trying to cash cheques. One day he tried four or five places and got four or five polite refusals from shopkeepers who knew him. By this time the cheque looked somewhat crumpled and dilapidated. His final try was at the laundry. 'Would you be so good as to cash me a small cheque?' he said. 'I'm sorry,' came the reply, 'but we still have an old one of yours that bounced.' 'Oh well,' said the actor, 'could you at least iron the bloody thing?'

> ### Here's an idea for you...
>
> Keep your CV consistent with the job you're applying for. You may have to tailor it for different jobs. Once you have written the CV, get as many people as possible to look it over for you. Take it to business managers who hire people into their teams, and to someone who works in HR. In the end the same document has to work for both.

Nowadays, of course, it's highly likely that you'll send in your CV by email, but if they want hard copy make sure it's highly presentable, not like a well-thumbed cheque. It is up to you how complete your CV is, but you don't have to put anything on it that may damage your case. You can probably miss out the wrong job that only lasted six months, and a slight exaggeration of your role in your present company may help your chances of getting a more senior job with a competitor, as long as it's not too far from the truth. You'll have to substantiate it. Make the document fit in with the style of the job, formal and professional for the accountants, witty and outrageous for creative jobs.

What's in it?

Following your name in bold, write a first paragraph describing who you are and what you're like: 'An energetic IT project manager, with wide experience in complex projects, predominantly focused on bridging the gap between the business managers who generate the profits and the IT department who support their endeavours. Experienced influencer and coach. Decisive, commercially focused and passionate about service and quality. A proven record of delivering first-class results in major global companies.'

Now put down your career history starting with your current job and going back to your first. Make sure that each job has an illustration of the impact you had on the results, preferably financial, of the organisation you were working for. Don't just say what you did; say what it did for the company. Then put in your personal details, education and qualifications, contact numbers and addresses and outside interests.

> *Defining idea...*
>
> 'The only end of writing is to enable the readers better to enjoy life, or better to endure it.'
> SAMUEL JOHNSON

Research shows that a quarter of all CVs contain lies. Most firms don't test skills; so it's possible to get away with an exaggeration of your computer or other skills, but still quite dangerous. The humiliation when your boss uncovers your deception will give you a very rough start. A lie never ceases to be a time bomb, and it's so easy to forget what you said if it wasn't the truth.

If the job seems ideal for you, and you seem ideal for the job, don't pretend to meet a criterion set by the employer, rather work out in your preparation why the criterion is unnecessary and/or how quickly you could become able to fulfil it in any case. Use a covering letter to accentuate the particular experience you have to do the job. If there is an attribute in the advert or job description that you don't have, point the gap out and balance it with a strength that you do have that more than compensates for the lack. That way, forewarned by the letter they're more likely to read on when they hit the gap in the CV.

63. Look good on your CV . . . without lying

You must make your CV entirely consistent with what the interviewers will discover in interview. If you try to bluff them, they'll almost certainly trip you up and you'll have done yourself no favours.

This is a simple deal breaker. If they catch you out in a gross exaggeration or a lie, then you've probably blown it.

It's time to talk about bullshit. Take the example in the title of this Idea. If you've genuinely taken over for a significant length of time, then the statement is fair enough and you'll be able to substantiate it during the interview. If, however, the project manager had a couple of days off twice during the project, and you stood in for them at a couple of meetings, then your CV is misleading. The most you can claim is, 'I deputised from time to time for the project manager.' The Americans speak of a 'water cooler hero' when a junior member of a project tries to exaggerate their role by relying on the conversations the senior people had round the water cooler to bluff their way through.

The funnel technique

The way experienced interviewers expose such talk is to use the funnel technique. They stay very friendly as they ask one follow-up question after another until your cover is blown. It's extraordinary how often people fall at the first fence:

'I see it says on your CV that you measured the return on investment of sales campaigns before you submitted the proposal to the customer. How did that work?'

'Well, I had to work out the rate of return, taking into account the value of the sale and the costs involved in production, delivery and installation. It had to be at least 15% for me to be able to go ahead.'

'Was that just direct costs or overheads as well?'

'I'm not sure what you mean by that.'

'OK, let's talk about the rate of return. Did you do a cash flow and discount it, or how did you calculate it?'

'Well, actually it was the accountants who worked it out.'

'I see. What does a rate of return of 15% actually mean in your company?'

'Um, it was something to do with profitability.'

'Yes, of course. I understand. Next please.'

The key is to be able to substantiate every statement you make on your CV and in answer to questions. They're never going to take big claims at face value; they're always going to squeeze you down the funnel as they go from wide open questions to become more and more specific.

> **Here's an idea for you...**
>
> Go over your CV with a fine-tooth comb. Challenge yourself to substantiate every claim you've made. If you feel that funnel questioning will catch you out, change the wording. You won't necessarily weaken your case and you remove the risk of looking as though you were trying to pull the wool over their eyes.

Defining idea...

'O what a tangled web we weave
When first we practise to deceive.'
SIR WALTER SCOTT

Make sure that what they've seen is what they get

Your CV covers not only what you've done in your life but also how you behave and what you're like. Your behaviour at the interview has to reflect that pen portrait. So, don't give yourself an impossible task by describing a person you cannot be. If you describe yourself as energetic and enthusiastic, that's how you must act. If you talk about your careful analysis of situations before you make decisions then you should be very thoughtful in answering their questions. If you think that they're looking for an outgoing personality for the job, then by all means write down that you have that quality – as long as you can quickly overcome any nervousness at the beginning and hit a good conversational stride.

Defining idea...

'You told a lie, an odious damnèd lie:
Upon my soul, a lie, a wicked lie!'
WILLIAM SHAKESPEARE

When you're checking your CV, make sure that nothing that you've written could catch you out. Look out for adjectives; they're the words that trigger further questions. 'What exactly were the tangible benefits?' If you've described yourself as professional you've got to look and act the part. If you've written 'experienced coach and mentor', be prepared to discuss not only what you did but also the benefits to the person and the organisation of the coaching that you did.

64. Changing employers mid-career

If you make a move to a new company your fellow managers there have an advantage over you. They know the ropes and how to shine in the existing environment. It is therefore a very good idea to do something early on to question that environment and change it in a high-profile way.

When you are changing employer think long and hard about why they hired you.

If you are joining at a fairly high level it is likely that the people who hired you saw you as an agent of change, for a part of their business or culture which is underperforming – new blood, new brooms and all that. If this is the case, you can afford to take a few risks in the early days.

Make a splash, why don't you?

Here's a brilliant example of making a great splash early on in a new outfit. A manager I know moved from one telecommunications company to another much larger and longer established one. He knew, from his competitive

Here's an idea for you...

Even if you are staying put in your organisation have a long, hard think about change. What in your company really needs to be changed? Think deeply and don't be held back by things that seem to be cast in stone – nothing is. Right, if the change is within your authority, just do it. If it's not in your authority, but it wouldn't be a suicidal risk, just do it anyway. If it's too much of a risk to take on yourself, go to the person who could do it and persuade them to let you do it. Try not to give them the whole idea or they might pinch it.

knowledge and from things said at the interview, that senior management were implementing a huge programme of change aimed at knocking the old-fashioned corners off those managers who had served with the organisation since the year dot.

Many of these people were accustomed to a hierarchical, rather deferential culture where seniority counted highly. They were also struggling with the idea that the customer was king. On his very first day the new boy took action using the car park as his vehicle, if you'll pardon the pun. He removed every car parking space allocated on the basis of management seniority, and reallocated the best spaces to customers only. As he was doing this he realised that some areas were not only dark but also outside the range of the security cameras. So he allocated the next best spaces nearest to the entrance to those women who sometimes or regularly worked late.

At a stroke he got the support of those of his people who felt held back by the old guard, and of the more ambitious women willing to work long hours. His action also became high profile without his having to tell a soul – the old guard did it for him: they were fuming. They sent angry e-mails to the HR department and senior managers in all parts of the organisation complaining about this loss of their hard-earned privilege. They themselves gave him the oxygen of publicity. By the end of his very first day he had a very high profile. He had sorted the resisters to change from the enthusiasts for it, and impressed on senior management his grasp of what they were looking for in terms of cultural change. Senior management congratulated themselves, modestly of course, for hiring the right person for the job.

Defining idea...

'Most ideas on management have been around for a very long time, and the skill of the manager consists in knowing them all and, rather as he might choose the appropriate golf club for a specific situation, choosing the particular ideas which are most appropriate for the position and time in which he finds himself.'
SIR JOHN HARVEY-JONES, *former ICI chief*

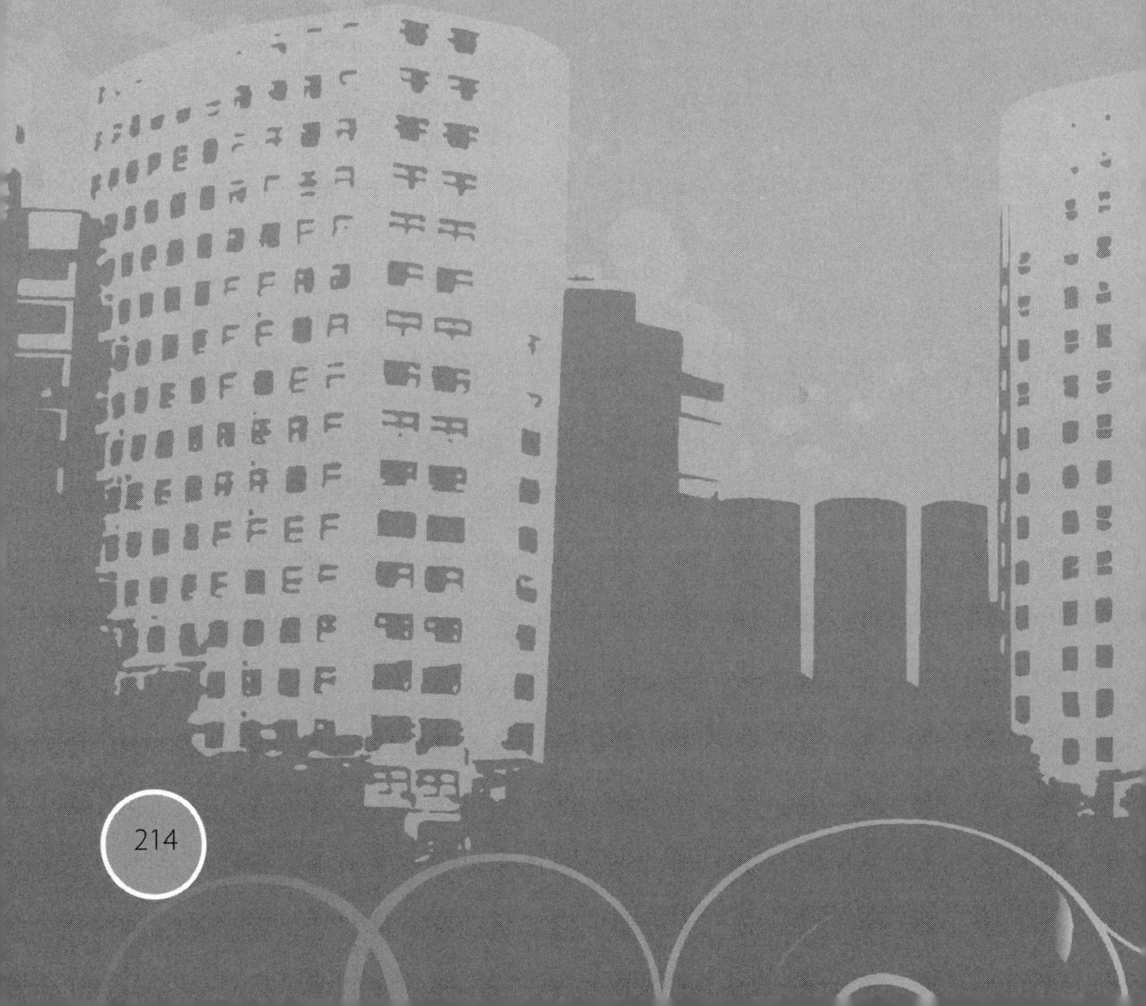

Stunning them at the interview

65. Great body language

Delivering great answers to the interviewer's questions is the main skill in impressing people and getting the job; but let's not underestimate the importance of the body language you use to get your nose in front.

Neurolinguistic programming can help you to develop rapport very quickly in an interview.

It includes techniques that can help you at the beginning of the interview when you're getting over your nerves and the interviewers are forming their first impression.

Matching and mirroring

Interviews are like speed dating. You quickly eye each other up and decide whether or not you're interested in taking things further. So you need to be able to build rapport with your interviewer as quickly and effectively as possible. You never have a second chance to make a first impression.

The key skill to use here is mirroring. Mirroring body language is based on the theory that we are more at ease, subconsciously, with people who are similar to ourselves. It's a bit like dancing. You can mirror most things:

Posture, for instance. If they're upright, so are you. If they cross their legs, so do you. If their arms are on the table, so are yours. If you're sitting opposite someone with their right leg crossed, you cross your left leg to make a mirror image. You're making the person feel comfortable that they're talking to someone with similar behaviours to theirs.

Listen to the tone and speed of their voice. If they talk quickly, try to answer at the same speed. Vary your tone in the same way they do. Is the language they use concise or detailed? If they ask long questions they're going to be more comfortable with you giving a detailed answer.

Pick up on their mood, whether it's humorous or serious. You will notice, of course, how formally or casually they dress and conduct themselves.

You can mirror their use of gestures to accentuate a point. If they change their posture, you change yours. (People who are brilliant at this technique claim to match the speed at which a person's eyes blink, but beginners shouldn't try this lest they look like a mole emerging into sunlight.)

Don't mimic them or copy their gestures too quickly. Mirroring is a subtle technique and interviewers who are not NLP proficient should not consciously

Here's an idea for you...

It's probably best not to try the technique of mirroring for the first time in an interview. First of all, observe people doing it naturally at social gatherings. That gives you visual evidence that people do it, even in groups. Now try it in conversation with someone you know well, and then try it in a business context. Just a few practices should make you proficient enough to do it at an interview.

217

Defining idea...

'She is the mirror of alle courteisye.'
GEOFFREY CHAUCER

notice what you're doing. They will just get the warm feeling that comes from dealing with someone on the same wavelength.

We all use this form of body language when we're relaxed with our friends. Watch people in a restaurant or a pub and you'll see how mirroring helps the group to feel comfortable in each other's company. Or maybe it's the other way round: when you're with someone you're entirely comfortable with, it's quite hard not to do it.

Anchoring

You're never at your most confident when you're about to try to be tested, professionally and personally. Anchoring can be very helpful in removing the signs of nervousness and helping to give you the confidence to give of your best. Anchor yourself to a memory of a time in your life when you felt really confident. Before the interview, perhaps outside the door, pause and bring that experience of total confidence into your mind. Hold it there, remember how you felt and what you saw and said. This reminds your brain of how to feel and look confident. At times of pressure in the interview, recall the situation again and you'll adjust your behaviour back to expressing confidence.

66. How do you balance risk and return?

Senior businesspeople see business as a series of decisions about risk taking, or the balance between risk and return. This question is one way of checking your knowledge of and attitude to risk.

Demonstrate here how you evaluate and sometimes reject risky projects even though you may be under pressure from above or from your team to take them on.

This risk/return attitude to business is pushing down the line at present, and middle managers are expected to have a reasonable grasp of the topic and to take appropriate calculated risks.

Know where they're coming from
First of all make sure you know what sort of company you're applying to. If a company is set up to take high risks in the hope of exceptional returns, they look for people who are comfortable in that environment and willing to take a gamble. Other companies settle for a lower rate of return and are generally considered to be more risk averse.

Here's an idea for you...

It's a good idea to get a detailed example of the company's attitude to risk. Look on their website or in their annual report for a subject where they are obviously risk averse and try to develop an example in that area.

Your industry knowledge should mean that you are aware of the general risk profile of a company working within that industry. However, you can research how the company you're applying to sits within the industry. One clue to this is how the company's price/earnings ratio compares with the industry average. The higher it is the more risks the company is expected to take. This gives you a good question in the interview: 'I see that your p/e ratio is higher/lower than the industry average. Does this mean that you are less/more risk averse than your competitors?' This knowledge flavours your reply to this question to suit the company. You don't want to apply to the local undertakers and look like someone prepared to put a month's salary on 36 Red.

Remember that risk aversion can be both good and bad. Being risk averse is often good when you're bucking the trend or the flavour of the month; when you're not getting involved when the high rollers are riding for a fall. (The telecommunications companies who didn't get into trouble during the internet bubble at the beginning of the century were the ones who were more risk averse.) The downside of risk aversion is missing out on opportunities and then missing out on the returns.

And so the demonstration

They've asked you for an example, so give them one. You could try a financial one. 'The IT people wanted my team to implement a new computer system that had heavy backing from top management. They made impressive demonstrations of the cost/benefit argument, but I had a huge doubt that the benefits would be as large as they claimed. And I knew of course that the costs quoted would be at best the minimum they would charge. I demurred and then watched as other departments implemented the system and then complained about the returns later on. IT had to lower the price and then we went for it.' This example has all the ingredients you want: not giving in to pressure, good judgement and the proof that you were right.

Or perhaps a people-oriented one. 'A salesman with a terrific track record wanted to join my team selling to the Ministry of Defence. He also had a reputation for flashy behaviour and sailing very close to the wind. My manager urged me to take a risk with him. He believed that the salesman's flair would overcome the rather formal approach of the civil servants and serving officers that we had to deal with. Rejecting that advice, and the salesman, did me some harm. People began to mutter about me becoming as stuffed shirt as my customers. Then they took the same guy on to work with another government department. He lasted three months before the customer insisted he was taken off the account.' Or you could give a personal example, such as not buying a house that would stretch you too much if interest rates went up.

> Defining idea...
>
> 'Rashness succeeds often, still more often fails.'
> NAPOLEON BONAPARTE

67. How do you work with difficult people?

You're bound to get something about your ability to handle difficult people. This is a very specific example. How do you make people change what may be the habits of a lifetime?

It's not particularly difficult to manage enthusiastic people who are self-motivated, keep to company procedures and are great members of the team. How do you pass on your drive and energy to someone who's simply not interested or is hostile?

A difficult person resists change, moans about everyone and is happy to tell the whole team why everything is wrong. Handled poorly, they're the bad apple that ruins the barrel. You've got to demonstrate not only how you'd try to get them to accept change but also how you'd prevent their becoming a creeping cancer in the team.

Why are they difficult?
Sometimes people resist change because they lack some of the skills and knowledge involved in doing things differently. So you need to find out whether this is the case and at the same time show that you're willing to help

these people develop. It's your job to get to understand the difficult person and why they're like what they are. Having said that, you can often get people to change by tackling them head on. Discuss not their behaviour itself but rather the impact that it's having on what they do and how other people see them.

Here's an idea for you...

If you don't have experience in this area find a manager who has. Get a good example of how the problem was handled and use this, attributing it to a mentor or colleague manager.

Give an example something along the following lines. 'I had a person who absolutely refused to accept that she had to work in a different area to the one she had been in for a while. Her work was producing less and less return, and we desperately wanted her to move her attention to another product. She categorically refused to start working in an area where the younger, newer people were happily operating. I had a difficult conversation with her and she got upset; but it was useful because I found out the real problem – because of her seniority she hadn't attended the induction course where new people had found out about the new product and its potential. She was unwilling to go on a course with a bunch of rookies; so I organised for the training department to give her a one-to-one briefing on the topic and she came back changed and ready to go.'

Others are just very cynical. They see any management initiative as bound to fail and by their attitude can help to make that into a self-fulfilling prophecy. (They even have a word for it: 'BOHICA' standing for 'Bend Over Here It Comes Again'.) In this case it might be useful to say that you would make sure in the first place that they aren't right and that the change is necessary and will be effective. If this is the case, then you have two weapons – business processes and peer pressure.

Defining idea...

'Aye, he's a difficult person, and that's on a good day.'
BOB FRASER, ICL *Account Director*

'In my experience such people always stay just inside obligatory business processes. They may ignore some less significant ones but never give you a simple opportunity to prove misconduct. So I would look for how I could build the new way of working into their job; I'd try to make it impossible for them to carry out their function and resist change at the same time. I've also seen that simply ignoring them tends to leave them more and more isolated. Then peer pressure might bring them on board.'

Don't let them rock the boat

Now demonstrate how you would prevent the difficult person infecting everyone else. 'There can be a way of making such people look for positives rather than negatives. I might try going to them frequently and asking for their advice. Their challenge becomes to look for what should be done rather than complaining about what is being done. If I can get the rest of the team cheerful and energetic, that should bring them along with the tide. If it really doesn't work and I haven't solved the problem I would try to maintain friendly relations but I would keep this very business-related. Having protected the team, I mustn't let the person get to me either.'

If the interview is going really well you could take a flyer by hinting that you've heard of head shunting where you use a friendly headhunter to attract the person somewhere else. But be careful with HR people in this area; if a case like this is not handled within the rules it could lead to an unfair dismissal claim or to the duped company suing.

68. So, why do you want this job?

Turn a question like this into a selling opportunity by using a double answer — balance what you'll get out of the job with what they'll get out of hiring you.

It should be reasonably easy to answer this one as long as you're going for the right job. If it's very difficult, then ask yourself if this is the right employer for you before you go in.

An employer wants people to join them with enthusiasm for the challenges they're about to face. Similarly you want to get into an environment where your working life gives you joy rather than grief. Research and good self-insight will give you the right answer to achieve both aims.

What's in it for me?
It's probably best to start the dual answer with the straightforward answer to the question. It's another question that depends on your research. You've got to be able to reply in terms of the company's attributes as you find them. It doesn't really matter what the situation is; you can still paint it as ideal for you. 'Most people want to work for the market leader; I could use your name with pride' could equally be, 'I like the way you've made such progress in your industry over the last few years. A growing company like yours suits my energetic way of working. I really enjoy success.'

> ## Here's an idea for you...
>
> This question really is one to prepare for carefully. The time will never be wasted, since this question will always crop up in one way or other. The best way to prepare is to find someone to role-play the interviewer and then try out with them the actual words you're going to use. If you can get someone in the same industry that would be best, but anyone with good experience of organisations or business should be able to help.

Now try to get in something about their reputation. 'I understand that you can offer me a stable, challenging and inspiring work environment – you certainly have that reputation. I think it's the sort of environment that brings out the best in me.'

Now compliment the company on what it actually does. 'Many people regard your products and services as the best around. It's a pride thing again; I like to work for someone who is passionate about service and quality. I think we share those values and that I would enjoy fitting into your team.'

And what's in it for them?

Your unique selling proposition is you and your skills and experience. Try to work out a way of illustrating that everything you've done points at you being the right person for them. Perhaps start from specific experience. For a team leader in credit control: 'My experience in the credit control department of a builders' merchants was, frankly, a hard school. The building industry is always suffering from companies going under. I know about collection periods, credit ratings calculated from company reports and, of course, I've heard every excuse under the sun for not being quite ready to issue the cheque. I think that as team leader I would be able to help others to learn from that experience.'

226

Now relate the specific skills to the goals of the organisation. 'I understand the benefits to you of getting payment in on time or even before time because I've controlled cash flow for an organisation and seen the impact it can have on profitability.'

Defining idea...

'And so my fellow Americans: ask not what your country can do for you – ask what you can do for your country.'
JOHN F. KENNEDY

You can also be more open about your skills where you're sure they're appropriate. For a production manager: 'I've always scored well in problem solving and from what you've said you need to find some new ways of cutting down the waste at the end of the production line.'

Something more personal can emphasise your uniqueness. For a training deliverer: 'The fact that I've done a bit of amateur dramatics helps me to understand the "performance" side of running a training course.'

Now bring the three things together: 'So you see why I was excited when I saw your job ad; you seem to need a person with pretty much the experience, skills and interests that I've developed.'

69. What would your team change about you?

Knowing yourself, or self-insight, is crucial. The answer to this question tells the interviewers a lot about you, probably including a hint of your main weakness.

Pick the thing to be changed carefully – and turn a vice into a virtue.

Let's look first on the negative side. What they are probing for here is any trait of yours that really is a red light for them not to go ahead with you. So avoid showing them any problem that might be a deal breaker.

Use ancient history
Quite a neat way of handling this is to talk about a weakness that you've had in the past, that you've overcome but that you remain on guard for. 'A manager once pointed out to me that I was causing some discomfort to my team when I acted too precipitately when they came to me with a problem. I thought about it and realised that I sometimes listened to a problem and quickly proposed a solution. I might then volunteer to take the first action myself. At that point I'd pick up the phone there and then to put the action plan into progress. I talked to the team about it and they agreed that it was frustrating for them because

they wanted to go away, think about the plan and sort the problem out themselves. I think I've fixed it and don't do it now; but I'm aware of the tendency and watch myself carefully in those circumstances.'

Here's an idea for you...

Prepare for this type of question by actually asking it of your team. 'What would you most like to change about me?' With luck what they say won't be a surprise and you can work out an answer using the templates in this Idea. Perhaps it will be a surprise, in which case you've just taken a big step forward in getting to know yourself.

This is a reasonable answer and one that shows your ability to act on criticism. Which is pertinent to another question in the area of self-insight which often comes up: 'How do you react when your manager or a team member tells you that they don't like something you do?' Now, nobody's perfect and such criticism happens to everyone. It's crucial that you display real interest in the feedback and take some action to show that you are putting things right. There's no need, however, to suggest to an interviewer that such things happen very often.

'I've come to know that whatever the criticism that people are making, there is always something in it; so I never argue about it or attempt to justify my position. In order to learn from it, I've found that you need to talk it over thoroughly, to make sure that you're both talking about exactly the same thing. When I do that, it's normally pretty easy to modify how I behave. If I then invite them to point out any reoccurrences I find that the discussion ends up useful and amicable.'

Defining idea...

'The real solvent of class distinction is a proper measure of self-esteem – a kind of unconsciousness. Some people are at ease with themselves, so the world is at ease with them.'
ALAN BENNETT, *British playwright*

Pick something they actually quite like

This depends on your function. Every job has a bit in it that people don't like or see as a low priority. For a salesperson it's easy. No one likes doing the paperwork. Often in a rather macho way, people regard it as getting in the way of the real work – the selling work. Once again present the issue as something you know you have to continuously overcome.

'I know I have a tendency to get a bit behind with the paperwork. I also know that that can upset the office people terribly and, if left undone for long enough, can lead to missed deliveries and customer dissatisfaction. So, I've put a severe discipline on myself to keep up to date every Wednesday afternoon when a lot of my customers are closed.' Whatever your function you can probably find your version of the salesperson's paperwork.

70. Why should we hire you over better qualified candidates?

Whatever the weakness that they probe, don't forget that they have invited you to the interview; so unless someone has blundered it's still possible for you to get the job.

It can be a good thing to ask a clarifying question at this point. 'Do you [all] think that only graduates should have this sort of job?' Once again unless someone's blundered they've got to say 'no' to this question; otherwise they're wasting their own time as well as yours. With a bit of luck one of them will be more certain that the successful candidate doesn't have to be a graduate. You may have an ally there. As you answer the question see if you can appeal to that person to help you out.

Here's an idea for you...

Generally, it's not your qualifications or even your experience in carrying out the tasks that'll get you the job. It's what they think of you as a person. Work out a little presentation that illustrates that you are interesting to talk to and keen to make your contribution. You'll find some way to work it into the conversation, either from your seat or using a couple of laptop slides. Some people have won jobs because they surprised everyone by giving an effective and witty presentation even though they hadn't been asked to prepare one.

It was my choice

Let's look at the graduate problem. The first trick in answering it is to avoid giving them the impression that you've got to the age of twenty-seven or whatever and suddenly realised that you need some sort of proper job and the possibility of a career. No, you chose to prepare for your career not by going into further education but by doing something else. Now work out what you learnt doing whatever you did. The main reason people like graduates, even when their subject has nothing to do with the job in hand, is that they believe that graduates have learnt to learn on their own. That's what you need to demonstrate here.

Anne Scott James, a journalist with a worldwide reputation for getting herself into the right place at the right time, used the following technique to get past customs officials and guard posts. She emptied out a huge handbag on their counter in order to search for the particular documents they wanted and she didn't have. She then acted the dizzy lady, smiled a lot and was incredibly successful in getting her own way. She didn't learn that at any university.

The thing you don't learn much about at university is motivating people and overcoming people problems such as those James faced. Concentrate on examples of this. 'I think my couple of years as an assistant in a wine shop taught me a lot about customer service, working as a member of a team and the importance of

Defining idea...

'My only qualification for being put at the head of the Navy is that I am very much at sea.'
LORD CARSON, *Irish politician*

being disciplined and trustworthy. From my understanding this job is a lot about all of those.' (Not many university students are entrusted with taking the entire takings of the student's union bar to the bank.) If rapport is good, you could try dropping a couple of names. Richard Branson didn't go to university and neither did the President of the Save the Children Fund. (Mind you, the latter is Princess Anne.)

You're not the most qualified for the job

Ask a line manager what they look for in all the interviews they ever go to and they will say some variation on the following: 'I look to see whether I trust them, whether we can work with them and if they are capable of doing the job – in that order.' Not much about qualifications there. So don't despair if you are less qualified; use the interview to prove that they can't do without you and show how you will work on any weaknesses they perceive you have. Ask them also about the company policy of helping people to go to night school, get trained, assist with day release or whatever is appropriate.

71. Role-plays and assessment centres

The use of assessment centres to evaluate potential employees is widespread. Don't think you can't prepare for them.

As with any interview, have in mind the precise impression you want to leave behind. The clearer you have this impression in your mind, the better will be the filter through which you pass the decisions you have to make during the exercises. Be a contributing member of the group but ration your contributions to times when they move the group forward. Be prepared to compromise and try not to go out on a limb unless you're absolutely sure you're right.

Ok, turn over your papers
Find out as much as you can about what the assessment centre will involve. Typically, you and the others will be given a group exercise where a team has to discuss a situation and come up with decisions about what to do next. The exercises will generally be relevant to the sort of job you're going for. If you're going for a sales job it will almost certainly involve a customer situation. If you're to become a team leader for the first time it's likely to involve handling a difficult team member. In all cases, look for an opportunity to suggest to the team how it might structure the discussion.

There are some basic communication rules for group discussion:

- It's easy to think that your contribution to a group discussion occurs when you're speaking. In fact in these group discussions it's often the person who says least who looks best. Listen to what people are saying, rather than spending your whole time preparing your next brilliant epigram.

- Don't interrupt people to get your point in. It's bad practice and rude, but you'll be amazed how much it happens.

- Look for occasions where you can support something that someone has just said: 'That was a really helpful contribution, Penny; thank you.'

> **Here's an idea for you...**
>
> Think about the impression you want to leave behind when the interviews are over. Write this down so that you have it really well expressed. A good example is, 'I don't make rash decisions.' This will tend to lower the risks that you take at the centre. Now practise it. You can do this in normal meetings in your current job or you can ask other people to role-play with you. Then ask for feedback on the impression you made to see how accurately it mirrors your plan.

- When someone has said something that you think has merit but needs more explanation, don't jump in and take it in your own direction. It's much better teamwork to ask them a clarifying question.

- When you know something about the group, you should be able to find an opportunity where, because of their background and experience, some people should be in a better position than others to make a contribution. It's very good team technique to invite such individuals to comment. This demonstrates skills in group discussion leadership: 'You know about the production side, Ellen. What do you think?'

Wait till you can see the whites of their eyes

Try not to jump into the discussion too early. It can be very effective to sit and listen hard to what's being said, asking questions and bringing people in

Defining idea...

'The reason we have two ears and
only one mouth is that we may
listen the more and talk the less.'
ZENO OF CITIUM

appropriately. Then form your view. Towards the end you can then give a comprehensive summary of the points that have been made and give your view or support someone else's view. With luck you may be instrumental in helping the group to come to an agreed decision.

They're role-playing; you're being yourself

Try to look at role-play exercises in this way. If you're the salesperson and that's your job, then you're not role-playing; you're carrying out your function. Use the preparation time they give you. We know it's obvious, but do read the scenario meticulously. Generally, there's not much padding in the briefing; all the sentences and phrases are significant. So try not to miss anything. Try to connect the briefing to a real situation you've been in. It may not be that similar, but anything a bit like it can be helpful in making it feel real.

You're not on your own. If there's time, speak to other people at the centre to see what they make of the briefing. Ask the interviewers if you feel there is a piece of information that in real life you would have. They may decline to tell you, but it's worth trying. Take some deep breaths before you start. Go as slowly as you can. The temptation is to say too much too fast. Use open questions and try to relax. That's all there is to it.

At the end of an assessment centre session, the organisers have a lot of valuable data about you. Ask them for feedback. In most cases they'll give you it if you ask, but possibly not if you don't.

72. What are your strengths and weaknesses?

This is a very general question that you should expect. It deserves a well-prepared answer. You need to demonstrate not only a high level of self-insight but also corroborating evidence from other people.

This is an example of a double question, often used by HR people: 'What's positive about…and what's negative about…?'

For each planned assertion of a strength or weakness, think of a supplementary question they might ask. Often the real test is these supplementary questions, so you have to prepare for them.

I'm good; I'm very, very good
Start with a general statement of what you are and what you do. Then show what strengths you had to have to achieve the results you have: 'I'm an energetic IT professional with experience in running complex projects. I have a proven record of delivering the benefits of technology to a business. I have run teams as big as thirty and have had to involve many other people in the organisation in order to implement computer projects. During that time I developed my strengths in a number of areas. First, I'm very commercially

Here's an idea for you...

Good interviewers are adept at getting to your strengths and weaknesses – through what they've read about you and through the interview process. It's vital, therefore, that you do have good insights into the real you. Take all of your appraisals – you have kept them, haven't you? – and list the strengths and weaknesses that the appraisers have picked out. There will be a pattern that you should take very seriously. When you've finished your preparation for this question, go over your answer with somebody senior to you who knows you well. You may as well have their insights too.

minded. I never forget that IT is there to serve the financial performance of the organisation. (I've had to convert some people who start from the opposite position – that the organisation is there to benefit the smooth running of the IT department.) After I delivered my last project the managing director went on record as saying that the project had saved the company millions of dollars in currency transactions.

'I have strong project management and control skills; but I recognise that all the project management tools in the world don't get the work done. People do that. I enjoy leading teams and I have skills in involving and motivating the people in them. My last boss will testify to that and two of my referees are people who've been in teams I've managed. Most of the projects I've done have meant that a lot of people have had to change how they work. There's often heavy resistance to change and my tenacity when things are difficult has been fully tested. A departmental manager for whom I implemented a new system believes that I had at one point more people trying to hinder my delivering the system than I had helping me. Having said that, another strength I have is flexibility. If I have to change course I can do so rapidly in order to meet a new demand.' Notice the pattern: the result, the strengths necessary to achieve that result and finally the evidence from a third party.

Another way of putting the question is, 'What would you say are your outstanding qualities?' You can probably structure your answer in a similar way. If you choose to talk more personally try not to give them a simple list. It's much stronger to pick out one or two qualities and tell a story illustrating the benefits of those particular qualities.

> *Defining idea...*
>
> 'O! it is excellent to have a giant's strength, but it is tyrannous to use it like a giant.'
> WILLIAM SHAKESPEARE

But if I have a weakness...

Choose weaknesses that are based on truth. Remember they're looking for self-insight, but choose weaknesses that in fact will probably benefit the organisation rather than hinder it: 'I've discussed with my manager a couple of areas that I need to think about and work on improving. If I have a team member who's struggling with something, I tend if I'm not careful to jump in and do the job for them rather than leave them to develop their skills. I do this sometimes when time is short. I need to put in place good training and development plans to make sure I don't do this. Although I appreciate the importance of my work/life balance to both the quality of my life and my accomplishments at work, I do sometimes overbalance towards work. Both I and my family are working on this.'

Finish off by using the term 'weakness' in its alternative meaning to end with a bit of humour. 'I also have a weakness for the Scottish rugby team. It's sad, I know, but I'm afraid incurable.'

73. Is there anything you want to ask me?

This often comes near the end of the interview. If everything's gone well then make sure you don't at this point snatch defeat from the jaws of victory. On the other hand, if you think there's a problem, here's a good opportunity to go back into an area where you think they have doubts about you.

The worst answer here without any doubt is 'no.' It can look as though you're not much interested in the job, and it can indicate poor preparation.

By this time you ought to be having a sensible and interesting discussion with good rapport. So give two answers to this question: an open question that keeps the discussion going and a closed or more specific question that will elicit more insight into what it's like working for these people. After all, there are two decisions to be made here: they make the first decision, whether to offer you the job; then you have to decide whether to work for them.

More about the industry and their position in it

Start by illustrating your preparation. Use something as up to date as possible. 'I'd like to hear a bit more about the industry and your position in it. There was an interesting piece in *The Times* about this Christmas being the worst for the retail industry for ten years, despite the fact that overall sales increased by 2.5%. Can you explain that and how do you see the next few years for retail generally?' You may think that question a bit too specific if, for example, you think they might struggle with the first bit. So go even more open. 'This industry has been very successful for a while now. How do you see it maintaining that progress?' This should get one or two of them going and you will listen and show that you're learning.

Another good area to probe around at this time is their competition. It's good to join an organisation that recognises it's in competition and that most companies in their industry have strengths and weaknesses. (Be careful here. Don't let yourself down by looking as though you know nothing about their industry. If you've prepared this question, don't ask it if the ground has already been covered.)

> **Here's an idea for you...**
>
> You can strengthen most of the questions you want to ask by using your research. If, for example, you've read the recent press about the company you can ask the competition question much better. 'I understand your main competitor is X. Is that right and who do you feel are the main players making progress in the industry?'

Defining idea...

'Holding hands at midnight
'Neath a starry sky,
Nice work if you can get it,
And you can get it if you try.'
IRA GERSHWIN, *US songwriter*

'Who do you regard as your main competition and who do you see becoming a bigger threat in the future?' It's a great idea to ask a question that's broader than the job itself. For example, if the job's in Europe, ask something about the worldwide performance or strategy. The point is to show your interest in the future as well as the present.

And specifically...

Be careful. Silly as it may seem, this simple question has sunk more strong interviews than many more sinister-sounding salvoes. Don't focus too much on salary reviews, promotion prospects, type of car you get, parking spaces and so on. If there are important questions you want answers to, by all means ask them. Make sure, however, that you don't look as though these things are all that's important to you: ask some softer questions about the environment in which you'll be working. 'If you had to sum up in a few words the type of person who likes working here and the type of person who gets on well, what would they be?'

You can always turn a dual question back on them: 'What would you say are the main benefits of working for your organisation and the main frustrations?' 'Can I ask you if you have any reservations about my suitability for the job which we could discuss at this stage?' 'I am applying for other positions; but I'm particularly keen on this one. Is it possible to tell me when you'll make a decision?'

Final note: don't look as though your one and only reason for wanting to join them is to make money!

74. Panel interviews

Aha, you're in a panel interview. There are special techniques for handling a group of people in a more formal environment.

The difficulty in panels is maintaining the interest of all the members at all times.

As an example of panel interviews, we'll take a type that many organisations use. They put a hurdle in place that all potential managers from all parts of the business must jump if they are to move into management at all. This is not an interview for a specific job, but a check to ensure that you have what it takes to make the first rung of the corporate ladder. You need to pass such panels first time and preferably easily and unanimously.

Keep everybody interested

The panel interview is a more formal process and less of a conversation. Prepare thoroughly and try to be precise in your answers rather than more conversational. Use questions to establish quickly the role of each panel member. Try to make all the members of the panel speak, and then listen to what they say. All the clues will be there. The HR person will know when in interviews it's right to hold their tongue, but the line managers will often respond, particularly if they have already listened to a number of enthusiastic talkers who listen very little.

Here's an idea for you...

As part of your preparation speak to a wider section of people than just your boss. The latter will be helpful, true, but their experience of these matters could be out of date. You'll gain more from speaking to people who've recently passed a panel and, if you can find one willing to help, someone who's recently failed. Make sure that in the interview you display the preparation you have done; that puts you ahead of the crowd.

Let's look at possible pitfalls. 'How will you go about the technical side of a project?' This one could take you into your comfort zone and make you go into too much detail. It's always possible to check that you're at the right level: 'Is this answering your question or do you want more detail?' should get an honest response from the chairperson. If you're answering a technical question that one panel member is interested in, still check on the others: 'I'm conscious that I'm going into some detail on this. Is that OK?'

'Why do you think this is the right time for you to go into management?' Square away your current job, and then show your ambition: 'We're coming to the end of the second phase of my current project; so it's good timing from my boss's point of view. Rather than moving on to another project, I feel that I'm ready to go up a gear. I think I've shown that I'm at my best when I'm given more and more responsibility and that's what I'm looking for in my next job.'

They're almost certain to ask about poor performers, since managers have to deal with some tough situations: 'What would you do if one of your team members was really not performing?' You need to show you have the authority to handle such a situation, but don't jump in with, 'Well, sack them.' Know the rules and procedures for what has to be done. Your answer needs to show them that when you've exhausted coaching, training and all the HR procedures, you will have the assertiveness to do what needs to be done and move the poor performer on if it's necessary. 'In the end it's not just me and the team who are in a bad situation; it's also the poor performer. It's in their interests as well to resolve the problem once and for all.'

Remember your body language

How do you keep in with everyone? First and foremost is eye contact. Keep it flowing across the whole panel all the time. It keeps everyone involved in the conversation and gives you the chance to pick up on their reactions. It's very tempting to limit your eye contact to the person who asked the question you're answering, or, probably worse, to speak almost exclusively to the senior person in the room. And there's a sex trap here. Some men dodge eye contact with the women on the panel and concentrate on the men. Nothing can be more guaranteed to make a female manager seethe, and quite right too: it's bloody rude. And it works the other way too. Some women interviewees keep more eye contact with women panel members. The men may take this as a sign of weakness – you're obviously looking for feminine support.

Defining idea...

'The function that distinguishes the manager above all others is their educational one. The one contribution they are uniquely expected to make is to give others vision and ability to perform. It is vision and more responsibility that, in the final analysis, define the manager.'
PETER DRUCKER, *management consultant*

245

75. How will you know when you've found the right job?

This is a useful question for both sides. Preparing for it gives you a huge insight into what you're really looking for. The interviewers may see a deal breaker in your criteria; or they may give them clues how to present the job to its best advantage.

The work you do in this area will pay off, not only in answering this question, but also in weighing the merits of any offer that may come along later.

You need a comprehensive set of criteria for your decision as to which job you want to take. You can really impress an interviewer when you answer this question if you demonstrate that you've used a logical system to come up with the criteria. You should also show that you've talked to everyone useful in deciding on the importance of each criterion.

What are you going to measure?

First of all impress them with your organisation and preparation: 'I've taken four headings as my criteria: the type of organisation I want to work for, logistics such as remuneration, the impact of my job on my family and last but certainly not least the job satisfaction I think the role offers me.'

'OK, what type of organisation are you looking for?' Because you've come this far, it's likely that the one you're talking to has a lot of the attributes you've identified. Keep to the criteria for the moment and fill in the details when they ask the supplementary questions that are bound to arise. So, don't offer a heading if you can't substantiate it. Here's an outline of a possible response: 'I have to easily identify with the objectives of the organisation and the sector they operate in. I believe very much in "cultural fit". I've found that there are some organisations that I can easily operate with and others that are more difficult. I also want to go where there is success. I also need to feel that I can make the sort of contribution to that success that will stand out in the crowd.'

'So how do we measure up against those criteria?' You might answer, 'Very well. I like your long-term strategy of collaborative projects with other European companies and the fact that you're a leading light in the aerospace sector. From what I've gathered you operate a pretty free and easy, open and consultative culture. That suits my enjoyment of finding innovative solutions to problems. So, if I've read you right I think we could get on well and that I could really help the company to meet its financial and other goals.'

Here's an idea for you...

There's a simple but very useful spreadsheet you can use in this area. Put potential employers across the top of your table. Now give each criterion a weighting, again between 1 and 10, where '10' is a very important criterion and '1' a 'nice to have'. Mark each employer as usual on the scale, but add another column for each employer and use it to multiply the score by the weighting. This enables you not only to check each job but also to compare it with others in a logical manner.

Now move on to the other three. Keep the logistics bit short at this time. Unless they want to go into detail, it's better to impress them with the other bits of your research:

Defining idea...

'When you can measure what you are speaking about, and express it in numbers, you know something about it; but when you cannot measure it, when you cannot express it in numbers, your knowledge is of a meagre and unsatisfactory kind.'
LORD KELVIN

'As for logistics, I do want to use this change of job to improve my remuneration. I want to do my share of the travelling your people have to do; but I want to be home most weekends, and I'd like to be based in an office within, say, a half-hour's journey from home. In terms of job satisfaction, I want a stretching challenge and to work in a team that's enthusiastic about getting the job done. I want to use my project management skills as well as my engineering training and experience.'

How will you measure them?

Now compile your list in a table under the four categories. Measure the importance of each on a scale of 1–10. Only use 10 for real deal breakers. You should have about four criteria in each area marked as particularly important. However, try not to put everything down as high priority. Most jobs will require some sort of compromise on some criteria.

76. What are your salary expectations?

The interviewer seems to have moved into negotiating mode. In answering this type of question remember that they're in a competitive position too — you could go and work for someone else.

Interviewing is not an exact science and interviewers aren't necessarily rocket scientists. They go on their emotions as much as anyone and when they've decided they want you they'll do all they can to get you.

Let's assume that this question is asked when they've pretty much made you an offer and you're talking terms and conditions. In this situation it's good technique to move the selling job from you to them. This is probably the strongest position you can be in to get the best deal out of them.

What's in it for me?

Interviewers take to people who have the confidence to make them do some selling too; so don't beat around the bush. It's never wrong to keep it simple: 'Why do you think that your company might be best for my career?' Keep in mind that it's you they want and, you never know, there may be more than one opportunity available. It's not infrequent for people to be offered a different job

Here's an idea for you...

By using recruitment agencies, the internet and the personnel department you should be able to work out the salary range for the position you're applying for. Now work out why your experience and abilities mean that you deserve to be in the top 25% of the band. The top 25% is normally reserved for the real high-fliers in the organisation.

to the one they were interviewing for. So, if in these circumstances there is something about the job you don't quite like, not just the salary, talk about it now.

Perhaps the job description lacks something you like doing. 'I was rather hoping that there would be more contact with the product development people in this role. Who actually does the liaison work between research and development and the production department?' A question like this may well make them start to think of other ways they could organise things, or even talk about a different role for you. Don't burn your boats. For whatever reason, you may have to come back to the role as it is. But in our experience interviewees are more likely to err on the side of not pushing as hard as they might.

It's terms and conditions you need to discuss

If you're disappointed by the starting salary, don't just accept their first bid if you think it's less than it should be. 'Well, that base salary is below my expectation. I don't want to reject it out of hand; but I'll need to think about it. Could I ask if you have any flexibility in this area?'

If you have got another offer then you can certainly use it as a lever. 'I have another offer that's 20% more than yours. If you could offer to halve that gap I would be delighted to join you.' If they will not move, you can try to make the first salary review much earlier than it might have been, particularly if you can tie it into a performance result. 'If I join at that salary and bring in five new customers in the first three months would you be prepared to review my salary at that point?'

> Defining idea...
>
> 'Let us never negotiate out of fear. But let us never fear to negotiate.'
> ROBERT KENNEDY, *US politician*

They may convince you, probably erroneously, that company guidelines prevent them changing the salary that comes with the job. In this case, look at the rest of the package and see if there is anything else that could be improved: leave days, pension contributions, type of car or whatever. Just make sure you get as much out of them as you can at this advantageous point in the relationship.

4

Be the boss

253

The ultimate career coach

Start your own business – be your own boss. It's the dream of millions, but how do you go about it? Luckily, we've got the answers.

Born entrepreneur or born employee?

Some of us are born to be entrepreneurs. Some of us have to work at it a little harder. No matter how brilliant your business idea, check if you have some of the vital qualities needed for your own business. Imagine yourself in each of these scenarios.

1. You've just learned to drive but you still can't parallel park well. You:
- ☐ a. Practise every chance you get.
- ☐ b. Avoid parking whenever you can.

2 You're lagging far behind in a race and have no chance of winning. You:
- ☐ a. Finish.
- ☐ b. Head home.

3. You go shopping but the crowds are horrendous. You:
- ☐ a. Shop.
- ☐ b. Go to the movies.

4. You're trying to work out a mental problem with your statement in your bank but the darned background music is deafening. You:

☐ a. Concentrate so hard that you don't notice the music.
☐ b. Complain until they turn it down – it's too distracting.

5. If you nearly knock someone over on a zebra crossing, it is likely that:

☐ a. He darted out without giving you sufficient time to stop.
☐ b. You didn't see the zebra crossing.

6. You have become so engrossed in a work project that you have lost complete track of time:

☐ a. Doesn't everyone?
☐ b. About once that I can remember?

These questions measure tenacity and focus – both essential for starting your own business. If you scored more than one (b) in questions 1–3, read idea 103 to help you make a plan. If you answered more than one (b) in questions 4–6, read idea 91 to make sure you've thought it out thoroughly.

77. Read this first

Setting up your own business can be highly lucrative... or a total financial disaster. Here we'll focus on the key financial issues involved in kissing goodbye to the corporate life in order to do your own thing.

It's said that sometimes you can be too busy earning money to be making money.

Except for an élite few, those of us in a salaried job are unlikely to see our pay increase by 25 per cent this year. It's not the way things happen. Pay scales, salary review processes and the like are not the backdrop against which dramatic pay rises tend to happen.

This can make heading for the open road of self-employment – where there's no inherent cap on earning potential – seem like an attractive alternative. As organisations continue to downsize, outsource and generally give growing numbers of staff the boot, there are increasing opportunities for us to trade the company car for the mixed joys of working for ourselves.

Look, it's not my job to give you career advice in this book about whether this would be a good move for you personally, but you do need to be aware of the financial implications of going self-employed…and it's not all good news.

Oops, there go my pension and my life assurance

A move from salaried work to fee-earning work carries with it greater autonomy and the promise of increased income, but without the security provided by an employer's remuneration and benefits package.

When you stop working for a company, they stop paying you a salary. Alright, that may hardly qualify as a revelation, but have you thought about the whole raft of benefits that disappear along with your final pay cheque? The company pension goes, your death-in-service benefit goes, and you are no longer covered by group insurance schemes for public liability (the 'health and safety' insurance that protects you and visitors to your company in the event of accidents).

You'll also be saying goodbye to the world where the monthly salary cheque is for a predictable amount and hits your bank account on a predictable date. In its place will be…well, who knows what? Chances are that your income stream will flow in fits and starts, at least initially. Do you have a financial cushion in place to underwrite your living expenses until your business picks up momentum?

What are your chances?

According to a report by NatWest Bank, around 400,000 new businesses are launched each year in the UK. You've doubtless heard some of the horror stories about the number of new businesses that fold within a few years, sometimes

> **Here's an idea for you...**
>
> When you set up on your own, there will be nobody to insist that you put in place a new pension plan, increase your life assurance cover and so on. It becomes your call, and your call alone. Don't forget these, and check what insurance is compulsory. Some public liability insurance will probably be required if the people need to visit your premises. You may also need it if you visit the premises of your clients/customers, say to service equipment.

Defining idea...

'Your career is literally your business. You own it as a sole proprietor. You have one employee: yourself. You are in competition with millions of similar businesses: millions of other employees all over the world. You need to accept ownership of your career, your skills and the timing of your moves. It is your responsibility to protect this personal business of yours from harm and to position it to benefit from the changes in the environment. Nobody else can do that for you.'

ANDY GROVE, *Only the Paranoid Survive*

just a few months. The stories are pretty much true. On average, 20 per cent of new businesses crumple within 12 months, with over 50 per cent disappearing within three years.

Why you might fail

There are a number of finance-related reasons why your new business might go to the wall:

- Overestimating sales and underestimating how long it takes to achieve them
- Underestimating costs
- Failing to control costs ruthlessly
- Losing control over cash, i.e. carrying too much stock, allowing customers too long to pay, paying suppliers too promptly
- Underpricing

Cheer up, it might never happen

Look, there are financial upsides to being self-employed, not least of all because the tax regime is still a very favourable one. And if you make a roaring success of your business idea, you definitely have a big opportunity to put your corporate salary in the fiscal shade. The point I'm trying to get over is that the financial dice aren't entirely loaded in favour of self-employment. Please don't underestimate the benefits of salaried work in a rose-tinted rush to be your own boss. There may be gold in them thar hills but it will still need some digging out.

78. Raising the funds

If you are looking for capital from outside sources, it's not enough to show you are passionate about the idea — you must have a business plan and the prospect of a good return for your investors.

You do lose some control by inviting others in to finance your business, but often there would be no business without their help; investors may bring useful skills along with their money.

Investment capital will make or break your business. Get your hands on as much of it as you possibly can, even if it means telling a few white lies.

When you have a great idea for a business, it is often quite difficult to understand why everyone is very happy to talk to you about it until you mention that it needs some funding. Suddenly there is an awkward silence and people make their excuses and leave.

The best possible scenario is that you are launching the business with your own capital that you have just lying around in a deposit account, but the chances of this are very slim. You may have to sell assets to raise cash, or you may have to borrow or seek outside investors.

It is important to exhaust your own means of raising cash before asking for any more from anyone else. Every penny counts because the more you borrow from others the more you will have to pay back, and the more control over your business you will lose. If you can reduce that amount by even a small sum, it will help.

Do not sell yourself short and pretend that if you sell the car to raise money, you can always buy another one once the company gets started. This won't happen and you will be without a car for a long, long time. Only sell assets that you can really do without. Look to raise money by selling off unused items you own, such as old CDs, DVDs or furniture. Many of us own a lot of extra stuff that we do not use that is sitting in boxes in our own or, even worse, other people's houses. Make these items work for you and sell them. There are the traditional routes such as car-boot and garage sales, but with the glut of online auction houses and Amazon's marketplace program, you can start selling very easily.

No matter how generous your friends and family are, they will all think very hard and long before deciding to become involved. It really isn't distrust of your ability to set up a business and make it happen, or revenge for all the times you left your friends to pay the bar bill. There is something inherent within us all that makes us wary of investing in start-ups. The statistics back this up; a staggering number of start-up ventures fail.

Here's an idea for you...

Take time to set up the right bank account for your business. A common mistake is simply to go with your personal bankers. Personal and business accounts work very differently and are run by different staff – so your twenty years of loyalty may not be rewarded. Choose the bank that the offers best product for the lowest cost.

If they are happy to invest, you must provide them with the same information that a professional lender such as a bank would require: a business plan and some financial projections. In your own mind, treat them as a lender and set up a realistic payment plan through direct debit, so both parties know how the relationship will work out. Again, if your lender is looking to recoup their capital and receive a return on profits, it is in everyone's interests if a solicitor formulates this relationship professionally – a gentleman's agreement really isn't enough if things go a bit sour.

Banking On It

Banks are a safe way to borrow money. Although their interest rates are very high, everyone knows where they stand. The bank will insist on forms being signed and, if the loan is taken out by the company, they will ask for some security (depending on the amount), which could be your home or other assets. They may also require that the directors agree to take on loan repayments should the company fail. By going through a bank, you will be asked to provide the all-important business plan and financial statements which will have been completed prior to the money being paid over – so at least you will have a clear plan that you can start implementing the moment the cash comes through.

Defining idea...

'Drive-in banks were established so most of the cars today could see their real owners.'
E. JOSEPH CROSSMAN, *poet*

79. Influencing the bank

Don't even mention my bank — head, meet brick wall! We will, because we are going to show you how to get exactly what you want from them.

Banks! Don't you just hate them? Most of us do – unreasonable charges, slow responses, constantly selling us stuff we don't want, arrogant, no personal touch.

We get introduced to our 'small business adviser' who, we're told, will look after us for at least the next twelve months. We ring up two weeks later and he has moved on. That's really not on. We are sort of vulnerable, because most of us need help with our finances every so often, even if it's just a mortgage and the occasional overdraft. So, how do we influence our banks – or, of course, any financial institution or big organisation that doesn't seem to be helping us as they should?

We play the game. And what does that mean? We work as they work. Let's be honest, there's one element of this you may not like to hear, so we'd better get it over and done with straight away. Actually it's best expressed in this comment made to a customer by a London bank: 'Mr Smith (name changed to protect, of course), we [the bank] would like to go back to the more usual arrangement where you bank with us rather than the other way around.' Okay, it's an old gag, but it gives us something to think about.

Here are some things to bear in mind about banks
– or any major organisation – before we start
ranting and raving at them:

1. Banks are in the business of managing and
   making money, not giving it away. Traditional
   high-street banks – which most of us deal with
   – are not in the business of risk. That's why
   they are constantly after security.

2. There are rules. Those rules are clearer than
   ever (e.g. when and what you will be charged
   for an overdraft). If we break these rules we will
   be punished and the simplest punishment is a
   charge.

> **Here's an idea for you...**
>
> Keep a special file for all of your dealings with the bank. If they are a typical bank, they will make mistakes; if you are human, you will forget things. Keep everything and put everything in writing; check everything. In the file, build up a structure-chart of the bank: who is your manager and who is their manager? Get e-mail addresses; don't allow them to be a large unfamiliar organisation. Get close and get what you want.

3. Nobody likes being ignored, so if you do ignore communications, like notice
   about breaking an overdraft limit, then you will be punished even more.

It probably does seem unfairly biased to the bank, but that's the score. If we are
going to be great at influencing, we must break this chain of thought which just
says 'all banks are b*st*rds'. To influence your bank, you've got to do what most
people don't do:

● Be well-behaved. Find out what you are able to do with the account you
  have and do not break the rules. Friends can be flexible. Banks cannot be. If
  your account does not do what you need, ring up the bank and make an
  appointment to see how you can get what you want.

- Keep records. Keep your statements and check them. If you have a meeting, ask for an e-mail address and put your conversation in writing and ask for the e-mail to be confirmed. Leave nothing to a verbal agreement – e-mail is quick and easy.

- Point out mistakes quickly. Provide the evidence and ask for mistakes to be rectified immediately.

- Be assertive; don't get aggressive. The person you are speaking to only has a certain level of authority. If they can't help you, ask to speak to the person who does have that authority. If you are blocked, put it in writing. All written correspondence has to be answered.

- Be polite and persistent.

- Do stick with one bank. Build up a track record and keep your files up to date. Sadly, though, you must accept that the days of developing a long-standing relationship with one manager are long gone.

Banks love people who are willing to work to their rules and who understand that the bank is not a charity. Once you can do that, you can start getting what you want.

Defining idea...

'One rule which woe betides the banker who fails to heed it ... Never lend any money to anybody unless they don't need it.'
OGDEN NASH

80. Who are your customers?

For the business to work you need customers. Do you know who your customers will be? Are you sure you know? What proof do you have?

Many people start a business because they are looking for a lifestyle change and a chance to do a job properly. The best reason, though, is because you feel it will be profitable.

Customers are a bit scary and some of them may not be people you would like to meet in a dark alley, but you need to explore their needs and behaviour. It is important to decide on your stereotypical customer, both in your own mind and for the purposes of defining your consumers within your business plan. What you write will not be set in stone – there will always be consumers buying your products that you would never have imagined (octogenarians buying sportswear to run a marathon, for instance) – but the vast majority of your customers will fall in to a standardized category. Once this has been defined you will be in a better position to know exactly what it is you are researching and, once the business has launched, how best to market yourself and your products to that group.

Here's an idea for you...

Identify your target customer. If you can define it precisely as, say, a 16- to 32-year-old cash-rich male, you are on the right track. You will not be painting yourself into a corner or alienating investors or consumers by acknowledging this.

The internet can provide you with a vast amount of information, ranging from the entirely useless to the highly informative, to help you in your quest to start a business. Use the internet tirelessly to uncover stats and numbers for a better understanding of who is currently buying the products or services that you are considering providing and who is likely to want to consume if you were to let them know about your existence. Start with government sites and consumer groups that can provide you with demographics, average spend, trends and patterns found in the area of business that you are planning to enter.

Whether you are looking to borrow from the bank, or from other sources, you will require a bank account and therefore you will be booked in for a meeting with a business manager. During this meeting give as much information as you can about your business and your target audience. Many banks provide fact sheets on starting specific businesses (especially in certain areas of retail and catering) if you ask, which can sometimes be useful.

There are top-level research reports you can buy (they tend to be expensive) that will provide you with huge amounts of data and information about specific products, industries or consumer trends. It is well worth investigating what organisations such as Mintel hold on the area you would like to investigate – their reports are costly but they take a lot of the hard work out of research.

If you don't have much business experience, you may be overoptimistic about how many customers you can acquire. Remember that demand is what drives sales. In some businesses, such as being a landlord, it is quite easy to assess the demand for your offering by studying rental property in a certain area. In others, such as

Defining idea...

'Research is the process of going up alleys to see if they are blind.'
MARSTON BATES, *American author*

marketing consumer products, it is much more difficult to know whether any customers will buy, especially if you hope to sell through major distribution channels that may not have your best interests at heart. Make sure that you have really good evidence that people will buy before you launch the business. One way to do this is to try small-scale pilot schemes; one small business I know tried several different ways of marketing their products on a small scale and discovered that only one method was profitable. This kind of information could save you a fortune if you discover it early on.

81. Getting to grips with finances

You will need to determine how many customers you can expect per day, month and year and how much each of them will spend on your products and services.

Although nobody is expecting absolute accuracy, very few people will be fooled by sheer hope. Picking numbers out of the sky is one sure way to complete your projections quickly – but the document will be useless.

Dust off the calculator and prepare yourself for the joy of profit and loss sheets! In some respects you can get away with producing any old figures to present in your business plan – but the only person that you will be deceiving is yourself. No one can project figures completely accurately, but it is better to take an educated guess, based on the hard facts and the research that you have conducted, than to just make them up.

A huge mistake is to view both the creation of the business plan and the financial statements as a chore that you need to complete for someone else's benefit. Primarily they are both documents that you need to create for yourself and revise religiously; other people will need to see them along the way, but the primary audience is you. The best business plans are referred to again and again.

These documents should become the benchmark by which you judge yourself, not abandoned files that are demoted to the third drawer of your filing cabinet. They will act as anchors to stop you vying off on a particular tangent and they will be a great indicator as to whether things are going as well as they should be.

If it turns out, very quickly, that the figures you have projected have become either unachievable or desperately under actual performance, then you can alter your future projections accordingly.

Here's an idea for you...

If you have three routes to market, say high street retail sales, internet sales and mail order, revise the figures so that your original focus becomes secondary and you are now dependent on one of the other routes (say, mail order instead of high street retail). How does this alter your sales projections and customer spend?

Get out of the mindset that your projected sales are merely figures you need to create in order to secure finance and get the project off to a start. They are your future and the more accurately you can predict future success, the more chance you have of securing the finance that you require in the first place; and making your business a resounding success.

If the data exist, then you will quickly be able to determine the size of the market from websites and paid-for research. Next, decide how much of the market you intend to command after one, two and three years of operations. If you know the value of the entire market, you can work out the value of your projected market share.

When creating your financial spreadsheet you can break that figure down into the number of customers required and the average customer spend. It's not exact, but you have a starting figure that indicates how much you feel is achievable; this is the number of customers expected to buy from you, and how much they will be spending.

Defining idea...

'All progress is based upon a universal innate desire on the part of every organism to live beyond its income.'
SAMUEL BUTLER, *19th century author and critic*

Now consider the factors that could affect your plans: the time it will take you to get up to speed; what if the competition raises their game? What if there is a sudden depression in the market? How would it affect your particular line of business, if interest rates suddenly sky-rocketed and consumer confidence was shattered? Would you be the first or last industry to feel the pinch? These are valid questions that you must consider, not ignore. Notice that you have moved forward, away from guessing wildly just to make the business plan visually exciting and attractive.

82. Effective budgeting

If you spend more than you have before the business is even launched, you're setting yourself up for disaster.

If you overestimate how much revenue you expect to make in your first year then there are still a few options open to you that will mean the books balance at the end of twelve months.

The most successful businesses are those than plan expenditure right down to the last penny, and stick to it. Sticking to a budget is as hard as sticking to a diet – but to run a fit and healthy business you need to avoid eating all the pies before breakfast is served. You will grossly underestimate how much even the basic things cost to buy – coupled with the desire, every now and again, to break the budget on one or two items that you just must have to make your business a resounding success. Then there are the items that you accidentally hadn't budgeted for and come in as emergency purchases the weeks, or days, before launch. Added together, you are likely to go 5–20% over budget – and that's with sound planning!

Here's an idea for you...

Look to save on the ancillary costs of running your premises. Just saving half a per cent on your electricity and phone bill will make a big difference to your expenditure and therefore your bottom line. There are a glut of providers out there, desperate for more customers – so negotiate hard and remember that they need your business.

It is tempting to massage your sales figures to appease investors and your own ego, but trying to convince others that your idea is the best thing since sliced bread, whilst guessing at, or rather underbudgeting for, business expenses is setting yourself up for failure. Remember, if it all goes wrong then you will still owe your investors and they won't care what went wrong; they'll be just looking for their money. When planning expenditure, do it primarily for your own benefit, and include absolutely everything.

Your wage bill will always be your largest outgoing, closely followed by your stock – though if you are a service rather than a product provider, then you have slightly more room for manoeuvre. Although including these costs into your projections is absolutely key, ensure that you add on the other costs that every business faces – and find out exact figures, never rely on a rough guess. The surprise costs that start making a hole in your finances are all the ancillary costs. Look at how much electricity you will be using both when you are working in the business premises and when the place is dormant. A massive cost for small businesses is paper and ink – whether it be copying, printing or scanning, it all adds up. Postage should be a major concern no matter what type of business you are planning to launch, and then the shock of running an internet connection, water, phones, rates and machinery all rear their ugly heads.

Even the big bills are not set in stone. Whatever salaries you are planning to pay, add on about 15% to cover the cost of employee NIC and PAYE in the UK, not to mention health, pensions, gym membership and travel loans, if these are perks you are considering for your staff. The more accurate you can be with the true expenditure your business will incur, the more accurate your projections will become. These bills are constant and spread evenly throughout the year. Even if the business you are starting is seasonal, you must still leave enough, and budget, to cover the monthly or quarterly barrage regardless of your own sales performance.

> *Defining idea...*
>
> 'Annual income twenty pounds, annual expenditure nineteen six, result happiness. Annual income twenty pounds, annual expenditure twenty pound nought and six, result misery.'
> CHARLES DICKENS

83. Number crunching

Many of us fear numbers, or see working with them as a terrible chore, but working accurately with spreadsheets will quickly show you, and others, if a business is viable.

These financial documents can be a prophetic vision of your financial future; when the hard graft is over each month, those figures you have entered under salary will be your reward.

When creating your financial spreadsheet, you really should be looking to prepare for every possible eventuality that you can foresee over the next three years. Even if your business is going to be in an office or a shop and you are looking to run a transactional website as a bit of a sideline, it could be that web sales will be your major route to market in eighteen months' time. Create a row for each and every route to market, even if you are projecting sales to be zero for the first year. Include everything like bank interest rates for loans and overdrafts, even if you are self-funding the business at launch – you may have a bank loan in the future and it is much easier to alter the rate of interest and enter an amount that you will be paying every month than it is to create a new spreadsheet.

Break It Down

As well as preparing for all foreseeable eventualities, it is good practice to be as specific as possible with your financial projections. If you are launching a hairdressing salon employing experienced stylists and apprentices, there will be different rates charged to the customers and differences in the cost of sales. Keeping your entire sales figures in one row makes it hard to analyse profits. It is better to create a row for each type of sale. Although the volume of sales through the stylists may be high value, your cost of sales (their salary or commission) is also going to be high. The apprentices will not charge as much for their work, but equally they will not be paid as highly, meaning more profit for the business – so it might prove better for your bottom line to employ one stylist and three apprentices than the other way around. The more information that you can present on your financial plans, the better you will be able to understand the full picture.

Pretty Pictures

Presenting the data can be done by simply printing off a copy of the spreadsheet – but very few people (apart from maybe an accountant) will be happy with this document. Once the numbers are in, use the software to create

Here's an idea for you...

Create a spreadsheet to present the following data as a graph:

- Sales projections for the next twelve months
- Sales projections for the next three years
- Expenditure since launch
- Monthly bank balance for the next twelve months

This should show you how easy it is to produce good visual data and make it clear where you should be in twelve months.

Defining idea...

'It is a very sad thing that nowadays there is so little useless information.'
OSCAR WILDE

more viewer-friendly versions and excerpts of the data. Graphs help readers 'picture' the business and understand the data far more easily than looking at an enormous spreadsheet. Although the viewer might need to refer back to the source document, your message can be displayed very quickly and accurately with a graph. Likewise, in your business plan you should summarise the data with simple one-line statements of fact or intent, e.g. 'with 47,000 investment we intend to create a business turning over 390,000 with a net profit of 61,000 within our first twelve months of operations.'

Defining idea...

'It is the responsibility of the sender to make sure the receiver understands the message.'
JOSEPH BATTEN, *business guru*

When presenting data it is important to show when cash is actually going in and out of the business. If the rent bill is 12,000 per annum, display the outgoing funds, broken up into payments, as they will occur, not forgetting to account for deposits and legal fees. Managing cash flow will be the key to making your business a success. Find out what terms your suppliers offer, and always try to negotiate more favourable terms. Suppliers are often wary of new businesses – and rightly so, as so many go out of business leaving big debts unpaid. No matter how good your negotiation skills, some suppliers will demand a year of good relations before allowing more generous terms, or for the value of orders to exceed a certain level. The long-term goal is for your business to be selling products or services to your customers, and receiving the cash, before having to pay your suppliers.

84. How to be an entrepreneur

The world needs entrepreneurs. The world needs constant, fresh money-making ideas. Whether you head up marketing or facility management or run your own business, here's how to be an entrepreneur.

The New World of Work brings many challenges created by seven drivers of change:

- Driver 1: acceleration. This is the increasing rate of change in the very different commercial world of today.

- Driver 2: automation. This is the move to replace any possible process with a chip; to go high-tech rather than high-touch.

- Driver 3: alternative shores. There is always somewhere cheaper in the world. And with the advent of the Internet and the global market 'alternative shoring' is now a valid possibility.

- Driver 4: abundance. So much choice – and in everything, from mortgages to vegetables.

- Driver 5: ambiguity. The death of long-term planning, and the unreliability of planning in general.

279

Here's an idea for you...

Take a product you use a lot (your mobile, your kettle, your car, your washing machine). What's a frustration you have with it? There's bound to be something; your mobile's battery needs constant recharging; your kettle gets hard-water stains; your car has two serious blind spots and your washing machine has too many options... Now ask outrageous questions. What would it take to create a phone that never needed charging, a kettle that couldn't stain, brand new cars configured to remove all blind spots or a three-option washing machine? You're thinking seriously about it, aren't you? That's your entrepreneurial spirit – get it to work.

● Driver 6: anarchy. Power is back with the people – the Internet, rising qualifications, one market…

● Driver 7: adrenaline. Fear – accumulate the above six drivers and you end up with a world of anxiety – or potentially do so!

You'll only survive in the New World of Work if you are entrepreneurial. To be an entrepreneur is to remember that ultimately it is down to you: if there ever really was any long-term security there certainly isn't now – it's the Wild West all over again. Time to look at some detail on how exactly you can become entrepreneurial in order to survive in the future.

Mindset: how you think

Entrepreneurs think in a certain kind of way, and everyone can borrow that kind of thinking.

● Adding value. Entrepreneurs know that one aspect of differentiation and making money is through distinction, through being different and that it can be done by adding value. They discover what their customers want – longer opening hours, less packaging, more crisps in the bag – and do their best to give it to them.

● No failure, only feedback. Entrepreneurs know that the world is too complicated to be able to plan and get everything right first time – or ever – so they are willing to try things and, if they go wrong, to learn and improve.

- There's always a way! Breakthroughs so often come when attention is given to what everybody else said couldn't be done – entrepreneurs recognise this.

- 'We can make this better.' Entrepreneurs believe in kaizen: never-ending continuous improvement.

- Qualifications do not (necessarily) equal success. Entrepreneurs realise that – whether or not they are graduates, have MBAs or left school as soon as they could – being an entrepreneur in the New World of Work is a state of mind and not a qualification-rich CV. The latter can help, but it can also hinder. And that goes for worrying about other aspects, like your sex, age, skin colour, creed, height…

Mechanics: what you do

How do entrepreneurs become good at their craft? By doing it. Be in no doubt: start something; start a small online business for additional income, reinvent your HR department. Keep asking the question 'If this were my own thing, how would I be managing it differently?' For instance, 'If my department were involved in a management buy-out, would it be a natural survivor?' Once you do that you will learn rapidly. Work hard to reduce any external dependencies so that you are not dependent on good market conditions or a favourable supplier, or vulnerable to a downturn or the loss of a market. That's great entrepreneurial action.

External/internal: the two aspects

There are, perhaps, two main kinds of entrepreneurs: those who are out there in the wilderness attempting to get their purest of juices established or their new totally biological organic nappies sold through the main supermarkets, and those who are within organisations. These are the people who realise that heading a fifteen-person support team was sustainable in profitable, great-product-margin days but is not so good when the economy is in a bit of a squeeze.

85. Business banking for beginners

Banks, we sometimes forget, are businesses looking to increase customers and profits — the same ideals as you've probably stated in your business plan.

Personal banking and business banking are two very different arenas, but there is a lot you can do to make sure that your business is enjoying a good service and a bit of personal attention.

Although a sawn-off shotgun will probably get you the cash you require, there is another way…Thankfully most banks do not try to tempt corporate customers with gimmicks and freebies, because they know it won't work. As a customer looking for a banking solution, you hold the power to take your banking wherever you please, based on hard facts: the charges. The charges that banks apply to business accounts vary from harsh to daylight robbery. Business banking is a cash cow. Don't be fooled by the glamorous welcome packs and glossy brochures; look at how much it costs to present a cheque, accept a credit card payment or transfer money by BACS or CHAPS. Banks can and do charge for merely opening an account or sending you a letter, and it's not cheap. In return, as a customer you are more likely to be able to arrange for a business loan or overdraft – but don't confuse this for benevolence; lending is also a way for banks to make lots of money, very fast, through the interest rate and terms they offer you.

On the bright side, banks provide a huge lifeline to businesses by offering a helping hand, especially in their formative years when it counts. Banks are very keen for your business to succeed because they will make money out of you for a very long time – in return for this expected 'loyalty', you are in a position to open an account on the understanding that you expect both a loan and an overdraft facility. Ordinarily you will be introduced to an account manager who will be assigned to your account. Charges for this service will vary, but it is very shrewd to befriend this person. Get them introduced to you and your business right from the start. Even if the business plan is at a draft stage, let them take a look and offer suggestions. The more exposure they have to your business and your thoughts, the more receptive they will be when it comes to giving you cash – be it loans, overdrafts or a reduction or waiving of fees. Your account manager will have you and many others on the books – ensure that you are their most exciting account.

> **Here's an idea for you...**
>
> Arrange an overdraft facility, even if you never intend to use it, rather than having to react to a cash-flow problem should it arise. Create a document that argues the case, explaining that it is better to prepare for all eventualities, and how the current arrangement is not related to the projected turnover of the business.

Biding Your Time

A new business without any previous history is always at a disadvantage. No matter what figures are put on a spreadsheet, until you start trading and the bank is able to build a profile, lenders will be wary. However, no matter what

Defining idea...

'A banker is a fellow who lends you his umbrella when the sun is shining, but wants it back the minute it begins to rain.'
MARK TWAIN

opening loan or overdraft facility you are offered, within six months of trading a profile begins to form and you are able to look at your bank as a potential source of second-round funding. A bigger loan or overdraft facility is more likely to be granted once the business is set up and operating. Once the bank sees money coming in and out of the account, and you have shown your account manager the PR, advertising and CVs of key personnel you have attained since launch, all the odds begin to stack up in your favour. Show the bank that your business is really taking shape, along with detailed plans about how you intend to use the money, to the last pound, and justify why there is a sudden need for it now when there wasn't before. The bank will probably look for security on the loan. Make sure you are certain that the money will indeed lead to increased business – don't pump more good money after bad.

86. Business angels and venture capitalists

Sometimes banks are unwilling to lend large sums of money, especially if the money is unsecured. This is when you need to call in the big guns.

To say dealing with venture capitalists or business angels is like selling your soul to the devil might sound a bit strong – but it's not far off…

If you require larger amounts to realise your business objectives, then a route to raising the capital could be through either business angels or venture capitalists. Business angels tend to be individuals looking to invest their money in new businesses, or businesses seeking a second round of investment to help growth. It all sounds incredibly benevolent, but angels want a better return than they would receive through a bank (currently approximately 5% p.a) or through investing in stock (currently 10–14% p.a.) and therefore will be encouraging you to make as much money as quickly as possible. Angels are usually found through business networks or online and often tend to invest only in businesses operating within a sphere of their expertise.

Venture capitalists (VCs) tend to be corporate organisations that invest heavily in new businesses and like angels will be looking for a high return on their investment – quickly. Both angels and VCs will most probably want a share of

Here's an idea for you...

Wasting valuable time pitching to the wrong angel or VC is not going to help, as responses can take weeks if not months. Target those with a track record of investing in your industry. Once you have identified a short-list of potential investors, tailor your business plan accordingly – when and how much profits you are going to make. VC firms don't want the marketing fluff, they want the cold, hard figures along with an explanation about how you will make it happen.

the company in return for cash or a share of profits and will often insist on placing a few of their own people on the board. Accepting this level of funding does come with a price – the loss of some control – but by accepting their money you can often tap into their wealth of experience about all sorts of issues. After all, both types of investors will want to make sure your business succeeds.

Business angels can be just that: heavenly angels providing the capital to make an idea work and kick-start a business into an innovative, exciting and profitable enterprise. But this level of financial assistance does not come easily or cheaply. A business angel, or group of angels, is looking for a healthy and safe return on the investment that far outweighs the more obvious routes to letting money work for them – i.e. savings accounts and share dealing. To entice a business angel something must be so striking or unique about your offering that it really makes people sit up and take note. Opening a hairdressers is unlikely to attract this kind of investment, but an innovative software product or organisation that is trying to set new precedents with technology are very high up on the list.

Venture capitalists usually have significant amounts of other people's money to hand, over which they have free-reign (or certainly a lot of influence) to invest in businesses they feel are worth pursing. This is purely and systematically for financial gain. During the internet boom of the late 1990s, venture capitalists seemed more active than ever, with literally billions being pumped into internet-based businesses around the world. Some of these investments paid off tenfold, but a large majority failed to achieve any return whatsoever on the capital employed. The net effect was that venture capitalists pulled the plug on internet investments and started looking elsewhere.

Choosing the route of venture capitalist investment can be both good and bad for your business. In the short-term it can actually cost you money to look for investment because a lot of the charges, such as accountancy fees, legal fees and consultant rates, are borne by your business until the deal is done, in which case it is paid back.

Therefore, this route of fund-raising is simply not viable for many businesses mainly because you need to have a large amount of disposable capital to spend in the first place.

Defining idea...

'Everybody likes a kidder, but nobody lends him money.'
ARTHUR MILLER

87. Choosing your company's status

Deciding upon the legal identity and status of your business can be tough, but remember, the status of a business can bring 'high status'.

Becoming CEO of a PLC does sound great, but floating a company is not always best for your business. Choose wisely and ensure that you remain in control.

Limited companies

The limited company is regarded as the best thing that the Victorians ever did for us, although I would argue that the flushing toilet was equally important. A limited company is a completely separate legal entity from those who run or work for the company (thus the directors have limited liability). With that definition come a number of benefits and disadvantages.

By creating a limited company you can give the impression of size and experience very easily, even if the business is completely new. Customers will be happier writing cheques to XYZ Ltd. than to John Smith. However, some suppliers are less keen for small companies to be limited because it can give the impression that you are protecting yourself from risk, which ironically makes you a risky bet. Banks tend to feel the same and in a bid to ensure that any money they lend to a business is in some way protected or secured, will ask the directors to sign a mandate ensuring that if the business is unable to meet repayments, you as directors will. In the UK, filing accounts with Companies House is a legal requirement if you become a director of a limited company and there are knock-on costs if you require your accountant to prepare these documents for you.

Partnership or Limited Liability Partnership

A partnership works for a number of industries and types of businesses exceptionally well, and not so well for others. The classic examples of partnerships are law firms and accountancy firms. With a standard partnership the partners have unlimited liability and this means you would be liable for the business debts of your partners even if you were unaware of the debt. There are, however, tax advantages to forming a partnership. A recent invention is the limited liability partnership, which is almost a fusion of partnership and limited company in that the partners enjoy the protection of limited liability but remain partners rather than directors.

Sole Trader

A sole trader is on the bottom rung of the status ladder. With that come quite a few benefits and a few disadvantages, but most importantly it speaks volumes about the perceived 'size' of your business – which can work both for and against you. A sole trader has unlimited liability and so is responsible for all the debts of the business; however, more and more large firms are happy to deal

> **Here's an idea for you...**
>
> Take the time to speak with an accountant to help you decide which status best suits your own business. Your accountant will be able to advise on which status will help you achieve your long-term goals as well as recommending which is best at this stage to help minimise your tax and VAT liability. These are huge decisions and not to be made on the spur of the moment.

Defining idea...

'A static hero is a public liability.
Progress grows out of motion.'
RICHARD BYRD, *explorer*

with sole traders because they appreciate the risk that the individual is taking and feel they are more likely to get a good service and value for money.

Plc

Going public is often seen as the king of the status pile – 'publicly owned' immediately conjures images of size and access to capital, even though the truth of the matter may be far different. PLCs work very well for creating a buzz and interest in your company, but with the extra cash raised from the flotation and shareholders come your commitment to being scrutinised and having to appease shareholder sentiment and the need for return. It is important to understand that the shareholders own a PLC, not the directors of the business. You could be voted off the board, but equally you could be managing director of a multi-million pound international conglomerate far quicker than through running a partnership or limited company.

88. Why you need a solicitor

Going it alone is very risky when it comes to launching a new business. Bring a solicitor in on your project as soon as possible.

Solicitors charge for their services but they look out for you and your interests. Employing a solicitor to help you get started will be far cheaper than employing one should you get into legal difficulty later.

Before you buy or lease property for the business, be sure to request a land registry search through your solicitor. Although everything might look fantastic on the estate agent's information sheet, they are only acting on the word of the vendor, and not everything may be true. The search will reveal important information about access, by-laws, parking and if the property is sitting on any dodgy radioactive pockets of gas. Most importantly it will confirm that the person asking for the money is indeed entitled to sell or lease.

Solicitors have template contracts available at the touch of a button. Unless your company is employing permanent legal staff or happens to have a qualified lawyer on the board, this information and their knowledge of current law is absolutely vital to your business and continued good relations with your staff. Employing somebody to work for a business is more of a commitment than it has ever been. Staff obviously help bring the business to life and help you achieve your goals; they're also your most expensive drain on resources. In a small business this can cause all sorts of problems, not least of which is long-

Here's an idea for you...

To fully appreciate the worth of employing a solicitor for the business, test their skills by requesting a standard staff contract particular to your industry. For a single fee you will now have a company contract, which can be simply altered for every employee you hire. As you will have to issue yourself a contract if you become a limited company, this is money well spent.

term illness. Protect yourself and your staff with a bona fide contract of employment.

If you plan to launch a website it is paramount that you have a legal statement on the site. The pages should cover your contractual agreement with users and their agreement when using your site. Is it clear who owns the copyright on text, images and other content found on your site? It is well worth the cost of having a legal expert read over your statement. Pinching another website's statement and altering it to suit you own needs is not good enough – you will be caught out either by the originator or by a user finding loopholes.

It will quickly become apparent during the creation of a business plan that you are likely to need the services of a law firm. Depending on the need and the cost, it might be wise to set up a fixed monthly or quarterly payment that is offset against their invoices. The monthly charge will be easier to manage and much better for cash flow than reacting to varying sized bills as and when they are presented. The firm itself will be able to suggest a suitable amount – if it is incorrect you will both soon realise and the situation is easy to resolve.

To build up a good working relationship fast, it is well worth putting any private work you might have through the firm of solicitors you plan to use for the business. Something simple, like a will, will cost you very little, and is something that you should have organised anyway. Because you have a number of reasons to call, your name will soon register with the solicitor and, sometimes more importantly, her secretary; if you do need to talk urgently you are far more likely to be top of the list of messages, not bottom.

Defining idea...

'Lawyers, I suppose, were children once.'
CHARLES LAMB

89. Choosing and using accountants

Accountants are highly skilled individuals. Getting the right one will save you and your business hundreds or thousands a year. Get the wrong one and you will be paying through the nose for bad, even dangerous, advice.

If you don't get a buzz out of crunching numbers, don't worry, these people do. They might not be much fun at the Christmas party but they will make sure you can afford to have one.

Many businesspeople regard accountants as though they are the enemy. This is not the case if you have a good working relationship with an accountancy firm. Very few of us like working with numbers (those who do are accountants!) but it is an intrinsic part of running and operating any business. A good accountant is on your side to ensure that the business is able to make, and more significantly keep, as much profit as possible – and this is not a bad thing. A good accountant needs to be brought in right from the start, to get to know you and the proposed business right from its infancy. You will not be scored badly for offering an incomplete plan, just helped in the right direction to make it right. By allowing accountants to give you feedback on early drafts of the business plan, they quickly learn about what it is you are trying to achieve and can tailor their service to suit you and the company – saving you needless meetings and expenditure.

Accountants come in all shapes and sizes. Choosing an accountant is a major decision, so you should never just reach for the telephone directory and pick a name that sounds quite good. As a rule of thumb, don't contact firms that advertise in the local papers, or who drop flyers through your door, or worse, who cold call you – although they have every right to advertise, it does beg the question 'why do you not have enough clients?' The best way to choose a firm of accountants is through personal recommendation. If someone you know runs a business and they've been happy with their accountant for a few years, it's a safe bet that they will work well for you too. Unlike solicitors, it also pays to use a local firm. Not only will you get a more personal service, it will be much better when it comes to preparing the company accounts if you are able to transport files and documents by hand or car than trusting them to the mail.

A good habit to get into from the moment you start planning your new business is to keep records of absolutely everything. An organised office is immediately obvious from the number of box files taking up every available shelf. Leave nothing to chance. You can always destroy it in a year's time if it

> **Here's an idea for you...**
>
> Make a shortlist of three firms who you would consider employing as your accountants. Prepare your questions and meet with each. The firm that is most keen for your business should be your first choice. Over the coming years they will be charging you for their services, so make them earn their money right from the first meeting.

Defining idea...

'It is better to know some of the questions than all of the answers.'
JAMES THURBER

really is useless. As a bare minimum, every business should have a box file for:

● Bank statements
● Credit card statements
● Invoices received
● Invoices issued
● Staff (contracts and income tax information)

There really is no upper limit on the number of box files you use over the coming years, but happy indeed is the accountant who can ask for a document and the client knows exactly where to look!

Accountants vary enormously in the methods they use to produce your accounts. Remember, there is no single correct answer in accounting issues. In general, they prefer to understate profits rather than overstate them because optimistic accounts tend to lead to more problems later. You can picture the scenario: gung-ho businessman puffs his accounts, borrows money and attracts investors, and finally, a few years later, goes broke. Who does everyone blame? The accountant, of course! Every time there is a big business scandal, from Robert Maxwell to Enron and Worldcom, the accountants are brought shuffling out to explain how they allowed the managers to bamboozle them. From an accountant's point of view, a 'conservative' attitude towards profits is highly desirable – and it means you pay less tax, too.

90. Getting the right people

Ugh! Don't you hate that term? Let's get back to people — how to find them, keep them and motivate them.

It's been said many times of course: people are your greatest asset, but you'll also be aware – being truthful – that they can also be your greatest nightmare!

Essentially, you want to do three things with people. Firstly, find the best; secondly, get the best out of the best; thirdly, keep the best doing their best. You'll notice that that challenge gets harder from first to second to third, so let's take a look at each of those challenges in turn.

Finding the best

Whatever business you are in (or in which you are advising/consulting) – service or manufacturing, high tech or low tech, sweet shop or call centre – the business is the sum of the people in it. So you need to have the best and that starts with getting the best.

Begin by making this a core activity in the organisation. Make everyone keen to find the best people to work alongside them. Create a simple reward scheme for finding good employees. After all, those who already work in an organisation tend to know what sort of people are good for that organisation; it can also be a lot cheaper than a big recruitment campaign. And however wonderful HR are,

> **Here's an idea for you...**
>
> Take five people in your team (or one of your client's teams). What motivates each of those people now? What do you believe will be motivating them in eighteen months' time? The same factors or something different? What does that imply for the way you currently manage and lead them?

they often don't fully understand all the roles in an organisation. Any other recruitment process should be subsidiary to this 'people find people' process.

Secondly, ensure that any contact with your organisation can allow those who are impressed with you to enquire about positions which are vacant. Thus it should be clear wherever you have a presence – on your website/blog, at an exhibition, on any publications – what someone should do if they're interested in joining you.

Once the organisation lives and breathes the concept of 'everybody recruits', you need to be clear on what the best actually is. Consider three factors: knowledge, skills and attitude. For any person you seek, define those three aspects of the job: the knowledge (what they need to know), the skills (what they must be able to carry out with consistent competence) and finally attitude (the way they think). Remember that ease of trainability is generally considered to be in the order of knowledge, then skills, and then attitude – and yet too little time is often given to seeking someone with the appropriate attitude. Knowledge can be the easiest to develop, but people are often recruited on the basis of just that; consider giving more attention to finding people with the right attitude instead.

Get the best out of the best

Once you have the best on board, how do you get them to consistently deliver their best? Begin by ensuring that they go through an induction programme. At the very least this should equip them with whatever they need to do their job on a daily basis. It will also introduce them to names and faces so they can ask the right people for help when necessary. What are known as 'hygiene factors' should be sorted out. Will they be paid on time? Do they have a computer? A desk? An email account? A job description? Then check that they know their objectives and how they are being measured. Finally, make sure they get things like positive reinforcement and appropriate praise. Are you reinforcing the best by catching them doing things right?

> *Defining* idea...
>
> People are not lazy. They simply have impotent goals – that is, goals that do not inspire them.
> ANTHONY ROBBINS, *from a seminar*

Keep the best doing their best

You got the best on board, you stopped them getting dulled and cynical within the first few weeks. How do you get them to perform to their best for several years at least? By understanding what motivates them, which is not the same for all people all of the time, or for an individual all of the time. You intuitively know that. Most of us want money, but money rarely compensates for a job we hate, so there must be more to it. Abraham Maslow developed a model called the 'hierarchy of needs' which details the items we all require to keep us motivated. At the bottom of the hierarchy are the basics – food and shelter – in the middle are growth and challenge and at the top is 'self-actualisation' or 'being the best version of ourselves'. Can you help people be the best version of themselves? If you can, they'll stick with you. If you can't – well, at best they will be dulled, at worst they will leave.

91. The business plan

Creating a business plan is like baring your soul to the world because what is contained within the text will expose your aims, goals, aspirations and level of motivation for all to see.

Write the document for you, not others, and use it as the blueprint to success. Remember you're not writing a novel – less of the flowery prose and idealistic diatribe and more on the facts and figures.

A great business plan is really simple. No matter how complex your business, the end product should give any reader, no matter what their background, a huge insight into the business, your market, your goals and how you intend to succeed. A business plan should not be an excuse to confuse and wow readers with excessive use of management talk, industry lingo and overwhelming statements – it should outline your intentions in plain language. In terms of length, the business plan need only be as long as it takes to explain the proposition. Don't set yourself a page count and work towards that – write the plan, and if anything try and edit it down to 75% of the original size. A very long document will not help in raising funds, or encourage staff, or prove to be particularly useful in the future. In fact you will just bore people and maybe convince them that you are hiding insecurities about the business behind reams of stats, figures and a few poems thrown in for light relief.

Business plans really do reveal all, namely your own company's strengths and weaknesses, and are highly confidential documents that are not for public consumption. Be very careful who gets to see it and understand fully why a certain person needs to see it. Be sure to number each version and destroy older versions so that confusion does not arise.

> **Here's an idea for you...**
>
> Before embarking on your business plan, obtain as many actual business plans as possible. Although there are no hard and fast rules about layout and style, as you begin to compare you will begin to see patterns. Use existing plans as a template.

A business plan is not a marketing document only comprising of forward-looking statements that will be nigh on impossible to achieve. A business plan is a working document, one that a good business refers back to again and again. It should lead your business to success and be followed, not locked in a filing cabinet once the seed capital has been secured.

What readers are looking for in a business plan is to be taken on a journey, from start to finish, of how you are going to make this business work. It's all very well concentrating on how many units you plan to sell and at what price, but don't lose sight of the fact that whatever industry you are planning to work in will have established competition. Acknowledge the competition and show categorically that you have researched the market. List your competitors' strengths and weaknesses.
If you are able to obtain financial data (try the annual shareholder reports), quote this and show where your business fits into the market.

When planning how you are going to tackle the marketing aspect of the business, don't just list what you intend to do, work out a timeline (for yourself more than for others) and give people a point of reference of when certain

Defining idea...

'It had only one fault. It was kind of lousy.'
JAMES THURBER

projects or campaigns will begin and how long they will last. Break down the costs for each individual campaign and explain the rationale behind the expenditure and timing.

When the plan is complete you will need to test it on someone you trust but who is not involved in the business or the same industry. Can it be read and understood by someone completely removed from the business? Whatever terminology or areas they find difficult to understand must be revised or explained – your plan must have universal appeal.

Once complete and fully edited it is time to make sure that the plan itself is well presented. Nobody is expecting gilt-edging, but having the document bound, or at least placed in a colour co-ordinated folder, will make you and your proposal all the more attractive – and the reader is also less likely to lose random pages, which helps too.

92. Know the opposition

When you are constructing your business plan and when you are actually operating the business, you should always watch what your competition is doing. Imitate their successes and avoid their mistakes.

You don't have to wear a balaclava and spend your evenings suspended above buildings trying to break into a competitor's office – although this could be a lot of fun… There are easier ways!

Sun Tzu teaches that if you study the enemy intimately, you will win the war. Waging war and competing in the commercial market are not dissimilar. Although you are unlikely to lose your head if you fail, it is much better to be the winner and have your enemies begging for mercy at your feet – or at least conceding some of their market share. A simple way to monitor your competition is to test their service as much as you can – have members of your staff phone them up, order products, return products, check their email response times and their website availability. They will be doing the same to you. This should not be vindictive or malicious; you are testing their service and hopefully improving your own through the outcome. If there is a weakness in their service, obviously you don't let them know about it, you simply ensure that your service is far superior.

Here's an idea for you...

If you use sequential numbering on your invoices/receipts – stop! Have this altered immediately; someone out there is monitoring your business. Place some orders with competitors and see how they number documents. This intelligence is frightening, both in terms of what you can learn about your competition and how easy it is to obtain.

Never give away your position and strengths but know their weaknesses – use the trade press to keep abreast of competitors' machinations. Who are they doing deals with? How are they advertising? From adverts alone you should be able to make an educated guess about how much is being spent on marketing. Does your competition run any promotions with clients? If so, get the details of the deal and explore, as best you can, where their products/services are selling and to whom.

It is reasonably straightforward to monitor their staff retention through how many adverts they are placing for staff vacancies. Note that to disguise growth, some companies advertise for a temporary position due to maternity leave – or even paternity leave now. This can be a very clever way to both bring candidates in on a short-term contract and, if they are suitable, make their contract more long term, thus protecting the company from having to retain unsuitable staff and hiding the number of new employees from competitors' eyes.

When I was with Amazon I was given a budget every week to buy books on the internet from our competitors. Why? Well, I would like to believe that Amazon were incredibly benevolent employers and they knew how to retain a bibliophile; however, the reason was much more clever, and nothing to do with me at all. Every

> ### Defining idea...
>
> 'All you need in this life is ignorance and confidence; then success is sure.'
> MARK TWAIN

Monday at 11.00 a.m. I would place an order with five competitors and over the week the orders would arrive. On each of the shipping notes/invoices there was a shipping number or reference – and all of these companies were using sequential numbering. So, for the cost of a few orders, we were able to see how many orders the company had shipped ever, calculate an approximate value of their entire business and see the number of orders they received a week – priceless.

93. Maximising your company potential

Variety is the spice of life. From the moment you start creating your business plan you should be exploring every possible way that the business can make money.

This isn't about having fingers in every pie and getting in a mess. It's to ensure that you are maximising profit for you and your business.

Although the strongest business planning revolves around a business's core values, shrewd entrepreneurs do not put all of their eggs into one basket. It may be that you look at adding a website or a mail order capacity to your business plan as a way to seem like a multi-channel, 'with-it' sort of business. Or you may include the other sales channels as serious money earners but not be truly committed to them, by not allowing enough for staff recruitment and development. But these simple activities could prove, sometimes very quickly, to be your main strengths and they must be planned from the outset. Despite your confidence in your retail outlet selling x number of chess sets per week, it could be that you really don't have the footfall (passing custom) to support the business. Your website, designed and built for a few hundred pounds at the insistence of your nephew, could turn out to be the resounding success story of the company if sales exceed expectations. Don't sell yourself, or your sales channels, short. If you are planning to have multiple routes to market, plan each of them with as much care and attention as your main business objective.

Staff skills

Treat your own skills and the skills of your staff with a completely mercenary approach. If you or a staff member is a skilled writer, farm out your talents to other companies – by using the infrastructure of your business to pitch for work, you can charge a far healthier fee for the work and justify a split in revenues between the author and the business.

Is your business such that you could spare a staff member one afternoon a week to talk or present at tradeshows or to other organisations? Again, using the resources of the business to promote these talents means a larger fee for all involved.

There are so many ways to earn extra cash by selling your staff's skills to other businesses; remind them that although they might earn more by freelancing full-time, it could take them several years before they developed enough contacts to get a steady flow of work. By working for you in this way, they increase their income at no risk.

Here's an idea for you...

If you are planning to operate a retail or catering business, produce flyers or mini-catalogues showcasing a selection of products or promotions. Now negotiate an insert into the next edition of the local free paper. If you promote the business address, phone number or web address (or a combination of all three), it will quickly show whether there is a potential market for a mail order business or, in the catering arena, home-delivery and large group bookings. This could open up a number of new sales channels for your business.

Defining idea...

'If we don't succeed, we run the risk of failure.'
DAN QUAYLE

The space around you

When buying or leasing premises there is often a price point that, once breached, means for very little extra cost you can acquire a tremendous amount of extra space. If the space is surplus to requirements, sub-let part of the building to another individual or organisation at a competitive rate. Proportionately you will be recouping a large amount of rental income whilst only sacrificing a small amount of space. But watch out – if all your small tenants go broke in a recession, you'll end up having to pay the entire rent. This can and does happen, so be careful with your selection of tenants and the agreements you make with them. Often retail premises are easier to let than offices during hard times; it matters less if you lose a tenant when there are others eager to take their place.

94. How to make a profit

There are various forms of money. And the danger with business schools is that it can all get too theoretical...

I'm going to ensure your understanding of this topic is so good that you are standing up and shouting for profit!

Here's how to make money. I thought you would like the sound of that!

What is profit?

In its simplest terms, it's the money from sales of the organisation less the costs of the organisation. Importantly it is distinguished from revenue, which is simply the money from the sales which the organisation makes. It is also distinguished from cash flow, which is the coming in and going out of cash. An organisation can fail, even when ultimately it should be profitable, because it has not managed its flow of cash and runs out of it. And, clearly, revenue alone is not an indicator of a viable business.

Profit is important to an organisation because, firstly, it is a clear, visible and ultimately published measure of how well a business is doing. For good or bad, people will measure your success to a certain extent by looking at your profitability. Secondly, it is a reward to those who run the business. They have taken risks with their time and money and resources. If there is no reward, what is the incentive to continue taking those risks? Thirdly, profits provide funds for expansion in the future and, finally, a business that does not make money will ultimately fail.

Here's an idea for you...

Talk to three groups of people either on the phone or by email. The three groups are your customer or your client's customer, your client (or ask yourself) and your bank manager or those in the world of finance – for instance, your accountant. Ask them this simple question: what makes for a successful business in their view? Summarise the results in fifty words or less. You'll notice a dilemma. Customers want great product at low cost, business people have a dream or vision to execute, the financial person wants growth, excellent shareholder return and profit. You have to balance those three demands.

How to make profit...

Here are six straightforward – but often neglected – ways for your business or those of your clients to make profit.

- Pricing. Profit will originate from the money made on products (hard) or services (soft). The money made, of course, is arithmetically calculated by price less cost. To a certain extent there may well not be a lot you can do about costs, but you can often be more imaginative about prices. Do not be frightened to increase your prices, for example. If there is a lot of customer resistance you can always lower them later. Consider having some premium price products. By all means give discount for volume but ensure your accountant has done the calculations; it can take a surprisingly large increase in volume to make up for even small discounts.

- Manage costs. Do whatever you can to keep costs down by choosing your suppliers well, managing your infrastructure, measuring costs and encouraging your employees to keep costs down. Ensure expenses policies are documented and adhered to. If there is a loophole which allows someone to fly business class, then they will. Don't begrudge them the extra comfort if it is appropriate, but that's a heck of a cost compared to economy.

- Measures. Ensure profitability is measured, especially to the level of detail which allows you to identify something like a product which is very profitable or is not price sensitive, or a product line which is not profitable and should be removed. Identify which customers or markets or countries are profitable for you. Understand the reasons behind those results, too, as that may well allow you to create more products with extra profitability.

> **Defining idea...**
>
> The promise of every product and service is a better life. Profits are the prize for delivering on the promise. PATRICK DIXON, *Building a Better Business.*

- Manage cash. Without cash it doesn't matter how profitable you are. You need cash to work the business on a day-to-day basis.

- Training and development. Teach everybody to realise the importance of revenue, profit and cash flow, and to understand the essential differences between them. In particular remove the naivety that some employees can have that 'revenue is all'. Run a negotiation course and teach them how to sell value and not be defensive about prices.

- Devolve responsibility. Give responsibility for profitability to all concerned. It is a common mistake to reward sales people simply by the revenue they've generated, for example. That may well encourage too much deal making, discounting and consequent low profitability.

311

95. Get the best advice

With any new idea, we naturally want to do as much as we can on our own, but being too proud can lead to disaster. Look for others who offer good advice for free; if you don't, your competition certainly will.

Look to experienced business development organisations for advice, and read serious technical books about corporate finance and investment decisions. Business is one area where theory really does turn out to be applicable in practice.

Letting go

There should be an element of secrecy involved in setting up a new business. The fewer the people who know the finer details, the more likely that your idea will not be hijacked by another individual or company. But you also need to build awareness of your business right from day one. You will not divulge sensitive information to random members of the public, you will be entering into discussions with professionals who are either paid or volunteer to offer advice to businesses. There is an important difference between the two!

What's on offer?

Depending on where you are and the nature of the business you are planning to launch, you may be able to obtain anything from a cash grant, tax breaks and access to qualified staff to financial advice and moral support. It is your responsibility, as the person driving the business, to research every option and, if possible, meet as many potential helping hands as you can.

From whom?

A search on the internet is your best place to start. Very quickly you will begin to appreciate the myriad organisations out there that exist solely to support businesses. Some are for profit and some offer their services gratis. What you pay for may not necessarily be more valuable to you than what is given for free. In the UK, a few searches to start you on your way should include 'business link' 'DTI' 'Chamber of Commerce' 'British Embassy [name of country you are planning to trade in]' 'British Council' 'Business Learning & Skills' and your local government website.

> **Here's an idea for you...**
>
> Make a point of contacting at least one organisation in your local area and setting up a meeting to determine how useful they could be in helping your business achieve its goals. During your half hour chat you will probably be given sound advice and the contact details of individuals or organisations who will also help you move the business forward.

Why?

So much of setting up a new business comes with a price. It may feel strange that individuals or organisations are prepared to be so benevolent – but remember they receive funding from somewhere (usually from the government through taxation) and therefore in a roundabout way you have been paying for this assistance for years; you'd be crazy not to 'cash in' now. We can also become a little blinkered about our own abilities. Whilst it is good to be confident and passionate about a new business, involving a third-party can mean even more good ideas are thrown into the mix. Why not give your business an even greater chance of success?

> **Defining idea...**
>
> 'Good advice is something a man gives when he is too old to set a bad example.'
> FRANÇOIS DE LA ROCHEFOUCAULD

313

96. The rainy-day fund

When every penny counts it may seem strange to leave a large percentage of your working capital aside for a rainy day, but that's what you need to do.

Here's an idea for you...

Take some time to scan the jobs in the national press and look for the skills and experience required for the roles you would be interested in applying for were you in the market. Is there something that you could be doing now (training through the business, for example) to ensure that you improve your marketable skills?

Be too cautious of course and the business won't have a fighting chance of succeeding at all – tiptoe rather than crawl.

Any monies borrowed, if at all possible, must be secured on some of your assets, even if the lender is not asking for such a provision. Yes, you could declare yourself bankrupt if it all went terribly wrong, but if you truly believe in the business that you are creating, you should never get into the position of having to declare yourself bankrupt – if you are paying enough attention to essentials such as your cash flow, you'll see the downward spiral before or whilst it is happening and react accordingly instead of reacting after the event.

There are times when the risk of launching a business involves you putting absolutely everything on the line, including your car, house, kids, family pet and every last penny of savings. This is unwise. If the idea is that good, there are other areas of investment open to you. Although you will be well regarded for showing such commitment, especially by banks, they won't be there to applaud if it all goes wrong – in fact, they will probably be the ones repossessing your vehicle and house. Avoid this at all costs.

Defining idea...

'First weigh the considerations, then take the risks.'
HELMUTH VON MOLTKE, *German army general*

As the months become years and you are able to say that you run an established business, don't lose sight of the ever-changing market. When creating your business plan, a lot of time and effort probably went into researching the market into which you were entering and the competition as it stood then. Over a period of months and years the market alters; consumers change allegiance and react differently to pricing models depending on what else is going on in terms of interest rates and earnings. Competitors consolidate their position and sometimes fold. All this jostling around alters the picture at any given time. Keeping a keen eye on the industry should be an ongoing concern for everyone in the business. Something you would rather not think about, but nonetheless a very valid exercise, is to imagine the worst-case scenario. If, for whatever reason, the business is gone, you may be back in the job market looking to keep a roof over your head and your family fed. How would you do it?

Defining idea...

'Take calculated risks. That is quite different from being rash.'
GEORGE S. PATTON, *US army general*

315

97. Keeping on top of cashflow

In an ideal world your customers would pay you before you had to pay your suppliers, but it rarely works that way. To stay afloat, you need to manage your cash flow.

In the majority of businesses, the pressure is on you to spend before you get paid. Effective cash flow is about ensuring that you have more money coming in than you have going out.

For sales to take place you will need to order products and materials, supply them to the customer, invoice them and, in many cases, wait to be paid. For this you will need a trading platform (a shop, office or website) and staff, which all costs money.

So how does it really work? You order the materials and services you need and sell them on to your customer, but it is the terms you have arranged with both that will determine your cash flow. Good cash flow management enhances profitability and is a key element in ensuring that your business survives.

Your mission, quite simply, is to try and use other people's money to cover your expenditure. If you can manage this you will be cash rich and in a very healthy position. If at all possible, obtain immediate payment from your customers before providing the product or service. If, at the same time, you can pay your suppliers over a longer period – usually 30, but sometimes 60 or 90 days – you will have a very healthy cash flow. Crack this and maybe retirement and the front cover of Time Magazine are not so far away.

Here's an idea for you...

Try to tighten the credit you offer to customers. For retail businesses, most payments are instantaneous, but there is still the option to take deposits for stock you haven't even ordered. For commercial businesses, drop your terms to 7 or 14 days rather than the standard 30 days – it's amazing how many companies will pay up without causing a fuss.

On occasion, it is possible to spread your banking custom and thus your ability to borrow more. By setting up separate accounts to handle each of your routes to market, such as internet sales, mail order sales or international sales, there is the possibility of creating multiple relationships with banks that will allow more access to lending and credit. As long as the business is not overstretched, and the loans are overdrafts that can be covered by the revenues from each of the sales channels, you are not breaking rules, just giving your business more options.

By definition, a new business has no track record and no sympathy from the firms it deals with. Even if you are bringing years of personal experience to the party, the sad truth is that when it comes to paying bills you will be hit the hardest in your first year. Suppliers may demand that your first order is paid for pro-forma (in advance). The bank may be reluctant to grant the overdraft facility you require. Much, if not all, of the business machinery must be purchased and

Defining idea...

'It is better to have a permanent income than to be fascinating.'
OSCAR WILDE

you will pay deposits on your premises, hire-purchase items and other leases. In short, your first twelve months will be expensive, but you need them to be cheap until you get your income up. The net result is that you may need to earn much more in your first year than in subsequent years just to break even. Budget for being taken to the cleaners in your first year; the business world, it seems, is geared up for making the life of a start-up as hard as possible. The trick is to make it through to the other side and start earning more than you spend. You must make the difficult journey to the fabled world of profitability!

It's time to put your negotiating powers to the test and try and get the most favourable terms for your business. Although you will have trouble convincing your suppliers in your first year to give you any special dispensation over and above their standard terms,

Defining idea...

'When a man tells you that he got rich through hard work, ask him: "Whose?"'
DON MARQUIS, *author*

there is no harm in asking. Whatever their terms are, be sure to pay up on time; if you don't, you are asking for trouble.

98. Reinvent. Regularly

One of the major banks said recently: 'if we were launching today, there is absolutely, categorically no way we would design a bank like this'. So what's to be done? Reinvent...

How to turn around a business: rapidly. New, struggling or failing – you are the person to do it.

Stage 1: review the 'hot spots'

- Hot spot 1: marketing. Review the '4 Ps': product, price, place and promotion. Ask yourself the tough questions: what's the product, who are our customers, how will we talk to them and why are we different? Those questions can either be present (i.e. who are our customers now) or future: who might our customers be? Keep the tense, present or future, consistent across one session. Don't leave the room until those questions are fully and properly answered. When they are, a sustainable business is born or reborn.

- Hot spot 2: tough decisions. You are going to address what everybody else has been afraid to do: where the money is going to come from. Who do you need to fire? Who do you need to hire? Where will you be based? What are the plans? You have got a whiteboard and all of these are listed, ready to be ticked when they are actioned.

Here's an idea for you...

Do some scenario planning. It's great fun (after the initial 'do we really have to?'). Ask those from your planning group to write a 500-word story of what your company will be like in three years' time. Emphasise that you want detail and narrative rather than bullets – something like 'We will be a player with 60% share of our chosen financial software market: 100% of our transactions will be executed online which will allow us to have a minimal but passionate and dedicated staff...' Ask each of your team to read their stories and then discuss the output. Capture actions for future sessions.

Hot spot 3: money decisions. Get all the money stuff sorted: a decent profit and loss account, serious cash flow, the necessary pricing calculations, things like guidelines to the sales force on discounting. Ensure invoices are issued promptly and bills chased immediately.

Hot spot 4: processes and systems. You need great working processes and systems and the more you can automate the better. Who is responsible for a tidy reception area? Quite.

Hot spot 5: people. You need to develop your best. Recruit more excellent people, brief them, empower them, train them. Get them focused on the new direction of the business.

Hot spot 6: facts. You need facts, facts about who and what makes the money, which salespeople are worth three of the others, what the markets are doing. Too many businesses, too much of the time, work on guesswork. Not you: knowledge is power.

Hot spot 7: being brilliant at the basics. Ensure people know how to sell rather than just take orders, how to negotiate rather than just give discounts and how to forecast not just guess; that they know how to manage their time and how to wow the customer. Above all, ensure there is a simple planning round which regularly reviews this list and gives particular attention to innovation...

By the way, without innovation the majority of businesses will die in the New World of Work. This is not hyperbole; what was brilliant rapidly becomes only OK. Innovation is not a choice: it is a necessity. So what is innovation? It's creativity plus action; both are vital and the challenge is that they are almost contradictory skills – free-flow versus discipline; open-ended versus closure; 'off the wall' versus acting within the rules. Address

that challenge and yours will be one of the rare truly innovative organisations.

> **Defining idea...**
>
> The difficulty lies not in the new ideas, but in escaping from the old ones, which ramify, for those brought up as most of us have been, into every corner of our minds.
> JOHN MAYNARD KEYNES

Stage 2: action the 'hot spots'

- Step 1: take the above list and highlight all the areas which you need to address. What needs to be done in your business? Who can action it? And what's the priority? What is the delivery date?

- Step 2: get the management team (perhaps just you, of course) together. Review your thoughts. Get full buy-in. Assign every action to an individual with a report-back date. Set the date for the next meeting when those actions will be reviewed.

- Step 3: keep that cycle going. Every quarter.

If you want to survive, you should carry out the above processes regularly, and think and act differently.

99. Routes to market

The more routes to market you are able to tap into, the more chance you have of gaining revenue. Know what you want and go for it!

Talking about your great ideas for world domination down the pub is all very well, but your time would be better spent actually putting them into action.

Listing every possible sales channel may make for a healthy looking business plan, but don't spread yourself too thin. Each route to market will require expenditure, expertise and serious commitment. Know exactly why you are entering each route to market and what you expect to achieve from each sales channel. Many retailers never consider the possibility of mail order. Mail order, if you are already holding stock, is a relatively cheap way to expand your customer base. Start off small and local and test the market. If it works, grow to regional or national exposure at your own pace.

Web Fest
The World Wide Web is an ever-growing phenomenon, and even despite the massive bursting of bubbles in 1999/2000 that many thought marked the end of a relatively short time in the limelight, selling through the internet can be a profitable endeavour. Research the web intensely, invest well in a website and reach a global audience at the switch of a button.

ReSellers

You can also pay resellers or lead generators to help you sell products or services to customers, for a commission. Whether your resellers are web-based, 'real' people knocking on doors, or based in an office and drumming up trade by phone, it makes no difference – they are exposing your product or services to customers you were unlikely to come into contact with. Customers get what they want, the reseller earns a commission and you make money.

> ### Here's an idea for you...
>
> Seriously consider creating a part to your business that will explore either a reseller/lead generator scheme or a network-marketing scheme. There will be a cost associated with researching the market and carrying out the viability study, but sharing in what is already a multi-billion pound sales channel in the UK (and growing) has got to be worth it.

Building A Pyramid

Network marketing has become the new black in terms of alternative retail. From the early days of Avon ladies to Tupperware, we have moved on in leaps and bounds to the halcyon days of the noughties where we can now buy everything from perfume and bedtime accessories to cleaning products in the comfort of our own home, with very little effort. Effectively the shop is our living room and the sales assistant is a lifelong friend earning a bit of pin money on a Thursday night (or for the very successful, new cars and holidays).

> ### Defining idea...
>
> 'What we have to do is to be forever curiously testing new opinions and courting new impressions.'
> WALTER PATER, *19th century writer*

Setting up a network marketing scheme is well worth consideration, as long as your margins allow for the various commission structures and a multi-tiered hierarchy. Some products lend themselves very well to this, such as small items like perfume with a high margin,

323

Defining idea...

'If you don't know where you are going, any road will take you there.'
LEWIS CARROLL

and others don't, such as large high-value items like rocking horses. Have your solicitor create the vendor contract and your accountant work with you on commissions and the organisational structure. Decide on the product and pricing and send your army off into the night to sell.

100. Create a brilliant experience

It's not about service — it's about the experience. Disney got it. Starbucks gets it and, increasingly, so does M&S. Do you get it and, more importantly, can you create it?

A wow experience, that is. Something which causes your customers to feel a positive tingle, to come back and back and back. And you just take more money to the bank.

It's a tough old global market out there: the competition gets tougher and tougher. Customers get choosier and choosier. And product differentiation is harder to maintain. But, wait: at the 'hard' product level that is certainly true, a latte is still a latte. A small hatchback is just a small hatchback, a bank is a bank. OK, you can add an extra shot to your latte or free SatNav to your hatchback or new, faster ATMs to your bank, but how long can that differentiation be maintained? You're right, not long. Do remember, though, that differentiation is about three factors – company or brand, products and people. And it's the people which can create the real difference, who can create a wow experience. You see, everyone knows that's no longer about the commodity. It's no longer just about the brand. It really is about service, of course. But it's actually about more than that: it's about experience.

Here's an idea for you...

Write a story, write a scenario about your company or product. Take a few of the basic ingredients, tell a story and see where it goes. The most important thing is to write. Don't plan or prepare. Don't, at this stage, worry about syntax or grammar; simply write. If you do this you'll be amazed at the ideas which are revealed from your deeper consciousness. Wondering how to tackle it? Think about Levi Jeans – what would you do with them? After all, what a story – cowboys, men who were men, great girls in great trousers. How could you create differentiated experience from that?

You know the Disney story. A man has a dream, a dream to create a perfect theme park – one which is safe for children and a delight for their parents, a place where there would be no litter and all the staff would be courteous. True, the rides are fantastic, but what's really different is the people. (Remember how there were initial problems in Euro Disney as the staff didn't get the idea?)

What about Starbucks? Is it about coffee? Sort of. It's great coffee, of course, and their lovely, well-designed shops. But the staff and the music and the aroma all pull together to create Howard Schulz's 'third place' experience. Not home, not work, but a place where you can go to chill.

There are plenty of other examples. How about Innocent Juices? Is that really all about fresh fruit juice? No. It's about the friendly 'banter' of their bottles, about their quirky website, about things like the banana phone. It's a total experience, and so is the new M&S too, with their amazing advertisements for food. The stores are now a whole lot fresher, and the whole thing is a much better 'experience'. Of course.

Here's the bottom line. To pull ahead in what's known as the New World of Work, you must give your customers a powerful and positive and enlivening experience, one which is so good that they want to return. And how? Here are a few 'experience enliveners' you might consider for your organisation:

- Simplicity: less is more. In a busy world people appreciate it if things are really simple (forms to fill in, websites to navigate, airports to reach), elegant (where exactly are the English wines in this mess of a shop?) and straightforward (how do I complain?). This might be as basic as signage in a supermarket which helps people find the cereals or as sophisticated as your website. But less is generally more.

> **Defining idea...**
>
> Our brains deal exclusively with special-case experiences.
> BUCKMINSTER FULLER, *Operating Manual for Spaceship Earth, 1963*

- People: great people make such a good experience. How about helpful people on the end of a phone compared to robotic call centres? How about having enough baristas in your coffee shop? How about people so helpful that customers want to return? Yes, they are only buying a light bulb at the moment, but give them a great experience and they will come to you for their next dishwasher.

- Easy: stress-less. Here's a good example. There are plenty of trolleys at the airport and they're free, too. It's obvious where you need to queue, the signage is brilliant and clear, and the whole place has been planned to minimise walking.

- Design: great design. This creates an even better user experience – whether that's proper labelling and careful choice of colours or reduced wrapping and packaging and being more ecologically sound. Keep instructions helpful and provide simple start-up guides, as well as clear advice about where to go if it all goes wrong.

- Worthwhile: having purpose. Increasing numbers of people want to help the planet rather than damage it. How green are you? How fair trade are you?
- Lead, not just serve. Provide what people want, sure, but take it further and anticipate their needs.

101. Customers rule

Customers can be annoying, needy and very time consuming, but without them you would not have a business. Are you nurturing your customers?

The best people to judge how well your business is performing are those whom you are selling to. Take a deep breath and start proactively interacting with your customers.

Always keep questionnaires and correspondence to customers polite and well written, and answer their questions fully – you don't want your rude letters to be shown for all to see on some tough-talking consumer affairs programme on TV!

Many businesses deal with dissatisfied customers reactively – nothing happens until the complaint comes that orders have not been received, the product was faulty or the wrong item was received. Customers get upset if they perceive the staff to be rude or the service they receive to be less than satisfactory. The situation is usually dealt with and everyone concerned is happy for a very short period of time.

All of this additional customer contact time, whether it is additional phone calls, emails or full-blown rows in the shop or office, is valuable time when you or your staff are not getting on with the job.

It is much better to pre-empt your customers and ask them for ways that you could improve your business. Make their experience in dealing with you more problem-free and even fun.

A Question For You

When it comes to airing views, customers are often happy to give positive feedback as much as negative comments. The trick is devising a system that will coax the information out of them. But before you can start sending questionnaires to your customers, you need to know what it is you are asking. When approaching customers for feedback, be as specific as possible. Asking customers or clients whether they like your business will result in very bizarre answers, and although you will be happy that Mrs Dwyer thinks the young girl on reception is wonderful because she has the same colour eyes as her daughter, you have only succeeded in wasting everybody's time. Be clear what it is you are assessing. How satisfied are you with the service you receive from us? How satisfied are you with our pricing? Allow users to mark you out of 5 and also allow for extra comments at the end of the questionnaire. Try not to ask more than seven questions if you are not compensating clients for their time.

Create a questionnaire to gauge customers' opinion of your selection of stock. As this is probably the showpiece of the business, it's a good place to start. Your questions should not focus on the aesthetics such as the quality of your racking or shop fitting (although one question of this type is fine). Most questions

> **Here's an idea for you...**
>
> Any time you have contact with a customer, it is an opportunity to sell to them. Try to think of ways that you can use the customer complaints process in your marketing. For example, if you solve someone's complaint to their satisfaction, it is a great moment to ask them if they want to see a new catalogue, obtain a quantity discount on their next purchase, or come to a product launch.

329

Defining idea...

Defining idea...

'Your most unhappy customers are your greatest source of learning.'
BILL GATES

should be focused on the selection or ability to find the products they require, quickly and easily. Include space for customers to include their own comments and leave them with the question: 'If I could change one thing about this business it would be...'

The answers will be varied and strange, but depending on the size of your cross-section you will probably end up with over ten alterations that need to be made to the layout of the shop or warehouse. These answers are coming straight from your clients. Their reactions are real, if sometimes odd, and they will help give you an insight into who users are and why.

102. Creating time for reflection

Launching a business is hard work and can be all-consuming. However, we do have to take stock every once in a while and monitor how we are getting on.

Just as you would to cross a busy road, in business you should stop, look and listen every now and again to put it all into perspective.

Business is constantly changing. With technology becoming ever smarter and smaller, the digital age is doing a lot more for us than making our music collections portable. We should see technology as our friend and use it to help us in more ways than writing fancy letters. Assessing your own progress can be as scientific as you like, but there's no point in spending time and effort on the exercise if you are not reacting to the results. Just as the business plan you are writing will alter over the coming years, so should your projections. Once you begin trading you should capture the actual results and match your income and expenditure against your projections. If your projections are wildly high or far too low, you need to work on them again. Outperforming or underachieving is not telling you anything other than the projections were wrong. Use spreadsheets as much as possible to both capture and present the data.

Here's an idea for you...

When assessing your progress, be sure to acknowledge your successes as well as your failures. Reward yourself and your team every so often for making the business work – throw a party!

Although you will have annual targets in terms of turnover and expenditure, it is very useful to break the year into quarters and sometimes even individual months or weeks. Even if the benefits are still to show through as savings, are you and your staff becoming more efficient in the basics? What is your performance in answering queries by telephone and email and increasing the number of clients visiting your office or customers entering your premises? Have your staff attended the training courses you thought would be beneficial? Have any problems been dealt with, or are you constantly fire-fighting? Take a long, honest look at your business. Fixing problems will improve the long-term financial well-being of the organisation.

You can learn a lot from your competitors, but this does not mean that by copying them to the letter you will become as successful as they are. They may have had first-mover advantage and now have a loyal customer base. They may have had four times more seed capital to get their idea off the ground. The market may have been different a few years ago, so the exact same tactics will simply not work now.

Many retail outlets selling similar products will look pretty similar to consumers, except for a different colour pattern and branding. There's a good reason for this: the pattern works. You can launch a completely unique business without having to be wholly original all of the time. Why go through a long and expensive learning process when other companies have spent the money researching consumer preference and trends? Assess what is going on in the market around you and adapt.

Have a third-party professional assess what you have achieved thus far. It could be a formal review or just a quiet chat over lunch, but it will not be a wasted experience. After about six months of operations it would be well worth buttering up your accountant or solicitor and giving them an update of where you are. If you involved these people in the formation of the business and talked through the business plan with them, then they will be more than familiar with the background. How do they feel about the progress you are making? Do bear in mind that they will only be able to react to the information that you provide – the more honest your account of operations, the more informed and accurate their reply.

Defining idea...

'Reflect on your present blessings, of which every man has many; not on your past misfortunes, of which all men have some.'
CHARLES DICKENS

103. What if everything goes wrong?

No matter how well crafted your plan, things can and often do go wrong; good business acumen is judged partly on how you minimise your risk but also on how well you deal with setbacks.

Despite the best will in the world and your best efforts, orders sometimes aren't what they should be. The question is, will you run or will you fight?

Quiet weeks quickly turn into quiet months and inevitably you have a lot more money going out than is coming in. There really is no point just hoping that things are going to turn out for the best and everything will sort itself out. It won't, not without a level of interaction from you. Keeping accurate records of your accounts is a minimum requirement for any business, but the trick is to actually read the data, try to make sense of the figures and look for tell-tale patterns. If you notice a downward spiral beginning to form, then react to it immediately rather than letting it get any worse. There are a number of options open to you if your cash flow is looking a tad negative:

Overdraft – Increasing your overdraft will be at your bank's discretion and may require personal guarantees from you that will mean you paying the debt off personally if the business cannot afford it. Assuming you can get the limit raised, this is probably the easiest way to cover the shortfall and can be the fastest way from realising there is a problem to being able to deal with it.

Loan – Borrowing additional funds when things seem to be getting bad can be a scary prospect, but it can also be the lifeline you need to ride out the storm and turn the business around. Whether you will be able to raise the money will depend on the amount that you have borrowed already, your likely ability to repay it and the amount required. A loan will mean additional monthly payments, which need to be accounted for, but it will also mean that creditors are kept happy and you have time to react to the situation.

Here's an idea for you...

If there is any way of ring-fencing funds for a 'rainy day', then do it. The funds do not have to sit in a separate account, nor is it a huge problem if you dip into the money occasionally to pay off invoices. Making this happen simply means negotiating hard on every deal and trying to cut costs wherever you can. If you can bring your expenditure down by 10% you'll have that much more room for manoeuvre.

Streamlining – Not a pleasant route at all, but one that must be considered. 'Streamlining' is a euphemism for letting staff go. There is often a short-term cost associated with making staff redundant – both financially and in terms of increased workload for others. In the long term, though, you will be saving significant amounts of money and it could be enough to fix your cash flow.

Selling off assets – Depending on what you have and how much of it is essential, you will soon decide whether this is a viable option. Although you will receive only about 30% of the original value of the items, it is probably the most painless of all the routes to regaining positive cash flow – and it's a lot easier to sell a couple of computers and desks than it is to let a member of staff go.

Defining idea...

'We are continually faced with a series of great opportunities brilliantly disguised as insoluble problems.'
JOHN W. GARDNER, *US politician*

Losing an important member of staff is a real blow to any business, no matter how big or small, but when you are a fledgling business the pain is all the more acute. There are numerous reasons why a staff member will want to leave and there is very little that you can do to stop the process. The most important thing is to always bear in mind that nothing is set in stone and no matter how well you get on with your staff, outside influences such as family, illness, rising house prices and, not least, better offers from elsewhere mean that on any day a staff member might resign from their position. Although you should not stay awake worrying about it, don't ignore it. No one is indispensable and therefore, whomever you deal with, in whatever capacity, from other companies or in your everyday life, they should always be assessed (privately, in your head!) as to his or her suitability within your business – one day you might just need to call upon them.

5
Supercharge your finances

Money, Money, Money. A source of joy or a source of anxiety? Survey show that 51% of us worry more about money than anything else – more than our relationships, our children or our future – so it makes sense to feel that when it comes to money, we put a bit of effort in to feel in control of it.

You can be earning a fortune and still be more worried about money than if you were unemployed. That's because money is about much more than survival. Our relationship with money tells us loads about ourselves, except we're too scared to look! But enough of the psychology. Whatever you earn, you can turn around your relationship with money so that you feel secure.

Are you scared of money?

Might seem a daft question, but often we don't realise how tricky our relationship with money really is. Ask yourself these questions. Where the situation doesn't apply to you, pick the response which sounds most like you.

1. When it comes to home repairs, you:
- ☐ a. Get repairs done as soon as you are aware there's a problem. Leaving it until they break or are ruined will only cost you more in the long run.
- ☐ b. Only fix things when they are unusable and/or life is pretty well impossible without them.
- ☐ c. Get them fixed if you have the money.

2. If you were given a first class ticket, you would:
- ☐ a. Not even think about using it, you'd trade it in for a cheaper ticket and pocket the difference feeling you've got one over on the universe.
- ☐ b. Enjoy it.
- ☐ c. Trade it in, it would feel so wasteful to use it but it would be lovely.

3. Would you drive a second hand car?
- ☐ a. Yes, if it was a good runner and looked ok.
- ☐ b. No, there's nothing like the feel and smell of a brand new car.
- ☐ c. Affording even a second hand car seems unlikely.

4. Do you know how much money you have in your main bank account to the nearest £50?

☐ a. Yes
☐ b. Not really
☐ c. Yes, nothing

5. Have you ever found yourself in a reasonably expensive restaurant or agreed to a big night out when you really didn't have much money at the time?

☐ a. Hardly ever or never?
☐ b. Often
☐ c. No, you just can't afford it.

Mostly

a. You are scarily good with money. **Try idea 112** – it should appeal

b. You are scarily unconcerned about money. **Try idea 113** – you probably need it

c. You are scared stiff by your lack of money. **Try idea 116** – you need to get positive.

104. Ditch the debt

Live on less than you earn. Hey, radical concept.

As I write this, press reports warn that there has been a sharp rise in people declaring themselves bankrupt. The stress caused by credit or, to call it by its old-fashioned name, debt, is well documented.

And if you've tried to remove the source of your debt you might well be even more stressed. Consolidating credit card debts into personal loans (at a lower interest rate) sounds like a good idea but financial coach Simone Gnesson has reservations. 'Lots of clients have done this but it only makes matters worse if you carry on spending and don't deal with the original habits that got you into debt in the first place.' (Hint: building up two debts is not the way to go.)

You've read it a million times before but here it is again. Get rid of credit card debt. There is no fast fix. It may well take you years.

Think about hiring a financial coach. The internet is a good place to look for one of these. You pay a flat fee to them and they'll help you sort through your attitudes towards money and change habits if necessary. If things have got desperate, you might need full-on debt counselling.

Move all your debt to a single credit card or two with 0% interest (and remember, these 0% deals may not be around for ever so don't think you can rely on them indefinitely to make the cost of your debt negligible). Check out the Saturday newspaper financial supplements for details of the best current deals. If you have a lot of debt, you will have to do this many times. Find out when your 'grace period' ends, and mark in your diary a month before you start paying interest. Start looking for a new deal then. Allow at least two weeks for the application to be processed and the transfers to be made, although internet banks are usually faster. Make sure you write to the old company cancelling your agreement and cut up the card.

> **Here's an idea for you...**
>
> Decide on an amount that you are allowed to spend each day. If by any chance you have any money left at the end of the day, stick it in jar and save it. This too can become a bit of a game.

Never have more than one credit card for emergencies. Hide this in your house. Some people wrap it in a bag and put it in a freezer. Do not carry it with you routinely.

Pay more than the minimum towards your debt. Aiming for double the minimum is a good rule of thumb. Believe it or not, you can start to enjoy the process – it can become a game, seeing how much you can pay off each month from money you save elsewhere. Try to pay off a little more each month.

How do you save more money?

Just writing down what you spend is enough to save money usually. But if you need 'special measures', try the following:

343

Defining idea...

'I am able to buy anything I want
[but] more than anything I hate
waste. Uselessness. The things you
buy represent how you see yourself
– how you wish others to see you.
You're a smart cookie. Let the world
know it.'
OPRAH WINFREY

- List the stuff you absolutely have to spend money on to get to your workplace and function at your job – so that's fares and oh, alright, you can have a daily newspaper. No money for lunches (take in your own).

- Allow yourself discretionary spending money. Decide on a reasonable amount for the week – you'll know how much you usually spend each week from writing everything down – try halving that to begin with. Now you know what happens next. Go to the cashpoint and take out your basic times five, plus your discretionary – that's what you have to spend in a working week. You can spend the discretionary on what you like but when that's gone, it's gone.

- Use the principle of carrying only what you need at all times. Going to the pub? Estimate how many rounds you'll buy and how much they'll cost and yes, take that with you. When it's gone, you go home.

105. Manage your credit

Credit limits are not virtual income — they simply reflect our capacity for debt. It's well worth exploring how well you use credit. We'll also look at the value of credit as a means of smoothing over short-term cashflow issues.

George Orwell's book '1984' introduced us to the concept of doublespeak, i.e. language that is deliberately constructed to disguise or distort its actual meaning. When it comes to the language deployed by credit card companies and banks to 'help' us manage our personal finances, we hit the gold standard of weasel words.

So here's the reality behind some financial doublespeak. *Credit is simply another word for debt.*

As linguistic sleights of hand go, it's pretty good. After all, think of the connotations that the word 'credit' has: phrases like 'to their credit' or 'creditworthy' or a 'creditable performance' makes the word seem like a desirable thing to have. But substitute our likeable chum 'credit' with its ugly alter ego 'debt' and it's a whole new ball-game. Imagine getting a letter from a credit card company saying 'Good news! We've decided to increase your debt limit.' Or

Here's an idea for you...

There are some nifty offers out there encouraging you to transfer outstanding balances from one credit card to another. Often, these offers come with low or no interest charged for maybe six or nine months or – if you're in luck – until the transferred amount has been repaid. Be careful not to spend on these cards. If you make any purchases, the credit card company will almost certainly clear the cheapest debt first, leaving you to accumulate interest at the higher rate on any subsequent purchases.

picture a shop that offers 'interest-free debt for six months'. Doesn't seem quite so tasty does it?

When a credit card company increases your credit limit, what it's really saying is that you are considered to be a reliable payer of the extortionate rates of interest they charge.

So just reflect for a moment on how you tend to use your credit, sorry debt card. Unless you are some kind of credit card paragon who uses it purely as a convenient alternative to carrying around a wad of cash drawn from the plentiful reserves residing in your current account, the chances are you're using it when you can't afford to buy something outright, and so you buy the item on credit.

A question: when you don't have the money in your current account this month to pay for the item in question, does it occur to you to consider whether you're any more likely to have the money next month to pay off this new debt? If you have a bonus coming through next month, then fine – a month or two's interest may be a small price to pay for the benefits of having something now rather than later. But the chances are that you are going to be equally strapped for cash next month, in which case you're in danger of heading inexorably into a world where it will take you an age to clear the core debt. And even that assumes that you're not continuing to purchase new stuff from time to time.

Don't get me wrong. I'm not saying that credit cards are the devil's spawn (although if you're using them to spend money you don't have on things you don't really need, there's something unholy going on), but they can tempt us into spending habits that are beyond our real means.

Defining idea...

'Money is just the poor man's credit card.'
MARSHALL MCLUHAN, *Canadian writer and theoretician*

However, it doesn't have to be like this. It's possible to use credit cards so that they work to our advantage and not the other way around. Here are some tips for making best use of them:

- If you can pay outright without using a card, do so.

- Always try to pay off 10 per cent of your balance every month on your credit cards – if you only pay the minimum it will cost you loads and take an age to clear.

- Do not, whatever you do, build up the amount you owe on store cards. With one or two exceptions, their annual interest rates are extremely high.

Defining idea...

'A check or credit card, a Gucci bag strap, anything of value will do. Give as you live.'
JESSE JACKSON, *preacher and politician*

- Used intelligently, credit cards can be useful sources of free credit. Used rashly, they can bring about an imperceptible slide into long-term debt.

106. Be realistic about debt

I suspect we've all been there. Don't despair. Here are some positive techniques for getting out of debt.

I always smile when I think of that interview on an episode of the Alan Partridge show in which Steve Coogan's comic creation turns to the father of a unendearing child genius and asks: 'Do you ever sit alone at night by the fire with your head in your hands and think, God have mercy on my soul, I have spawned a monster?'

Although 'spawning a monster' may be putting it a bit too strongly, it would be nice to think that the banks, building societies and credit card providers who have fuelled the current spending binge are suffering at least one or two pangs of guilt.

Many of us have been making the most of historically low interest rates to borrow money and to rack up debt on our credit cards. Our level of collective debt is unprecedented. It's reckoned that around an average 12 per cent of our income is eaten up by servicing debts.

And that figure is based on current interest rate levels. How would we cope if our bills suddenly went up by 20 per cent? It only takes interest rates to rise a few percentage points and it could happen.

Part of the trouble is that the older of us have forgotten the years of double-digit rates, and the younger of us have no real experience of the cost of borrowing rearing up. OK, we can bang on about how the credit card providers should be more responsible about unsecured lending. We can criticise them for setting low minimum repayments which can tempt customers to repay little more than the interest on the amount owed and so never pay off the debt. Ultimately, though, we are the ones who have to dig our way out of the debt hole. Waiting for a lottery win, or for a bequest from a distant relative, is no strategy.

Here's an idea for you...

This is strong medicine but if you're not convinced that you have a problem, try producing a consolidated debt statement. Every three months, compile details of all the money you owe anybody, including credit card debt, the outstanding balance on any loans you have, overdrafts, even the tenner you owe your best mate. This will give you an all too clear picture of the state of your finances.

Techniques for getting out of debt

- Stop the rot. If you have multiple credit cards, identify which one has the most draconian interest rate and shred it. Don't tuck it in a drawer and rely on your willpower not to use it. History suggests this is not a great tactic. If you can, consider transferring the debt on this card to the one carrying least interest.

- Talk to your creditors. Let them know you're having problems. Depending on the extent of your debt, you may want to agree a strategy for clearing the debt. Work out how much you can realistically afford to pay. Focus on the most important monthly payments – mortgage/rent, council tax, gas, electricity, etc.

- Don't panic but don't ignore the problem. You may have seen nature

Defining idea…

'Anyone who lives within their
means suffers from a lack of
imagination.'
OSCAR WILDE

programmes where creatures stay very, very still in order to evade predators. Your debt won't go away; in fact, ignoring it guarantees that it will get worse as the interest builds up and your creditors start to hound you. Don't ignore court papers.

- Don't pay for advice. There are plenty of sources of free help and counselling. Talk to your bank, ask your employer for advice, try the Citizens' Advice Bureau.

Getting into severe debt is horrible – I know, I've been there (it happens when you write for a living!). The crucial first step back to solvency is to face up to the fact that you're in debt and to recognise that you need to adopt a conscious strategy to get out of it.

Defining idea…

'I can get no remedy against this
consumption of the purse:
borrowing only lingers and lingers it
out, but the disease is incurable.'
WILLIAM SHAKESPEARE

107. How to deal with severe debt

Hopefully, you'll never get so seriously into debt that you are dealing with credit management agencies. In case you ever do, though, you need to know how to manage the situation.

Most of us have been strapped for cash from time to time. Generally we are able to dig ourselves out of trouble with a bit of financial belt-tightening or some creative use of credit cards. It's not always that easy.

Remember the character played by Kevin Costner in the movie *Field of Dreams* who felt impelled to build a baseball stadium in the middle of nowhere on the basis of advice from a mystical friend that 'If you build it, they will come'? There's a variation on this that applies to many people who get deep into debt and are unable to extricate themselves: if you owe it, they will come. The 'they' in question are either the people who are owed money or their appointed debt collectors.

Know what you're signing up to
If you should fall into serious debt, here are a few tips on how to handle the situation:

Here's an idea for you...

The days when lenders would send the boys around armed with baseball bats are largely the stuff of fiction and these days are confined to the extreme fringes of society. But watch out for the dodgy practices given above. They still happen from time to time.

- Don't panic or ignore the problem: unopened bills won't go away.

- Decide which debts take priority – like mortgage or rent – and which cost you the most through penalties or higher interest rates.

- Only agree to pay off debts at a rate you can keep up. Don't offer more than you can afford.

- Contact those who you owe money to as soon as possible to let them know you're having problems.

- Remember that's it's better to make a small payment than send nothing at all.

- Keep copies of all correspondence. You will need them if you want to seek help and advice from a third party.

- Seek advice if organisations won't accept your repayment offers.

Lenders have responsibilities too

Lenders and debt management companies have to behave properly. Examples of their (illegal) deficiencies include:

- Failing to investigate or provide proper details/records when a debt is queried or disputed.

- Failing to deal with appointed third parties such as Citizens' Advice Bureaux or independent advice centres.

- Pursuing third parties for payment when they are not liable.

Defining idea...

'It is very iniquitous to make me pay my debts. You have no idea of the pain it gives one.'
LORD BYRON

- Falsely implying or claiming authority – such as claiming to be working on court authority.

- Contacting debtors at unreasonable times and/or intervals.

- Claiming a right of entry when no court order has been obtained.

- Misleading debtors by the use of official-looking documents such as letters made to resemble court claims.

Lenders aren't allowed to ignore the dodgy practices of debt collectors acting on their behalf. If they do, their fitness to hold a credit licence can be called into question. Generally though, according to the Office of Fair Trading (OFT), complaints about debt management companies have dropped substantially in recent years.

So if you do get into debt, at least you shouldn't be unreasonably treated by the people you owe money to. Which leaves you free to concentrate on the task in hand, namely rebuilding your financial reputation.

108. Jump start your salary

Do you deserve a higher salary? Well of course you do. Let's look at tactics and techniques for making a persuasive case to your boss.

The prerequisites for getting your salary increased are that (a) you are reasonably competent, and (b) you're well regarded by your employers. If these basic elements aren't in place right now, then work through this book starting at chapter 1.

But taking these as read, here are some tips for negotiating your way to an optimal package. The first decision you'll have to make is, in the words of Joe Strummer, 'Should I stay or should I go?'

If you decide you want to stay where you are – for the time being at least – then you'll need to start gathering evidence that shows why you already deserve an increase. Perhaps you can make the case that some colleagues are getting more pay for doing the same work, or that others are getting more pay even though you do more work.

Before you fix a time to talk with you boss, make sure you know what you want out of your negotiation. This means having three figures in mind: your ideal salary (i.e. the most you dare ask for without alienating your boss), your bottom line (i.e. the lowest figure you'd settle for) and your realistic goal (i.e. the figure that you think you have a good chance of getting).

Armed with this information, prepare your case and book a meeting with your boss. Make sure you time the meeting to your best advantage. If you've only been with the company a few months, or if you've just made the mother of all cock-ups, hold off for the time being.

More precisely, go for a time of day which gives you a fighting chance of finding your boss receptive and in good humour.

> **Here's an idea for you...**
>
> Be prepared to be flexible. If your boss accepts the validity of your case but pleads emptiness of the department piggybank, come back with something like 'I can see the problem so let's see what else we can do. Maybe I could have an extra week's holiday and a company car as an alternative.' Bear in mind that your salary is only one part of the total compensation package.

When you go to the meeting, have all the facts and figures at your fingertips. Take along relevant reports, sales figures, performance stats and any other documents that support your case. It might even be worth putting together a supporting document to leave with your boss.

If there's nothing doing, don't despair. Career-wise, it might be an excellent time to position yourself for recognition when the money does become available again. You can ask for added responsibilities or a new job title. You're taking a risk, of course, that you might be working harder in the short term for the same pay, but you've bolstered your bargaining position down the line. If nothing comes through eventually, then, to be honest, I'd be looking for a new place to work.

Apropos of which, here are a few negotiating tip and wrinkles to deploy when you've been offered a position with a new company.

Defining idea...

'For they can conquer who believe they can.'
JOHN DRYDEN

- Always aim to negotiate with the decision-maker rather than through intermediaries.

- It's always preferable to negotiate on the basis of having received a written offer. Not only will this help to prevent misunderstandings, but it also helps to depersonalise the situation if you are negotiating over a piece of paper. Remember that you are often dealing with somebody who could soon be your new boss. It pays not to antagonise them.

- Keep the tone of the negotiation positive by reaffirming your real interest in joining the company, by emphasising how pleased you were to receive the offer, and by looking forward to working with the new company – it's just a matter of clearing up a few contractual points to everybody's satisfaction.

- Try to give the company a few options to respond to rather than box yourself into a corner.

- Don't let the process drag on. Negotiate crisply and settle quickly.

By the way, if you decide to reject the job offer, keep it courteous and professional. Remember that the people you are dealing with are probably good networkers also. The last thing you want is to be bad-mouthed within your industry for buggering people about. For that reason, drop the company a line saying that you were pleased to have been offered the job, but that you regret that you can't accept the offer. Give your reasons why, thank them for taking the time to meet with you and wish them well with filling the post.

109. First save, then spend

If you find it difficult or impossible to save money, here's an approach that will enable you to divert some of your monthly discretionary spend into a savings account.

Let's be clear – building up your savings is a very good thing to do and an excellent habit to get into. Not least of all because we all find our wallets or purses ambushed at short notice by sizeable bills coming out of left field at us. You know the sort of thing: the central heating breaks down this evening, the roof springs a leak or the car starts making a noise like a Tuvan throat singer.

As well as warding off emergencies, savings can enable us to plan for the future. It might be something coming up relatively soon – your next holiday, upgrading the computer or replacing the car (that Tuvan throat singer thing is not good news, believe me). Or there may be a more distant blot on your financial landscape – children going to university perhaps.

When these things happen, you have three basic options: (a) draw on your savings; (b) go into debt; (c) write a snappy begging letter. If option (a) isn't available because you have little or no savings, you're left with unpleasant option (b) or unlikely option (c).

Here's an idea for you...

Set up a standing order from your current to your savings account, and make sure it goes out early in the month. (Wait until the end and you may well find that you've no money left.) Make it a reasonable amount but critically one that you can afford. To help avoid any temptation to dip into your savings, set up the savings account so that the money you've saved isn't too readily accessible. Use the building society across town rather than the one around the corner, and consider going for an account where you have to give notice before you can make a withdrawal.

You might be thinking at this point: OK, obviously having savings is a 'good thing' but what if there isn't anything left over at the end of the month to put into a savings account.

Don't get suckered into a 'not today, maybe tomorrow' attitude to saving. This may be an accurate description of your current situation but what I'd suggest is you could be experiencing a monetary version of Parkinson's Law (you know the one – it states that work expands to fill the time available for its completion). Most of us spend what we earn; if our pay goes up, we upgrade our lifestyle and we're soon spending what we earn again.

Against this backdrop, you can see the flaw in looking to save whatever is left over in your account at the end of each month. Chances are the sum involved will always be a big fat zero (and that's in a good month).

So spending and then saving what's left over will get you next to nowhere. Here's an alternative: try saving and then spending. In other words, set aside a certain amount each month as savings, and then make the remainder your budget for the month.

It's Parkinson's Law in reverse: reduce the amount of money you have available to spend each month and then adjust your lifestyle accordingly.

Is this possible? Well yes, when you consider that, on average, around 20 per cent of household expenditure goes on leisure. Think of the thousands a year that we can fritter away on lattes, newspapers and magazines, pricey sandwiches, DVDs, chocolate and so on.

Defining idea...

'Accumulating three months' income won't happen overnight. For most people who embark on a serious saving programme, it will take four to five years to reach this target.'
Alvin Hall, psychologist and presenter of the TV programme *Your Money or Your Life*

If you don't have a savings mentality, try setting yourself a goal. It might be to have three to six months' salary set aside for emergencies, or maybe to get hold of a plasma monitor in the next twelve months. Whatever you plump for, having a goal gives a bit of meaning and purpose to the idea of saving. It comes in handy when you next walk past Starbucks to remind yourself that passing up a take-out coffee is not just wilful self-denial, it's helping to bring that 42-inch screen just a bit closer.

Defining idea...

'Money is human happiness in the abstract.'
ARTHUR SCHOPENHAUER, *pessimist and philosopher*

110. Stick to your budget

Spend less than you earn. Easy to say, but harder to achieve when we're trying to keeping up with the high-livin' debt-ridden Joneses. It's time to focus on the challenge of coming up with and living within a budget.

'Annual income twenty pounds, annual expenditure nineteen nineteen six, result happiness. Annual income twenty pounds, annual expenditure twenty pounds ought and six, result misery'.

When Charles Dickens wrote *David Copperfield* back in the mid-19th century, few people would have disagreed with Mr Micawber's model of economic prudence. At the heart of it, of course, is the idea that we should strive to live within our means.

That is precisely what a budget is designed to help us achieve. If you looked the word up in a dictionary, you would find definitions along the following lines:

- An estimate of income and a plan for expenditure
- Total amount of money allocated for a specific purpose during a specified period
- A restriction on expenditure

So a budget is a financial planning tool, underpinned by the notion that there is likely to be some form of restriction on our capacity to spend. If we possessed limitless wealth, we wouldn't need to restrict our spending.

Unfortunately, these days, many of us suffer from a credit card mentality that seems to have banished the idea of living within our means to the realms of Dickensian quaintness. It's as though perched on our shoulder is a monstrous parrot of overspending that squawks in our ear: 'Debt's the way to do it.'

Here's an idea for you...

You really are storing up problems if you consistently overspend, even if it's only by a small amount. To give an example: your disposable income is £180 a week, but you're spending £200. On that basis, your debt is growing by £1,040 a year – and that's before adding in the interest, probably in the region of 15 per cent a year. It doesn't matter how high your income is if you consistently spend more than you earn.

Our capacity to use credit cards to gloss over shortfalls in the cash we have to hand has really undermined the concept of budgeting. In the pre-credit card days, if we had £100 to see us through the week, we would have had to adjust our spending accordingly.

If we really want to put together a budget that's going to work, then we need to take a clear-eyed view of our credit card usage. When we pay for something with a card, it's just a different way of spending our money. So if we have a budget of £100, and spend £90 in cash but have also put £20 on our credit card, we have gone over budget.

Defining idea…

'You aren't wealthy until you have something money can't buy.'
GARTH BROOKS, *Country singer*

The key here is to be realistic. You're unlikely to stick to a budget which allows you to drink one bottle of lager a month if your social life involves you being out three or four nights a week. Equally, your budget may fall apart if you drink seven or eight bottles every time you go out. You need to balance self-discipline with realism.

Coming up with your income details ought to be relatively straightforward. A quick compare and contrast between what you have coming in and what you have going out will highlight where you may have budgetary hotspots, i.e. points in the year when the numbers look a bit grim. The challenge now is to develop a plan for preventing those hotspots getting the better of you, maybe by adjusting down your spending plans, or perhaps by selling off your old stamp collection. The key here is that you have some time to sort out a sensible solution.

Defining idea…

'With money in your pocket, you are wise and you are handsome and you sing well too.'
YIDDISH PROVERB

111. Show me the money

How can you find out if you're underpaid or overpaid? And what can you do about it?

When you buy something for quite a bit less than you expected, you've got a bargain. When your employers pay you less than your market worth, they've got a bargain and the chances are you're being ripped off.

There's a great Tom Cruise film (and it's not often you can say that) called *Jerry Maguire* in which Cruise plays the eponymous sports agent whose job is to negotiate salaries and contracts on behalf of his clients (actually, client in this case – you'll have to watch the movie). One strand of the story follows an American footballer client of Maguire's who is very keen to realise his market worth and who is forever telling Cruise's character to 'Show me the money!'

So here's a question: are your employers showing you enough money?

If you've only just joined a new company, then the chances are you've had an opportunity to negotiate with them and you've ended up getting the going market rate. If you've been with the company for donkey's years, then your salary should at least have risen to the company's maximum pay for your grade. That might not be your market rate – for example if you work in a lower-paying sector – but it probably won't be too bad a deal.

Here's an idea for you...

If you follow any of the options set out above, just make sure you're comparing like with like. The salary packages that companies offer these days are sophisticated affairs. A particularly good pension scheme, perhaps coupled with other benefits and perks, might mean that the company offering the lower salary could be offering the better package. Try compiling a table of all the elements you'd like to see in your salary package – salary, share options, pension arrangements, car or car allowance, loans, special equipment like computers, etc. – and then use that as a basis for comparison.

You may be at risk if you've been with a company for a reasonable but not a very long time. Have you been in your current job for 3–10 years? If so, you may find that you're being paid less than your more experienced work colleagues (not unreasonably perhaps). However, you may also find that recent starters are either being paid more than you or are at least snapping at your heels salary-wise.

Most employers have to pay at or close to the market rate to buy in new people. Rather fewer employers pay at or close to the prevailing market rate to retain good people. Once you're in the company pay system, your pay increases tend to be linked to the level of inflation and across-the-board company-wide pay deals. Not all company pay systems are fluid and flexible enough to recognise what is going on in your specific job sector.

If you are not convinced that you are being paid the rate for the job, it's worth researching your market value before your next salary review so that you can make the case for what you believe you deserve.

> Defining idea...
>
> 'We all strive to earn our self-concept level of income. If you believe you are a £20,000 per annum person, then you will always earn close to £20,000. People who earn a lot of money are not necessarily more clever or more highly qualified than people who earn very little money. People who earn a lot of money…have a higher self-concept level of income.'
> RICHARD DOBBINS and BARRIE O. PETTMAN, *What Self-made Millionaires Really Think, Know and Do!*

112. Conduct an annual stocktake of your finances

So, all things considered, how well off are you right now? Do your assets outstrip your liabilities, or are you in debt overall?

Here are 20 questions that are designed to give you a pretty good handle on the general state of your 'finances':

- What's the state of your mortgage? Are you paying a competitive interest rate? If you have an endowment mortgage, review the latest information and make an informed guess as to whether this will pay off your mortgage when the time comes.

- If you are in debt, how much of it can you clear over the next 12 months?

- Do you have your credit cards under control?

- Can you reduce your outgoings?

- How's your pension looking? Should you be investing more?

- Does your investment portfolio need rebalancing? Is it appropriate to adjust the level of risk you're exposed to?

- What are your spending priorities for the coming year?

- Do any of your major possessions need upgrading or replacing? How do you aim to pay for this?

- Have you scored any financial own-goals over the past year that you can avoid in future? For example, have you incurred any late payment charges on a credit card?

- Have you made a will? Does it need updating to reflect changes in your life circumstances?

- Have there been any changes in your life over the past 12 months and are there any coming up? What's the impact on your finances?

- Are you on top of your tax commitments?

- Have you claimed all the allowances – tax, state, etc. – that you're entitled to?

- Do you need to talk to your accountant or financial adviser?

Here's an idea for you...

An important measure of your financial health is your net worth. Your net worth is the difference between your total assets and total liabilities.

You'll probably have three types of assets:
- Liquid assets. Assets that can be turned into cash more or less immediately such as current accounts.
- Personal assets. The current estimated market value of your possessions.
- Investment assets. Stocks and bonds, pension plans and investments.

And you'll (sadly) have two types of liabilities:
- Current liabilities. Credit card debt, and other short-term loans.
- Long-term liabilities. Your mortgage, and other long-term loans.

To determine your net worth, deduct your liabilities from your assets.

Defining idea...

'Never ask of money spent
Where the spender thinks it went.
Nobody was ever meant
To remember or invent
What he did with every cent.'
ROBERT FROST, *The Hardship of Accounting*

● When you review your income stream(s), do you feel you are being fairly rewarded?

● Are there other sources of income you might tap into?

● Do you have any longer-term savings challenges? Are you doing enough to meet them?

● What were your financial objectives this time last year? To what extent have they been met?

● What's your biggest financial fear for the next year? Is there anything you might usefully do to counter that fear?

● Can you take any pre-emptive action? For example, if you reckon that interest rates could go up later in the year, or if there's a risk that your income might suffer for whatever reason, trimming your outgoings now means that you might get away with a less draconian response down the line.

There may well be other questions that you could usefully ask. At the heart of this process is the need to come up with an action plan. Don't be like the lemming who says 'yep, still marching to the edge of that cliff' and does nothing about it. Be like the lemming who dons a parachute and a life-jacket.

113. Get thrifty

Our parents probably had the thrift habit. We can have it if we want it. Here's how.

The concept of thrift seems positively out of place in today's credit culture, a culture that exalts taking the waiting out of wanting. Nonetheless, trendy or not, thrift represents a state of mind that can save us money, and so it's an outlook that is worth cultivating. Here are some examples of thrifty thinking that will save you money relatively painlessly:

- Cook your own meals.

- Take a list when you go shopping and stick to it. Avoid impulse trolley moments. It helps not to shop when you're hungry because there's a real danger that you end up buying more than you need.

- Find cheaper cafés and restaurants.

- Buy your own drinks in the pub or club, but tell people beforehand that you are on an economy drive.

- Switch to own-label purchases in the supermarkets.

- Make your own sandwiches for lunch – saves around two-thirds of the cost.

- Find cheaper hobbies: go running, visit museums, go for walks, join a reading club.

Here's an idea for you...

Looking to pay off the mortgage early is a good aspiration but not if you end up struggling to make ends meet. There's no sense saving interest on your mortgage – one of the cheapest ways of borrowing money – only to end up paying higher rates of interest on overdrafts and credit cards that you don't have the financial resources to clear. You can always start overpaying on your mortgage once you have your finances under control. Alternatively, you could direct the overpayment amount into a savings account. This'll give you a reserve fund that you could use if needed.

- Find cheaper times to go places – cinemas, theatres, happy hours…

- Start buying clothes at charity shops.

- Grow your own vegetables.

- Use a bike or walk.

- Pay bills by direct debit: avoid late charges.

- Save money-off coupons and use loyalty cards.

- Shop around: often the best prices are to be had online.

- Switch any spare cash from your current account to a savings account. Making the money less visible and less accessible will help to curb your spending habits.

- Shred a credit card or two.

- Spend less time with big-spending chums.

- Share car journeys and taxis.

- Join the library.

- Cut back the amount spent on Christmas and birthday presents. Tell friends and family you have less to spend – you may even find a general sense of relief.

- Find the cheapest sources for books, CDs and DVDs – enjoy them and then sell them on.

Defining idea...

'Whatever thrift is, it is not avarice. Avarice is not generous; and, after all, it is the thrifty people who are generous.'
LORD ROSEBERY, *politician*

- Have a sartorial moratorium: i.e. stop buying clothes for a time. Remember that we probably only wear 20 per cent of our wardrobe regularly – the other 80 per cent is just festering.

- Review everything you spend: cable TV rental, mobile phone monthly rental, subscriptions to magazines, lattes, chocolate, etc.

- Have a serious look at your budget: be absolutely clear where your money goes every month.

Now come up with at least another dozen ideas of your own.

The key to thrifty living is to see the thrift experience as a challenge and something you can learn from. Remember that you are not making sacrifices, you are spurning fripperies and concentrating on the more important things in life.

Above all, try to keep positive. If you feel your existence is miserable and deprived, you are far more likely to yield to the occasional spending binge. Try promising yourself a small reward when you achieve a significant financial target.

114. The pros and cons of consolidation loans

Consolidating all your debts into one loan can either be an act of fiscal brilliance on your part or a financial disaster.

Here are some pieces of universal wisdom: never bother to go to see a movie that stars Vin Diesel; unless you actually are one of the stars of 'The Matrix', don't wear a long black leather coat and dark sunglasses because it will just look silly; never admit to owning a ferret or a Steps CD.

The world becomes a less certain place when it comes to deciding whether it can make sense for you to take out a consolidation loan.

Debt consolidation occurs when you take out a loan or other credit agreement in order to pay off two or more existing debts. You might do this via…

● An unsecured loan

● An advance from an existing mortgage provider secured against property but leaving the original mortgage intact

● A second charge mortgage (a loan secured on property, from a lender other than the existing mortgage provider, that leaves the first charge mortgage in place)

- A remortgage

- The transfer of balances to a credit card (including the use of credit card cheques to pay off non-credit card debts)

When the UK's Office of Fair Trading (OFT) investigated the debt consolidation market, it found that most of us do not shop around, even though this could save us money. Two-thirds of borrowers who consolidated debts obtained information from only one provider. The OFT also found that many borrowers, particularly those in financial distress, are unaware of other alternatives, such as negotiating with creditors themselves or getting help from free debt counselling services.

The OFT's final finding was that borrowers generally don't pay enough attention to the length of the term of the loan and the total cost of repayments.

So would debt consolidation be a good choice for you? It depends. If you're the sort of person who takes a perverse pride in telling your mates that you've maxed out your credit card (i.e. it's a boast not an admission of financial incompetence), then there's a real danger that

---

Here's an idea for you...

If you're interested in pursuing the idea of debt consolidation a bit further, you should take steps to find out:

- What debt consolidation is and what the alternatives are
- What the interest rate and APR is and whether it's variable
- What the overall cost of the loan is
- What the monthly repayments are and what you can afford
- Whether there are additional features which will change the rate at which the capital sum is paid back
- What will happen if you miss a payment
- What happens if you want to repay or refinance early
- If the loan is secured on your home, what are the consequences of not keeping up with payments and what happens if you want to move at some point

373

Defining idea...

'The interest isn't the most significant problem with consolidating your debts into a single loan. The biggest danger comes from the sense of relief that you feel when your monthly payment decreases. All too often this leads to further spending (which I call "relief retail therapy") and a spiral in an even worse debt problem.'

ALVIN HALL, *Your Money or Your Life*

you'll find yourself paying off the consolidation loan and still continuing to max out your cards. This of course puts you in double the trouble.

On the other hand, a consolidation loan will save you money (not to mention all the administrative hassle of paying off a number of monthly credit card statements) if you're extremely self-disciplined and if you are prepared to steer clear of shopping outlets – real world and online.

115. Staying on top of your finances

The biggest enemy of financial well-being is inertia.

In early 2004, it was announced that David Beckham, the England and Real Madrid footballer, had chosen the Queen's stockbroker to look after his fortune and that of his wife Victoria, the former Spice Girl. Beckham, the world's best-paid footballer, signed a deal for Cazenove to manage around £40m of the couple's wealth.

We don't need to have Beckham's level of wealth to recognise the principle that our finances don't manage themselves. They need to be monitored and reviewed on a regular basis.

Trouble is, all too often, our idea of a financial review is to check whether we have enough cash on us to fund this evening's drinking and maybe a taxi home. In other words, we fall into the trap of concentrating on the here and now at the expense of planning for the future. On the bright side, the fact that you're reading this book suggests that you'd prefer your financial future to unfold with intent rather than by accident.

So this final idea is about taking active charge so that you can manage your finances and they don't manage you. You might take advice from others but

Here's an idea for you...

We can probably all improve our ability to review, monitor and act if we choose to do so. An obvious next step would be to continue building our financial literacy. Generally speaking, we pay very little heed to managing our money unless circumstances force us to. There are plenty of things we can do to rectify this. Try browsing the financial sections of the weekend papers, attending a money management course, or taking up opportunities for annual reviews of your mortgage and bank accounts. It can also be helpful to build the financial literacy of those around us – why not pass this book onto somebody you think might benefit from reading it. Better still, get them to buy their own copy (I've got my royalties to think of, after all!).

ultimately it is your job to make sure you make it financially and no one else's.

At the heart of this book are three fundamental activities that anybody wishing to optimise their finances needs to undertake on a regular basis: namely to review, to monitor, and – critically – to act.

Here's an incomplete list of some of the things you might care to consider under these categories:

Review

● Undertake a root and branch review of your financial position at least once a year.

● Start to think five, ten and fifteen years – maybe even longer – into the future. What are your financial goals? How are you going to make them happen?

Monitor

● Know where your money goes every month.

● Check the accuracy of your bank statements and tax notices – everybody makes mistakes.

Act

● Avoid the loyalty trap. If your research shows that you're not getting the best deal from your bank, credit card company, life insurer, be prepared to move elsewhere. Remember that in the UK alone, you can choose between around 8,000 mortgages, 1,300 or so credit cards, and over 1,000 savings accounts.

> *Defining idea...*
>
> 'Most people say they're too busy…but we all have at least 15 minutes a days. If you use that time well, 15 minutes can matter.'
> DANNY SEO, *Heaven on Earth: 15-minute Miracles to Change the World*

● Try and save something every month – set up a standing order and then try to forget about it. Aim to have 9–12 months of your expenditure tucked away to protect you against unplanned events – surprise babies, job loss.

● Remember the 28-day list – don't spend without thinking.

● If you can pay outright for something, do so. Don't be tempted into a credit arrangement unless it is cheaper. Remember that putting something on your credit card, particularly if it is a store card, is one of the most expensive forms of borrowing around.

● Always try to pay off 10 per cent of your balance every month on your credit cards. If you only pay the minimum it will cost you a small fortune and take ages to clear.

The real point about taking control is that it involves a mixture of reflection and action. You need both – reflection without action is sterile, action without reflection lacks direction and mindfulness. To tweak a cliché: today is the first day of the rest of your financial life. So what are you going to do about it?

116. Love your money

And it will love you right back. When that happens life gets a lot less stressful.

Quickly, without thinking too much about it, write down three phrases that come into your head when you think about your finances.

(Hint: unless your three words are 'abundant, balanced, life-enhancing', then you need this idea.)

This idea is about respect. If you're disrespectful of your money, I'm prepared to bet that money is a stressor in your life. If you don't take care of your money, the chances are that, just like a neglected teenager, it's never going to amount to much. Worse, the relationship will probably deteriorate further. One day your money is going to do the equivalent of coming home pregnant with a crack cocaine habit.

Here's a quick test
Get out your wallet or purse. Check out how it looks. Is it neat with bills folded, receipts tucked away. Or is everything stuffed in higgledy-piggledy?

Here's a quicker one
How much money have you got in your wallet right now? If you're out by more than the price of a coffee, you need this idea badly. Your money is your friend.

You should love it like a member of the family. You wouldn't go to the shops and forget to bring home one of the kids. Well, why the hell would you misplace your money?

Here's an idea for you...

Go treasure hunting. Look for money down the side of sofas, in pockets, in foreign currency. How much money have you got stuffed in books. Or unrealised in gift tokens. How much of your money are you ignoring?

Look for your latte factor

Make a list of everything you spend in a day. Keep a notebook with you and write down how often you take money out of the 'hole in the wall' and what you spend it on. Every cheque you write. Every card you swipe. Every time you spend a penny. Literally. Keep it up for a week, preferably for a month. Now multiply (by 52 or 12). That's what it costs to run your life. Go through and highlight the big essentials – the mortgage, the essential bills. Now get out a calculator and work out what you spend on lunches, clothes, magazines, newspapers.

You're looking for what has been called 'the latte factor', those items that are completely expendable and add very little to your life but cost a fortune. It will frighten the bejasus out of you. My latte factor was £472. I needed that money a whole lot more than Starbucks. You also realise how much it costs to run your life. The very first day I practised this exercise I spent £197.45. All I came home with was a pound of cherries. The rest was debt I couldn't remember accruing. Shocking.

We're not going to talk about debt here but if you've got personal debt, do this for a month and you are going to work out exactly why.

Defining idea…

'The safest way to double your
money is to fold it over and put it in
your pocket.'
KIN HUBBARD, *American humorist*

Writing down what you spend is a fantastically useful exercise whether you're overspending or not. It sure as hell won't destress you in the short term but it will in the long term. It allows you to see almost instantly who or what you're spending your money on and then decide if you're happy with that. It allows you to take control, and every way you can find to foster the illusion of control is helpful if you want to be less stressed. Spiritual teachers tell us that money is neither bad nor good, it's simply a way we register our presence on the world. If you fritter away money as a distraction, you'll never focus long enough to work out what's really important to you. If you spend what you don't have, your spirit as well as your bank balance is going to be overstretched. Your bank balance isn't important. Your spirit is. Respect it, protect it – and you're going to make someone very happy and that someone isn't your bank manager.

6

Feeling better, faster

The ultimate career coach

382

You are doing all you can to sort out your finances and career, but you need a fast fix now. Trust us. Even if life is leaving you overwhelmed, there are ways of stopping the madness fast.

Are you living on adrenaline?

It starts normal and then goes completely nuts. Before we know it, we are living at such a pace that it's not blood in our veins but adrenaline. And the scary thing is we barely notice how we got there. Here's a reality check.

1. While you were eating breakfast this morning you were:
- ☐ a. Sitting at the table listening to the radio.
- ☐ b. Running around drying your hair and finding your phone.
- ☐ c. Breakfast is for wimps.

2. When you are deciding where to eat lunch you choose:
- ☐ a. The nicest place you can afford.
- ☐ b. The nearest place to your desk, indeed most often, your desk.
- ☐ c. Lunch is for wimps.

3. What were you doing this time last week?
- ☐ a. Give me a second, I can tell you.
- ☐ b. It's a bit of a blur.
- ☐ c. Why would I waste my time even thinking about it?

4. When you're forced to wait in a traffic jam or a queue in the bank, you:
- ☐ a. Daydream happily.
- ☐ b. Get fidgety.
- ☐ c. Start hyperventilating.

5. When you're watching a film on DVD, you're feeling:

☐ a. Absorbed in the drama, you use it to relax.

☐ b. Guilty, you should be doing something more productive.

☐ c. Irritated and restless. Why is it so slow? Couldn't the director pick up the pace?

6. Do you find yourself finishing people's sentences?

☐ a. Never – awfully rude.

☐ b. Yes, when they are people you know well.

☐ c. All the time. You've worked out what they're trying to say before they have.

If you answered mostly (a)s, you're safe from the dangers of overdrive.
But if you are still feeling that you aren't reaching a work–life balance, the ideas in part seven will help you out.

If you score mostly (b)s, watch out for stress levels rising. You are finding it harder to switch off. **Turn to idea 118.**

If you score a mixture of (b)s and (c)s adrenaline is the fuel that's running your life. **Turn to idea 129 before it's too late**

If you scored mostly (c)s. The only thing you need to do fast is slow down. **Turn to idea 121** and then read **idea 132.**

117. How to get rich on a not so rich salary

True wealth, both in terms of personal and financial wealth, comes from valuing who you are rather than how much you have deposited in the bank. All the money in the world won't buy you happiness.

Do you remember all those lottery winners who won millions and then lost it all? All the money in the world didn't make them rich. What if you could work out what you were worth that wasn't based on your financial net worth but was based on your Life net worth?

I first came across this exercise years ago in a book called *Money Magic,* written by Deborah L. Price. At the time I was in quite a lot of debt and wasn't making as much money as I would have liked to. I devoured the whole book in two days. As with everything, I skipped some exercises but others moved me to the page. The Life Bank exercise made sense. This is how it works. If it worked for me and for many of my clients, I am sure it will work for you. In your notebook answer the following questions:

How old are you?
How many life hours have you spent? That's your age (I'm 46) times 365 (days in the year) times 24 (hours in the day). For example, I have spent 402,960 life

hours. It certainly puts a different perspective on things when you look at your life in the context of the number of hours you've lived.

How have you spent your time?

Your answer to this question can include a list of all the things you've done in your lifetime that make you feel good about who you are and the things you have done that have been meaningful to you. This is not about the things you have. Next, make a list of all the things you would still like to do that would continue to give you great fulfilment and satisfaction.

> ### Here's an idea for you...
>
> Start a gratitude journal. Every day, write down three things that you appreciate and value from your day. Include the small incidents in your day, such as someone offering you a seat on a packed commuter train, or the bus driver who let you out on a very busy junction. Go from the least obvious to the more obvious. I promise you that as soon as you get started with writing your 'gratitudes', you won't want to stop.

Finally, how many days are you currently spending towards meeting these personal goals?

I found that it took me a few days to gather together all the things I wanted to include in my inventory. Once you feel you have a near enough complete list, spend several minutes really taking in what you've written. How do you feel about your list? How does it feel when you look at the number of hours of your life that you've already spent? Does it make you more discerning now about how you will spend your time and money in the future? Are you really getting to live the life you want or is the way you're spending your time actually robbing you of this?

This exercise stretches you to consider and appreciate your worth beyond the trappings of your financial identity. I have seen individuals on the brink of bankruptcy feel hope after completing this exercise and in many cases individuals have turned their lives around.

Defining idea...

There's a great difference between earning a great deal of money and being rich.
MARLENE DIETRICH, *actress*

Your goal is to coach yourself to value the time that's been spent and the time you have left to consciously decide how you will spend it.

Whatever you have gone through, you still have your whole life ahead of you. It's a joy when individuals in my coaching practice from all different income levels really get this. When they really get that what really matters is how they see themselves beyond what they earn. Hold on to the thought that your self-worth cannot be measured by your net worth. This recognition in and of itself often marks a huge turning point where money flows even more in their lives.

118. Find an hour a day to play

No, seriously, is that too much to ask?

Shut your eyes. Breathe deeply. Picture what you'd do today if you had a whole hour each day to yourself to spend doing exactly what you wanted.

'Yeah, right', I hear you say. Like there's any chance of that.

So here's a question worth asking

I think that the 'desirable' things we'd like to spend an hour doing fall into two categories:

- The stuff we yearn to do because it's relaxing and fun.
- The stuff that's usually prefixed with a sense of 'ought to' because we know the rewards are worth it

In the first category is lying in bed watching a movie, in the second going for a run or quality time with the kids. We need to find the time for both. But both categories tend to get shunted to the sidelines of our life because of general business.

Exercise especially is one of the things that goes by the wayside when life gets stressful. How many times have you said 'I'd love to go to the gym – but I don't have the time.' So here's the useful question to ask yourself: how will I feel in five years' time if I don't?

389

Here's an idea for you...

On the move and stressed? Running cold water over your wrists for a minute cools you down on a hot day and it works to bring down your stress levels, too.

More to the point – how will you look?

Nothing in your life will change unless you take action. If you don't take the time to exercise, if you consistently allow family and work demands to be more important than your continuing good health, then at best you'll be more vulnerable to illness; at worst you'll be fat (and still more vulnerable to illness).

This goes for 'life dreams' that fall into the first category, like writing a novel or learning Russian. These have been called 'depth activities' because they add meaning to our lives. If I had a fiver for every time someone said to me 'I'd love to write a book but I don't have the time', I wouldn't be writing this one. Wannabe authors miss the point that in just an hour a day, you can make a start. Here's the big question: how will you feel in five years' time if you haven't at least tried?

People who spend at least a bit of their time doing the stuff that they want to do tend to feel that they're in control, and that's majorly destressing.

First get the big picture...

Get out your diary and write down everything you're expected to make happen in the next month. This could take some time. Include everything from work projects, organising baby-sitters, buying birthday presents, decorating the bathroom, taxing the car, medical appointments.

OK, finished? Right, go through the list and mark the items that you can delegate to someone else. Be honest. What I said was the items you 'can' delegate, not the ones that no one else wants to do, or the ones that no one else will do as well as you. Don't worry. I'm not going to make you hand over all these tasks, just 10% of them.

Defining idea...

'Life is what happens when we're busy doing something else.'
JOHN LENNON

In a spirit of solidarity, I've done this too. And guess what? On a list of thirteen things only two of them have to be done by me. Actually, only one – writing this book. (I could ask someone else to do it but the publishers might notice; or maybe they wouldn't, which is an even scarier thought.) The other one is to take my youngest for an injection and I could even delegate this if I wanted. But I don't. By actively thinking about it and deciding that it's something I want to do I've turned it into a positive – a choice rather than a chore. Big difference.

Now you've offloaded 10% of your work for the next month, think about dumping 10% of what you have to do every day. Jot down your 'tasks' for tomorrow. Quickly, without thinking too much, run through them marking each entry.

A Must do
B Should do
C Could do

Now knock two of the Bs off the list and three of the Cs off and put down in their place an activity that you know would destress you or add depth to your life. Mark it with a whacking great 'A'. Soon, giddy with success, you'll be prioritising yourself all of the time. Well, at least for an hour a day. Life really is too short to wallow in the C-list – feeling busy but achieving nothing that matters.

391

119. Never procrastinate again

Procrastination is stress's best friend. It's not big, it's not clever but for most of us, it's a way of life.

But no longer. Here's how to get going when you have absolutely no motivation.

It was devised by life coach Mark Forster. An interesting man, he achieves more in a day than most of us do in a week. But he used to be disorganised and chaotic (he says!). None of the advice on procrastination ever worked for him (we all know that feeling), so he invented his own techniques. (You can read more in his brilliant book *Get Everything Done*.)

Mark calls this the rotation method. You need pen, paper and a watch but a kitchen timer with a bell works best.

1. First make a list of your tasks. (Here is my list for this morning: write two ideas for this book, organise dinner party, do washing, make phone calls to pay some bills.)

2. Against each item write 10, 20, 30. These represent blocks of minutes that you are going to spend on each item in turn. So my list would look like:
    Write book 10, 20, 30
    Organise party 10, 20, 30
    Laundry 10, 20, 30
    Pay bills 10, 20, 30

3. Start with the task that puts you off least. Set the kitchen timer for 10 minutes. Do the task for 10 minutes. (I choose the laundry – a mindless chore that I quite enjoy. I have my load on comfortably within the 10 minutes.)

4. When the timer rings. Stop. Wherever you are in the task. Stop. Take a pencil and score through the 10 next to the task.

> **Here's an idea for you...**
>
> Scan your diary for big projects coming up. Tomorrow spend just 10 minutes working on each project. By giving a tiny amount of focused attention regularly to projects, well in advance, you accomplish them without even noticing.

5. Set the timer for 10 minutes. Start the next task. (In my case, it's paying bills. It takes me the whole 10 minutes to get the paraphernalia together. Note: I'm no longer resentful about paying the bills, I'm irritated that I can't get on with it.)

6. Score through the 10 on the list and start the next task (Writing. The task that is most formidable, but buoyed on by the fact that I've made a start on the mundane tasks, I sit down, make some notes and start typing. The timer rings mid-sentence. Note: I'm disappointed that I have to leave my task and move on.)

7. Score off 10 and start the next task. (I look through recipe books for 10 minutes and make some notes on whom to invite.)

8. Score off 10 minutes. Now move on to the first task again but set the timer for 20 minutes. Repeat the entire process. (Laundry again. The first load isn't finished, so I sort the laundry so that it's ready to go in the machine. That takes 10 minutes but I score off the 20 next to laundry as there's nothing more I can do. I set the egg timer to 20 minutes for the bills. For most of that time I listen to Handel's Water Music played on a xylophone but I am halfway through paying the last bill

Defining idea...

'Procrastination is the art of keeping up with yesterday.'
DON MARQUIS, *American humorist*

when the timer goes. Score off 20. I move back to the writing with a sense of relief – that's the job that's most important but because of my 10-minute start I'm raring to go. When the timer goes after 20 minutes, I go back to the party, finalise the guest list and decide on the menu. Back to the laundry – 30 minutes. Unload and hang out the washing, set off the next load – well within the 30 minutes that they have now been allocated. Now I go back to my computer and complete another 30 minutes. After 30 minutes I pause and look at my list. All the chores have been completed. I don't need to do any more on the party – I've made a real start. And I'm where I want to be – sitting at my computer and enjoying writing, so I set my timer for 40 minutes and carry on, promising myself a cup of tea at the end. I'm so into it after 40 minutes that I bring the cup of tea back to my desk and carry on until lunch time.

Why this works for me when nothing else does

● It helps you overcome resistance. You can assign a task 5 minutes to begin with – although I started on 10 here. Anybody can do just about anything for 5 minutes.

● It has built in end-effect. This is the phenomenon well observed in employees in the two days before going on holiday – they get more done in two days than they usually achieve in a month. The rotation method keeps you focused because you build in artificial 'deadlines'. In other words, you'll get more done in 3 5 20 minute blocks than in an hour of unfocused grind.

● It has an innate momentum of its own. The easy tasks propel you into the difficult ones.

120. What's your Plan B?

Take the insecurity out of your life. All you need is a Plan B. It could be your best friend in stressed out times.

The life you're living is Plan A. Plan B is what happens if it all goes pear-shaped. Know how you'd get from A to B and you remove a huge chunk of the stress that is caused by worry about the future.

It was a former boss who taught me the value of having a Plan B. Magazine editors have one of the most glamorous jobs going – great pay, company car, free holidays, free clothes…

And they have one of the most insecure jobs you can imagine. The higher they climb, the faster they can fall. Their job is highly stressful and they routinely work their butts off for an employer only to be shunted to the side in a matter of hours if they don't deliver. 'How do you stand it?', I asked my former boss. 'Always, always have a Plan B,' she told me breezily.

Deciding on plan B
Every life has its fair shares of upsets and reversals of fortune. An essential of the Plan B is to be able to look at your life dispassionately and see potential stress lines – where your life is likely to come apart. For instance:

Here's an idea for you...

Tomorrow open a completely new bank account for your Plan B. Start a direct debit and pay in until you've built up your emergency fund total of three months' expenses. Knowing you've got enough money to finance your dream makes your present life a whole lot more fulfilling.

● If you work in a volatile industry, it's work. Your Plan B is what you'll do if your dismissal slip lands on your desk.

● If your relationship is struggling, your Plan B is what you'll do if you split up.

● If your health isn't good, your Plan B is to research methods of financing your life if bad stuff happens.

Now please, don't get cross. I'm not trying to rain on your parade or say that your happy world is about to fall around your head. I'm merely concerned with stress proofing your life, and Plan Bs are brilliant for this. No one says you'll ever need Plan B but having one is invaluable comfort when you wake in the middle of the night and can't get back to sleep because of catastrophic thoughts swirling around in your brain. You know those nights? Well, with a Plan B, you worry for about 30 seconds, go 'Oh, I remember, I've got a plan B', roll over and doze off again.

For Plan B to work it has to be a fantasy built on reality. By that I mean it's not just a vague 'Oh, I'll sell the house and move to France.' It's more concrete than that.

Building the dream
First, decide on your Plan B and start a file. Add cuttings, pictures, information to it. Suppose you were going to sell your house and move to France. Your file for this would include information on people who had done the same thing, and

research on how much you'd need to live on per year in France if you were mortgage-free. You'd also put in notes on the school system if you have young children.

Defining idea...

'Reality is the leading cause of stress amongst those in touch with it.'
JANE WAGNER and LILY TOMLIN, *comic writers*

Your Plan B should be realistic, but it should be awesome. It shouldn't be a case of 'Oh well, I could always move back in with Mum.' It should be training to become a chef, starting your own business, backpacking around Mexico. It should make your heart sing. Plan realistically but dream big.

Building an emergency fund

Think about the financial position you'd need to be in to make it work, and take steps to achieve it. The ideal sum for a 'just-in-case fund', whatever your Plan B, is eight months' worth of living expenses. Go through your bank statements, adding up your outgoings for a year – this is truly frightening – take the total, divide by 12 to get your average per month and then multiply by eight.

Still reeling? Yes, it does that have effect. OK, eight months is ideal but it's that – an ideal. However, I'd say that a priority for anyone who wants to stress proof their life is to build up at least three months' living expenses. That's the bare minimum that you should have easily accessible in a bank account according to the experts.

What happens when you spend more of your time thinking about Plan B than worrying about Plan A? Then it's time to move your life on.

121. Restoration day

When you're suffering from chronic, long-term stress. When your batteries are blown. When burnout is imminent, here is your emergency plan.

Book yourself a day out. By tomorrow, you will feel rested, stronger and more in control. (No, don't stop reading – you can make this happen.)

All you need is 24 hours. If you have children, ask someone else to look after them for as much of the day as possible. Remember that if you don't look after yourself, you will have nothing left to give to others.

The restoration day is based on three principles:

- Replenishing your body by giving it rest.
- Resting your brain by focusing on your body.
- Nourishing your soul with healthy simple food which will replenish the nutrients stripped away by stress.

Before you get up
When you wake, acknowledge that this day will be different. Today you are going to shift the emphasis onto relaxation and releasing tension and replacing what stress has drained away from your body. Stretch. If you feel like it, turn over and go back to sleep. If not, read an inspirational tome – a self-help book, poetry, a favourite novel.

Don't reach for your usual coffee or tea. Sip a mug of hot water with lemon: this, according to naturopaths, boosts the liver which has to work incredibly hard processing all the junk that goes into your body. Whatever, it's soothing. Every time panic hits because you're not doing anything – now and for the rest of the day – breathe in deeply for a count of eight and out for a count of eight.

> **Here's an idea for you...**
>
> Go to bed at 9.30 p.m. today and every day this week if you can manage it. Don't watch TV if you're not tired – read or listen to music. People who do this have turned around their stress levels in a week.

When you get up

Stretch for 10 minutes. A few yoga stretches are good, but it doesn't matter as long as you try to stretch every muscle in your body. You don't have to do this 'perfectly', it's not a work out, it's a reminder – you have a body: it carries tension and pain. Feel the cricks draining out. Finish with the yoga position known as the Child's Pose. Kneel with your legs tucked under you. Bend forward so your forehead rests as near to the floor as possible in front of you. A cushion on your knees might make this more comfortable. Take your arms behind you with hands pointing back and palms upward. Rest like this and breathe deeply. This is a favourite of mine because it releases tension in the neck and shoulders, which is where I store tension. I've been known to climb under my desk at work and do this for a few moments.

Breakfast

Try a fruit smoothie: blend a cup of natural yogurt with one banana and a couple of handfuls of other fruits; peach, mango, strawberries, pineapple. Thin, if preferred, with a little fruit juice. Sip slowly, preferably outside. Imagine the vitamin C zooming around your body replacing the levels depleted by stress. My advice today is to eat lightly and avoid (except for the odd treat) foods that strain digestion too much. Drink coffee and tea if you normally do; the last thing you

<table><tr><td>

Defining idea...

'Rest as soon as there is pain.'
HIPPOCRATES
</td></tr></table>

want is a caffeine withdrawal headache. But don't have more than, say, three caffeine drinks. Caffeine will make you jittery even if you're very used to it.

Morning

Get outside – in the most natural surroundings you can manage. Ideally, lie on your back on the grass. Stare at the sky. Let your mind drift off. Or walk in the countryside, the park, sit in your garden. If you really can't bear to be still, do some gardening.

Lunch

Have a huge salad combining every colour of vegetable you can think of – green, yellow, orange, purple, red. More vitamin C. Serve with a delicious dressing. This meal must include one absolute treat – a glass of wine, a dish of ice-cream, a piece of chocolate. Lie back. Indulge.

Afternoon

Go back to bed, or curl up on a cosy corner of your sofa. Watch a favourite movie, or a comedy show. A weepie can be great for this. A good cry is very therapeutic. Sleep if you can. Or if you'd prefer, listen to some favourite music.

Dinner

You should be hungry but feeling light. Eat another pile of vegetables – a salad or perhaps a stir-fry, following the 'eat a rainbow' advice given above. Have a fresh piece of fish grilled or fried in a little oil or butter. Think delicious but simple. Present your food beautifully; eat it by candlelight.

Go to bed early. Resist the temptation to watch TV. Read a book, listen to the radio or some music.

122. Crisis management

Facing the week from hell? Here's how to survive it.

This is the toolbox for navigating through those really stressful, busy times.

Don't catastrophise

Dorothy Parker, on hearing a telephone ring, apparently drawled 'What fresh hell is this?' We've all been there. On really busy days with multiple deadlines, I've got to the stage where I'm scared to answer the phone in case it's someone demanding something else of me. Then I made a conscious decision to stop being such a victim. My attitude became 'Why fear the worse until it happens?' Every time a negative thought crosses your brain, cancel it out with a positive one. This takes practice. An easy way to do it is to develop a mantra to suit whatever crisis you're in today and that you say to yourself mindlessly every time your mind goes into tailspin. Right now, I have to pick the kids up from school in half an hour. I have four weeks to my deadline for this book and I have done approximately half the number of words I promised myself I'd write today. My mantra is 'I am serenely gliding towards my deadline and everything will get done' and every time panic hits, I chant this to myself and feel much better.

Here's an idea for you...

Keep a time log of your working week so you finally get a realistic idea of how long it takes you to complete all your usual activities. This means you stop kidding yourself about how quickly you will perform tasks in an imperfect world – where you're interrupted frequently – and you'll reduce your stress levels hugely.

Master the only question that matters

The 'best use' question was taught to me by my first boss and it is invaluable in negotiating your way through any day with dozens of calls on your time. It helps you to prioritise 'on the run', sometimes quite ruthlessly. On the morning of manic days decide what you've got to achieve that day and if anything interrupts, ask yourself 'Is this the best use of my time, right now?' If the answer's no, take a rain-check and come back to it later. So if a friend calls at work, nine times out of ten, you won't chat then, you'll call her back at a more convenient time – unless, of course, she is very upset about something, then talking to her is the best use of your time. Nothing else is more important. By doing this, I don't let colleagues sidetrack me with complaints about their lack of stationery, unless of course it's the best use of my time. (No, you're right, so far stationery has never been the best use of my time, but you get the idea.)

Always underpromise

A lot of stress is of our own making. Thomas Leonard, who founded Coach University, the first professional training centre for life coaches, says 'One of the biggest mistakes is to tell people what they want to hear, give them what they think they want, without thinking if it's feasible for you. You overpromise results you can't deliver without a lot of stress. And of course, if you don't deliver, not only are you stressed, they are, too.' Leonard's advice is to underpromise rather than overpromise. That way your friends are delighted when you turn up at the party you said you couldn't make and your boss thinks you're wonderful when you get the report finished a day early rather than a week late. Make it your rule from now on to be absolutely realistic about how long it's going to take you to get things done. And until you get expert at this, work out the time you reckon it will take you to complete any task and multiply it by 1.5.

Defining idea...

'There cannot be a crisis next week. My schedule is already full.'
HENRY KISSINGER

123. Dealing with interruptions

Other people and their agendas — they suck the energy right out of you. But there are ways of dealing with interruptions.

It's been one of those days. This morning I had a clear day to get on with writing this. And then it all went wrong.

I've taken two phone calls and been side-tracked at the school gates by a friend wanting a coffee and a chat. I've agreed to pick up another parent's kid, which shouldn't be a problem but, somehow, now it is. It's now 12.45 pm and I've written 100 words. (That's not good, by the way.)

I'm reminded of the definition of an optimist: someone who believes that today will be better than yesterday. What's the definition of a fantasist? Someone who believes today will be better even if she doesn't make any changes. Sure, I can be an optimist, imagining I'll zip through everything I want to achieve today, but if yesterday was constantly hijacked by other people, and I don't do anything to change that today, I'm living on Fantasy Island if I think I'll get everything done. And that feeling of having wasted time is a total energy bummer. So it's time to start making some plans to ensure that I don't let other people interrupt me. My trigger points will be different from yours – as you've probably guessed, mine is being seduced by my friends into going offtrack. Below we explore some possible energy drains, and what hopeless cases – and that means me – can do about it.

You work in an office

The average office worker is interrupted every three minutes, according to research undertaken in California. It's a wonder that we get anything done at all. If you're lucky enough to have your own office space, how about operating a one-hour-door-open, one-hour-doorshut policy, when you can't be interrupted. It's also worth learning some great exit lines for bouncing the interrupter back to the drawing board until it suits you and/or they find someone else to help them. You could try 'Sorry, got to finish this project; can we talk about it tomorrow?' or 'Sorry, this week is impossible; what about next week.'

Your hobby is chatting

Yep, this is me. The answer is simple. Just say no. Personally, knowing how weak I am, I don't engage in conversation. Tomorrow, unlike today, I won't answer the phone but let the machine pick up. I'll check messages for urgency at noon and five o'clock.

> **Here's an idea for you...**
>
> Over the next week, note down when you were interrupted, by whom and for how long. At the end of the week, go through marking those interruptions that you couldn't put off because they were too important. how long did you have to spend dealing with them? next week be aware when you're planning your week's workload that that amount of time may 'disappear' from any day because of critical interruptions. keep a note to see if it's the same next week. planning for interruptions that can't be avoided means your week will flow more easily.

Defining idea...

'I choose to ... live so that which came ... to me as a blossom, goes on as a fruit.'
DAWNA MARKOVA, *poet*

You're a 'social e-mailer'

This tag is the invention of my friend Jane Alexander, a wonderful writer who admits that one of her occupations is 'social e-mailer'. She lives in the depths of Devon, so for her there's some excuse: e-mail is her window on the world. For the rest of us, it's probably nothing but a huge distraction. One radical idea that works for me is not to look at e-mails first thing in the morning. Instead, spend that first hour doing the most important task of the day. Often that first hour is the calmest you'll get, and what do you spend it doing? 'Chatting' to your friends – it's just that the written word fools you into thinking you're working. Or else you're answering other people's banal requests. Try ignoring your e-mails until you've done some serious work, and check them no more than three times a day.

You can't say 'no'

Perhaps you need to look at whether you are just being helpful or are hooked on being needed. Next time, when you're tempted to let yourself be distracted, ask yourself 'if I respond to this distraction, who am I disappointing?' It might be your boss, it might be you, it might be the child that you won't be able to take to the park at the weekend because you'll be making up time on a work project instead. Seeing the human cost of allowing yourself to be interrupted can help you decide if it's worth it or not.

124. Are you getting enough – pleasure, that is?

Jumping off the hamster wheel of relentless grind energises you very fast indeed.

The author of *The Attitude Factor*, Thomas R Blakeslee reckoned that at around thirty years old, we start to close down to pleasure, partly because we shut out new experiences and are less interested in new things. Basically we allow our ability to be adventurous to atrophy – and that directly impacts on how much pleasure there is in our lives. We stay in our comfort zone, and that comfort zone gets smaller and smaller.

Who cares, you might well be thinking (perhaps a tad defensively)? Who cares if my idea of excitement is a new series of *Celebrity Big Brother*? Big deal. Well, it is actually. If you're a couch potato, you are literally killing yourself. Traditional medics would say that it's because you're getting no exercise. Blakeslee would say it's because you're boring yourself to death.

To get you thinking, this is my much-simplified version of a quiz that's explained in full in Blakeslee's book and on his website. Base your answers on your usual behaviour and feelings in the last year, and pick the answer than is closest for you, even if not absolutely right.

Add up your score from the bracketed figures.

Here's an idea for you...

Make a list of the activities you used to love when you were around 17 or 18 years old – a pretty sure sign of what the 'real you' really loves. you're looking for a minimum of ten activities. pick one and carve out the time to do it in the next week. Work your way through the list of activities that still appeal.

1. Imagine you wake up on a beautiful summer morning without a care in the world. You feel happy. How happy?

   Slightly (score 1) Moderately (4) Intensely (7)

2. How long do these feelings last?

   Seconds (1) Hours (4) All day (7)

3. How often do you take pleasure in simple things such as a good meal or a conversation with a friend?

   Almost never (1) Weekly (4) Every day (7)

4. Look at your diary. How many events have you scheduled for the future that are guaranteed to give you pleasure?

   None (1) One or two (4) Plenty (7)

5. When you think of the future, how sure are you that you're going to have sensations of sheer pleasure in the future?

   Not at all (1) Pretty sure (4) Certain (7)

6. Think about the greatest pleasure you've ever had in your life. Do you think you'll feel that much pleasure again?

   Unlikely (1) Perhaps (4) Sure (7)

7. When you feel that all is well with the world, how strongly do you feel it?

   Minimally (1) Moderately (4) Intensely (7)

8. How often do you experience this kind of feeling of wellbeing?

   Almost never (1) Weekly (4) Many times in a week (7)

9. Think of the best you've ever felt in yourself. Do you think you'll feel that good again?

   Unlikely (1) Perhaps (4) Sure (7)

10. After feelings of pleasure and wellbeing, do you get negative feelings such as guilt or depression?

      Almost always (1) Sometimes (4) Almost never (7)

Add up you score and divide by ten.

If you scored 1–4. Your pleasure quotient is low, and your chances of being healthy and well in 21 years, are according to this research lower unless you start planning for pleasure now.

If you scored 4.1–6. This corresponds to the people who had a 45–55% chance of being healthy twenty-one years later. So pretty good, but could do better.

If you scored 6.1–7. Your score on this quiz corresponds to the people who had the most pleasure in their lives, and consequently the healthiest outcome on follow-up.

A two-pronged attack is needed

- *Plan for pleasure.* Dedicate time every day to simply enjoying life and planning for fun. Knowing you have something to look forward to, rather than letting life just happen, is a wonderful energiser. Plan something pleasurable for tonight, next Wednesday night, and one weekend in the next six months, just for starters.
- *Bust out of the comfort zone.* Why is this so important? Because it's the simplest route to intense pleasure. Anything we have to work for, we appreciate more. Start a conversation with someone interesting in the lunch queue, go to a foreignlanguage movie, book up to go abseiling. It doesn't matter how much you actually enjoy these things; you'll feel great after doing them just because you pushed yourself.

125. Aromatherapy masterclass

Think that aromatherapy is just for wimps? Wrong. Aromatherapy has attitude. Aromatherapy kicks ass. Aromatherapy actually works.

Here's a challenge. Next time you're writing your 'to-do' list, put 'Do something lovely for me' at the top of the list and give it top priority.

If you're laughing at the very thought of such self-indulgence, then you need this idea because it works – fast. Aromatherapy is a bit of a joke. How often have you read 'sprinkle a little lavender oil in your bath to destress you'? How often have you wondered how you'll find the time for a shower, much less a bath?

Let's face it, the people who can find the time to do the lavender oil stuff probably don't have too much stress in the first place. And I thought so, too, until I interviewed Judith White, an inspirational aromatherapist who believes aromatherapy can do a lot more than make your bath smell nice. 'Aromatherapy is perfect for those times when you have only seconds because it works in seconds and it is one of the most valuable tools we have to help us live a less stressed, happier life,' she says. She speaks from personal experience. 'I had to learn how to keep myself on an equilibrium when my previous business left me emotionally, mentally and physically stressed for an extremely difficult few years. My oils were my greatest ally. That, and taking responsibility for the situation I was in.'

Judith is very hot on the idea that it is empowering for us all, but especially women, to accept that they are not victims, that they helped create problems in their lives and it's up to them to change their situation for the better. 'When we take responsibility for our lives we automatically start looking after ourselves. We realise that it isn't selfish to put ourselves first now and then because we are taking responsibility for the effect our "victim" mode has on others. Think about the impact a woman's energy has within her home on her partner and kids. If a woman has a good day and her partner a bad one, he will soon be uplifted if she maintains her good spirits. On the other hand, if a man has a brilliant day, but the woman is down, then you will quickly watch his brilliant day evaporate as her energy dominates. Women have the energetic ability to sweep away everyone else's enthusiasm along with their own. Women's power over others is immense because we are the great intuitives and communicators and we can use these skills positively or negatively to affect others.'

She recommends you look for opportunities throughout your day to stick in a mini-multi-tasking treatment. Here are some I've found helpful. Oils

> **Here's an idea for you...**
>
> For days when you have to think fast, carry around a hankie with some peppermint oil sprinkled on it and sniff it to help you get focus. Studies have shown it aids concentration.

> **Defining idea...**
>
> 'Smell is a potent wizard that transports you across thousands of miles and all the years you have lived.'
> HELEN KELLER

Defining idea...

'Always remember essential oils are highly volatile, very powerful natural essences. Working with them is like working with magic. And what is magic? Magic is energy.'
JANINE MURPHY, *writing in Aromatherapy Today*

aren't just for baths. When showering, cover the plughole with a flannel and add 4–6 drops (in total) of a combination of essential oils to the shower tray. Add one drop of essential oil to your existing moisturiser. Inhale deeply as you apply it. Try soaking your feet in an aromatic footbath whilst reading or watching TV. For an immediate treatment put a couple of drops of essential oil into the middle of a hot, wet flannel, wring it out, hold it over your face and breath deeply.

126. Have a holiday at your desk

Imbue the old nine-to-five with a certain glamour and you'll be amazed at how much tension seeps out of your life.

You'll be raising your standards and that means lowering your stress levels.

Forty years has taught me that there are two ways to have a perfect day. One is in the grand tradition of the Lou Reed song. You hang out for a whole day with someone you really, really love who is loving you right back – or at least tolerating you. You don't have to do anything because just being with the beloved is so blissful it blocks out the boring little problems that usually stress you out. If you manage twenty days like this in your whole life time, you're doing pretty well.

And then there's the second way. You build a perfect day for yourself and by adding grace and glamour to your life, you remove stress. It takes a little thought. But it is more reliable than true love. You can have a holiday of the 'mind' on even the most mundane day.

Reboot your commute
Give your journey to work an overhaul. Set yourself targets. Instead of a drag, see it as a purposeful part of your day. If it involves walking, buy a pedometer. Learn

413

Here's an idea for you...

Clothes can play a huge part in improving the quality of our life. Every morning choose one thing that makes your heart sing – a colour you love, a fabric that embraces you, a piece of jewellery with sentimental attachment. Next time you're shopping buy clothes that help you radiate confidence.

a language. Use the time to repeat your mantras for the day. Be creative: write a page of free-hand prose on the journey in (not if you drive of course!). Start working up the characters for your novel. It's a terrific time to practice mindfulness, which can deliver the benefits of meditation. The list is endless.

Boost your environment

Your starter question: what five changes would make your work environment more pleasant.

Here's mine. Getting rid of piles of papers and magazines that need to be filed. Investing in a china cup and no more sharing the office's grubby, chipped ones. Cheering up my desk with a bunch of pink tulips. Cleaning my keyboard – so filthy it's a health hazard. Turning down the ringtone volume on my phone. Everyday find some way to make your surroundings more pleasant.

Beat the mid-afternoon slump

When you feel the slump kicking in, stop working and get away from your workstation if you can. Go for a short walk in the sunshine, or take a nap. If you can't, try this: palm your eyes in your hand for a few minutes and visualise a calm and beautiful place. See this in as much detail as possible.

The journey home

This needs a different mood from the journey to work. If you listen to music, make it different from the tunes you play in the morning – slower, deeper. Small stuff like that really helps to emphasise that this is your transition period. Have a project that you work on at this time (planning your holiday is good). And if you read, keep the tone light. If in the morning you read French verbs or the novels of Dostoyevsky, read P.G. Wodehouse on the way home.

Spread love
When you pass someone in distress send them 'serenity' or 'calm' as a thought. Spread good and happy thoughts wherever you go. Smile. Be gracious. Be kind, compassionate, a force for good.

Not every day can be a high day or holiday, but changing your mindset, looking for grace and sheer fun in previous black holes of misery turns you into a force for light and transforms your day-to-day grind – it's the art of living lightly and it gets easier the more you look for opportunities to practise your skill.

Defining idea...
'You can make more friends in two months by becoming interested in other people than you can in two years by trying to get other people interested in you.'
DALE CARNEGIE, *founding father of the self-help movement*

415

127. Zap those piles of paper

No, not those kind of piles. We're talking about the avalanche of paper, magazines, unpaid bills, flyers for pizza houses — the general detritus of 21st-century life that threatens to overwhelm you.

Not to mention your kitchen surfaces.

This idea is very personal to me. Following it has reduced stress in my life by a factor of 10. When my daughter, then three, was asked what her mother did for a living she said 'My mummy tears bits of paper out of newspapers.' Which is actually quite an accurate description of what I do for a living – it's called 'research'. I spend hours tearing out, but it's never enough. All my working life, piles of paper have dragged down my spirit and proven to be a stressor in my domestic life. My partner objects to hefting piles of magazines off chairs before he can sit down.

This is the system that works for me, culled from reading and interviewing just about every organisational guru on the planet. The only drawback is that it takes time to set up. But if you have a day to spend or ten free hours, give it a go. Ten hours can work magic. You will probably have to make a few adjustments to suit your life.

Step 1

Gather together everything that you will need to create order in your world. For me that's cardboard magazine holders, folders, pens, labels, stapler, a couple of hard-backed address books (personal and business) and a huge industrial-strength binbag. I also keep the family calendar and my diary at hand so I can put dates directly into them as I reveal the invites and school dates in my pile.

> **Here's an idea for you...**
>
> Chuck out files regularly: it's a good way to keep on top of paperwork. Every time you open a file, put a pencil mark on the corner of it. At the end of six months or a year, you'll be able to see in a moment which files you've barely opened. Most of their contents can be chucked out.

Step 2

Work systematically. You are going to go from one side of your desk to the other, or one side of the room to the other. Gather together one pile of paper and assorted junk and place it bang in the middle of the room or your desk. Start sorting. Every single piece of paper that you touch must be actioned.

- If it contains a phone number that you might need in the future, then put the number straight into one of your *address books*.

- If it is a bill that has to be paid, or anything which must be acted on immediately, then create a file for *urgent and unpaid bills*. (I carry this file with me, in my handbag and work through it every day when I have a down moment.)

- If it is an article or piece of information that you might need in the future but which is not urgent, start creating files for these (*named files*) such as 'pensions', 'holidays', 'general interest'.

417

Defining idea...

'We can lick gravity but sometimes the paperwork is overwhelming.'
WERNER VON BRAUN, *rocket engineer*

● If it is a piece of information that you need to act on or read or make a decision on but not now, put it in a file marked '*To Do*' and make an appointment in your diary sometime in the next week when you'll deal with it. This file should be somewhere accessible and you should clear it not less than once every two weeks or it gets out of control.

Keep a *tickle book*. Tickle as in 'tickle my memory.' Mine is an A4 hardbacked notebook. In it I note down the names of anything I might need in the future: the idea of an article I might write or a savings account offering a good rate of interest. The point is that I don't have to hold on to endless bits of paper just in case I ever want this information – there's enough in the tickle book to help me trace it. I also keep the tickle book by my side at work and if anyone calls me with a piece of information I may need but don't know for sure, then I scribble down their number and a couple of explanatory lines so that I can follow up later. Same with my emails. The tickle book means I have been able to throw out dozens of pieces of paper almost as soon as they reach my desk.

128. Have you burned out?

What is burn out? It's when a relationship — either work or personal — has got so bad that you just can't stand it any longer.

If the only route of action that appeals is hiding under your duvet until Christmas, it's time to reassess.

You're stressed. But just how stressed? Here are a few statements worth answering.

	Score
You fantasise a lot about your perfect life that doesn't include your dull/annoying partner/job	+1
You say 'I can't take it any more' at least once a week	+2
You feel unappreciated	+3
Tension is beginning to affect your health	+3
You wake up dreading the day ahead	+3
All you want to do in the evening is slump in front of the TV and sleep	+1

Score

4 or under = mild level of dissatisfaction. This indicates that the present situation is stressful but potentially saveable.

9 or under = life is not good and you know you need to act.

10 or over = burnout imminent.

> ## Here's an idea for you...
>
> Spend 10 minutes every evening planning your next day. It's proven that you get one-fifth more work done if you review what you want to accomplish the next day in advance. Plus what you do achieve will likely be of higher quality.

Dr Dina Glouberman, who has written on the subject of burnout, defined it as what happens when 'The love or meaning in what we are doing goes, but attachment drives us to carry on.'

It's this attachment that you need to question. It's clear that some situations are easier to leave than others but if you have tried all you can to fix your particular hell and nothing improves, it's time to admit the unhappiness to yourself and others, and move on. In our competitive world, it's hard to say 'I may have made a mistake.' The more time you've invested in the wrong life, the harder it is to give up on it. But the first step is simply admitting to yourself and perhaps a few trusted compadres that yes, you are human, you made a mistake.

There's nothing wrong with being unhappy with your life. See it as a positive. What it signals is that you have outgrown your present situation and that it's time to move on. Otherwise, the stress of living a life that isn't yours can be fearsome. You risk burn out – a state of collapse where you lose all joy in life. Your body gives out and your spirit gives up. It is extremely painful and can take months, even years to come back from.

But even if you do burn out, it's not an unmitigated catastrophe either. For many it's the beginning of a new more enlightened life. After spending their time in the metaphorical wilderness, they rethink their life and choose a new route.

Here's an exercise to help you get the process started:

Defining idea...

'Stress is an ignorant state. It believes that everything is an emergency.'
'O' MAGAZINE

● Lie down. Breathe deeply. When you're calm, ask yourself 'If I woke up and all my problems and worries had gone, how would I know a miracle had happened?'

● How would you behave, talk, walk, think – if the miracle had happened?

● How do you think your family and friends would know a miracle had happened?

● If you were to assess your life right now somewhere between 0 and 10, with 0 being your worst life and 10 a full-scale miracle life, where would this day be on the scale?

● What would need to happen for you to move one step up?

● How would other people know that you had moved one step up?

This exercise helps you realize that it's not so much miracles (externals) that determine your happiness, but your behaviour. You are in control.

129. Make life easy for yourself

Give up coffee, don't smoke, take exercise — we're always being told that unless we do our stress will become worse. And you know what? It's true.

Without a doubt, one of the main reasons our bodies and minds are buckling under stress is that our lifestyles are about as far removed from stress-relieving as it's possible to be. How do you fare? Answer these questions:

	Agree	Sometimes	Disagree
I'm happy with my body and I exercise regularly.	☐	☐	☐
When I suffer from stress I take steps to relax right away.	☐	☐	☐
I get enough sleep.	☐	☐	☐
I have a balanced diet.	☐	☐	☐
I don't drink more than one cup of tea or coffee a day.	☐	☐	☐
I plan regular weekends and holidays away.	☐	☐	☐
I don't over-indulge in anything bad for me – nicotine, alcohol or drugs.	☐	☐	☐
I have enough energy to do everything demanded of me.	☐	☐	☐

Score 3 for an 'agree', 2 for a 'sometimes' and 1 for a 'disagree'.

If you score 12 or under, you need this idea more than most. If you scored between 12 and 20, your habits could still do with some fine-tuning.

Follow each of these suggestions for a week or so, and when it's second nature add another.

Week 1

Drink a glass of water with every meal and every time you visit the bathroom. Self-explanatory. Just do it. There are lots of smart alecs who will tell you we don't really need all that water. But water is almost unique in being a substance with no downside. Drinking water means you're not drinking something else that is probably bad for you. It also gives you more energy, and that's got to reduce your stress levels.

Week 2

Swap one of your regular cups of caffeine for one healthy cuppa. Caffeine stimulates the adrenal glands to work overtime. It's been found that 4–5 cups of coffee a day raises stress levels by a third. Living on the adrenaline produced by tea, coffee, fizzy drinks and chocolate is just plain daft. Try rooibus tea – now easily available in the UK as redbush tea. Unlike normal tea it is good for you – bang full of antioxidants but no caffeine. Unlike herbal tea, it tastes nice. Aim for no more than one cup of caffeine a day.

> ### Here's an idea for you...
> Start your day with porridge: the best stress-busting breakfast is a bowl of the stuff. If you can throw in some yogurt or milk (for their stress-reducing nutrients) even better. Oats have been shown to keep stress levels lower throughout the day than other breakfasts and although muesli made with oats is good, cooking the oats as porridge works best.

Week 3

Eat breakfast every single day. Studies show people who eat breakfast are more productive – and slimmer, incidentally – than those who miss it.

Week 4

Every day eat: One orange – for vitamin C (or another helping of vitamin-C-rich food). One helping of oats, fish, meat or eggs (for vitamin B, necessary for beating stress). One helping of broccoli or one helping of carrots – just brilliant for antioxidants.

At lunch. One small serving of good-quality carbohydrate. Too much and you'll feel dozy but one slice of wholegrain bread or a fist-sized portion of wholegrain pasta or rice will release the feel-good hormone serotonin. Two to three servings of reduced-fat dairy, which is rich in natural opiates called casomorphins (have one serving with your evening meal if you have trouble sleeping).

At dinner. One small portion of good-quality protein (releases tryptophan which helps serotonin release).

This won't supply all the nutrients you need but it's a good start and it specifically delivers the nutrients you need to stay stress free.

Week 5

Exercise. It is the single best thing you can do to reduce your stress levels and the best thing you can do for your health full-stop (with the exception of giving up smoking). Aerobic exercise (walking briskly, running, swimming) burns off excess stress hormones. Yoga lowers blood pressure in a matter of minutes, and after half an hour, stress levels have dropped dramatically.

130. The energy drench

Convert your shower into a daily spa treatment
that will energise and revive you.

This will do you far more good than hitting the snooze button, or an extra cup
of coffee. It will take about two minutes longer than your usual shower, but it
does a whole lot more than get you clean.

One minute? invigorate your skin before you get in the shower
Buy a natural-bristle skin brush – not so hard that it hurts your skin when you
pass it over the back of your hand, but hard enough so that you feel it. Use this
brush prior to showering. Brush over your skin, working from your feet up your
legs, from your hands up your arms and over your back and torso, always
working towards your heart. The theory is that this works to boost lymph flow,
which means that waste products are eliminated from your body faster. There's
no evidence for this. What is for sure is that it causes blood to flood the surface
of the skin and thus increases circulation. It takes about a minute and it acts as a
powerful tonic.

30 seconds? rub away the old, reveal the new
Continue to stimulate your system with a body scrub using a sisal glove or a
face cloth.
Plain old soap will do but a cleansing scrub scented with a citrus scent will wake
you up even more. You can make your own scrub with a handful of coarse-grain
salt to which you add a few drops of lemon, grapefruit or bergamot essential oil.

Here's an idea for you...

give your insides an energy drench.
Take a glass of hot water and
squeeze a quarter of a lemon into it.
Sip first thing. This supports your
liver in expelling the waste that it's
been working on processing all
night.

Put some on your glove or cloth and rub your body vigorously. This action will get rid of the dead skin cells, softening your skin and invigorating you at the same time.

Two minutes? drench your body

Turn on the tap and wash away your scrub with some warm water. Then change the temperature gauge to cool. Quite cool. And stay there for one minute. Return to hot again for a minute or so, and then back to cool for a final minute. The shock of passing between warm and cool will also boost your circulation. The capillary walls (those of the smallest blood vessels) are strengthened and skin tone is improved. You should feel as if you've run about half a mile by now.

30 seconds? carry on the good work all day

Finally, 'mist' your body with oil. Make your own 'mister' by purchasing a spray bottle from a chemist, or recycling one that used to contain another product and has been washed out. For each 100ml of water, add half a teaspoon of olive or almond oil and ten drops of an energising oil. Bergamot, lemon or rosemary are all good.

An extra for the times you're washing your hair ...

3 minutes – get more focus Rosemary essential oil is fabulous for restoring focus and energy. Wash your hair as normal, towel dry then use rosemary to lift your mood. If your hair is short, add three drops of rosemary essential oil to a couple

of dessertspoons of almond oil and rub into your scalp. If your hair's long, add the oils to some conditioner and work into your hair. Now massage your scalp all over. Stick on a plastic hat or towel and follow the energy drench described above. When you've drenched your body, drench your hair and shampoo and condition again to get rid of the oils.

Defining idea...

'Energy is the essence of life. Every day you decide how you're going to use it by knowing what you want and what it takes to reach that goal, and by maintaining focus.'
OPRAH WINFREY

... And for those times when you fancy a bath

To maximise the restorative power of a bath at the end of the day, add one or two of drops of blue or green food colouring to your bath water along with your favourite bubble bath. Blue and green work powerfully on your brain to relax and calm you. Just a hint of green especially is very soothing. *Don't* overdo the colouring though.

131. A one-minute answer to mid-afternoon slump

Practically every medical system in the world (with the exception of our own) believes that energy flows around the body in channels. Suspend disbelief!

Lack of energy is attributed to a block somewhere in this energy flow. Release the block and you get increased energy.

You can do this by applying needles, fingers or elbows to specific acupuncture points around the body. True? Or unmitigated waffle? Here we're dealing with acupressure and there isn't scientific evidence that would pass muster with the *British Medical Journal* when it comes to acupressure and energy. However, there is evidence that acupressure works for helping with post-operative nausea and lower back pain – so working on the principle that if it works for one thing it may work for another, it's worth a try. I have derived benefit from the following facial massage which is specifically for tiredness and mental exhaustion. It was taught to me by a TCM (traditional

Chinese medicine) doctor about twenty years ago. There may be a placebo effect going on here, but hey, who cares? Whatever gets you through the night or, in this case, through the afternoon. This is brilliant for mid-afternoon slump. I've since taught it to friends – specifically those who spend a lot of time at their desk– and many use it.

Shiatsu facial massage for instant energy

● Lean your elbows on a table and let your face drop into your hands, with your palms cupped over your eyes. Look into the darkness formed by your hands. Stay there for as long as you feel comfortable or until your colleagues start to get worried.

● Place your thumbs on the inner end of each eyebrow and use your index fingers to work out along the upper edge of the eyebrow, applying pressure at regular intervals. When your index fingers reach the outer edge of your eyebrow, release all pressure.

● Return index finger to the inner end of each brow and work thumbs along to the *lower* end of the brows in similar fashion. Release as before.

● Place thumbs under ear lobes and apply pressure. At the same time, use the index fingers to apply pressure on points on a line from the bridge of the nose under your eyes, along the ridge formed by your eye sockets.

> **Here's an idea for you...**
>
> If mid-afternoon tiredness gets you down, combine the massage with this energising meditation – or do this instead of it. Empty your brain as far as possible, sit quietly, get an orange and concentrate on peeling it. look at it first – orange is an energising colour. Smell it – citrus scents such as orange, bergamot and lemon are revitalising. Eat it – vitamin c and fructose make a wicked combination for energy. After your orange, drink a large glass of water. you should feel better in ten minutes.

429

Defining idea...

'Shiatsu technique refers to the use of fingers ... to apply pressure to particular sections on the surface of the body for the purpose of correcting the imbalances of the body and maintaining and promoting health.'
JAPANESE MINISTRY OF HEALTH, Labor and Welfare, 1957.

- Touch fingertips to fingertips along an imaginary line running up the middle of your forehead from your nose to your hairline (no pressure is necessary). Use thumbs to apply pressure to points fanning out from the outer edge of the eyebrows to hairline. Repeat four times. (Feel for tender points and massage them. I find pressing on my temples when I'm stressed decreases tension in my jaw where, like a lot of people, I hold a lot of tension.)

- Use thumbs to apply *gentle* pressure in the eye sockets under the inner end of the eyebrow where you feel a notch at the ridge of the eye socket. (This is a very delicate spot. I was told by a doctor once that it is the major nerve closest to the surface of the body: I don't know if that's true, but go gently. You can really hurt yourself by pressing this point too hard.)

- Use one index finger to work up that imaginary line in your mid-forehead from the nose to your hairline.

- Now drop your head forward and, lifting your arms, work thumbs from your spine outwards along the ridge of your skull from the spine out to the point just under your earlobes. Do this four times.

OK, it's a bit of a faff to get the hang of the different points, but once you've practised a couple of times with the instructions, you'll have the hang of it. And it will be a good friend to your energy levels for the rest of your life.

132. Booking in peace

A good book can be a companion that lets you leave the workaday world behind.

Losing yourself in a book is one of the few times you can travel anywhere and not worry about baggage or passports.

Think about the history of the humble book. People have been killed for writing books. Some books themselves have been burned and banned. Despite this being the age of the ghost-written, 12-year-old footballer's autobiography, we still attach a degree of respect to books. We expect books to have substance and be somewhat timeless, in a way that magazines and newspapers aren't.

Worryingly, in the UK today, in some areas one in five children leaving primary school can't read. This is one of the greatest tragedies in our country as reading sets you free. If you're having a bad or boring time of it, picking up a good book is like Alice going down the rabbit hole – you're bound to have an adventure. However, the sheer number of books that are released each year can make choosing what to read more stressful than it need be. Should you listen to Richard & Judy or will your snobbish friends laugh at you for allowing TV presenters to choose your reading material? Should you ask at the local library what might be good to read?

Here's an idea for you...

Get a day pass for a seriously good library that covers the subjects you're especially interested in. Treat it like an outing and read not for work or study but for pleasure, surfing the books like you do the internet. I am interested in occult subjects and the Harry Price Library of Magical Literature is my library of choice. Find the library considered best for your own interests and immerse yourself in knowledge.

Books can change your life but they require the commitment of time, in both the hunting out of good ones and in the reading of them. So choosing the right book is a bit like choosing the right relationship, you have to like it enough to commit to it. I used to be a bit crab-like in both books and relationships; I'd cling on to the bitter, bitter end instead of abandoning and walking away if things were clearly not going to work out. I couldn't dump a book mid-way through, even if that meant dedicating a day to a book that I was clearly not enjoying. The day this all came to an end was when I spent a whole weekend reading a truly dreadful stream-of-consciousness number about an Indian woman and her Iranian husband.

The book rambled on and on like a bad dream until eventually we got some action on – and I kid you not – the last paragraph where after reams and reams of philosophical musings about love, sex, race etc., etc. the husband kills her lover. I cheered and wished that the husband had killed the protagonist too. And the author. And me, for having read it right till the end.

Apart from culling bad books from your life, actively seek out the good ones. Ask your friends for recommendations and note who was most successful in suggesting a book you liked and stick to asking them. Consider joining a book club. This is the age of the funky book club so pick one near you and it will be a chance to meet new people as well as read more widely. Keep a reading diary

and note what books you read and when, it
becomes like a journal of where
you've been in your imagination.

Defining idea...

'I have always imagined that
Paradise will be a kind of library.'
JORGE LUIS BORGES

It's a bit sad that everyone on the tube is usually
reading the latest big blockbuster and there's very
little variety. It feels like being spoon-fed things
from the publishing, retail and marketing industries. There is something to be
said for safe choices though. I adore self-help books but I'd never read them in
public as they have garish covers and titles like 'Feel the pain and rejection of
being dumped – and date again anyway' or 'He's just not that into you' (the last
one is a real title). Since I'm horribly judgemental about people based on their
reading material, I'm careful not to fall on my own sword.

Reading material is also a great way of judging whether you could ever fancy a
particular stranger on the train. A man reading Proust is trying too hard to be an
intellectual, a man reading Dan Brown is not trying hard enough to be an
intellectual and a man who's reading Terry Pratchett will force you to go to role-
playing gaming evenings and may disturbingly want you to dress up as Princess
Leia on occasion. I want a sexy, Nietzsche-reading superman.

Being able to read is a tremendous blessing and one that we probably overlook
when we're thinking of things to be grateful for. Exercise this fabulous skill as
often and as passionately as you can.

433

133. Stress is other people

Here's how to deal with the energy black holes.

Most of the time I wander through life in an agnostic muddle. And then, occasionally, life flows with such serendipity and I am so in the right place at the right time, that I think there must be a God.

One day I bumped into a woman I knew slightly, a refugee who has gone through more in her 27 years than anyone should have to in a life time. She was clearly upset, tears beginning to roll down her cheeks, and I stopped to see if I could help. Here was a woman who had walked stoically through war zones. What the hell had made her so desperate in central London? She told me she had been going through the ticket barriers at Oxford Street Tube station but hadn't been able to get her ticket to work the automatic gate. The inspector had started shouting at her, querying if she had paid for her ticket and accusing her of obtaining it illegally. 'It has made me feel like giving up,' she told me. 'I thought maybe it's because he's racist, and I'm black. But then I thought, no, it's me. I'm so stupid and my English isn't good. Total strangers hate me on sight. It's my fault. I'm never going to fit in here.' The shame and humiliation had ripped through her already fragile self-esteem and made her doubt if she could ever cope in the UK.

As I listened, my mind was whizzing furiously. My eyes narrowed. 'Was he tall, skinny, wearing thick glasses?', I asked her. She nodded. Clearly this wasn't the response she'd been expecting. What she didn't know was that only the week before I'd had a run-in with that very man at the same station. He had picked on me for no apparent reason. So I was able to assure my friend that it wasn't her. It was him. To hear that I – white, British and with English as my mother tongue – had been similarly abused by this bully changed around her day.

All around you are the energy black holes, people who are unhappy, negative or angry and who would like nothing more than to drag you into their stressful world. And there is absolutely nothing you can do about them. The only thing you can change is your attitude. (There is a proviso to this – if your life is littered with difficult people out to get you, then with respect I might suggest that it's got something to do with your expectations.) But sometimes, even most times, it's not you – it's them.

> ## Here's an idea for you...
> A lot of stress in our relationships with other people comes from trying to second guess what they're thinking or what their intention is. Try saying: 'What other people think of me is none of my business.' Think about that statement closely. When you start believing it, life gets a whole lot easier.

Some black holes are strangers
Other people have their own agends. You can't know what they are and you can't change them. Take a tip from Rosamond Richardson, author and yoga teacher. She recommends visualising yourself surrounded by white light, creating a protective bubble around you. Negativity just bounces off this white light and can't affect you. Sounds nuts, but it works. Try it and see.

Some of them you share a life, a home, a bed with...
Don't waste a moment dwelling on how less stressful life would be if John would only be kinder, Mum would cheer up a bit, Emily was more help around the home, or your boss was less aggressive.

435

Defining idea...

'A healthy male adult bore consumes each year one and a half times his own weight in other people's patience.'
JOHN UPDIKE

This is a surprisingly telling little exercise that you can do in five minutes on the back of a napkin. It may give you shock. Make a list of the people with whom you have regular contact. Then divide that list into three categories:

- **The energisers**   They look after you in every way. They give great advice. They bring happiness to your life.

- **The neutral**   They're OK. Neither great nor bad.

- **The drainers**   They're users, people who don't deliver, let you down, bring you down. They also include gossips, people whose conversation is sexist or racist and bitchy, sarcastic types whose conversation, no matter how entertaining, makes you feel bad about yourself afterwards.

And you know what I'm going to say. Maximise time with the energisers. Look for them when you enter a room and gravitate towards them whether you've been introduced or not. We all know these people when we meet them. If you have too many neutrals, think how you can bring more energisers into your life.

And the drainers? Your time with them should be strictly limited. And if some of them are your closest friends, your family, your lover, you need to think about that very closely. You may feel unable to cut them out now (although that is an option) but you can limit the time they are allowed to suck you into their world.

7

Make your life–work balance – work!

The ultimate career coach

It's the challenge for all of us in the twenty-first century – how to combine family, work and some semblance of a social life. Be challenged no longer. Here are ideas for managing your time, managing your work load and managing your kids.

439

What are your energy levels like?

You might be exhausted because you've got too much to do. Then again, you could be missing a trick by not taking really simple steps to restore your energy levels. This quiz will help you see in a moment where you can help yourself.

1. **Do you usually sleep for at least seven and half to eight hours each night?** Yes ☐ No ☐

2. **Do you usually sleep right through the night?** Yes ☐ No ☐

3. **Do you eat three well-balanced meals a day at regular intervals?** Yes ☐ No ☐

4. **Do you always eat breakfast?** Yes ☐ No ☐

5. **Do you eat at least two portions of protein foods every day (e.g. meat, fish, eggs, dairy, pulses) as well as two portions of wholegrain carbohydrates (e.g. wholemeal bread or pasta, or porridge)?** Yes ☐ No ☐

6. **Do you eat at least five portions of fruit and vegetables a day?** Yes ☐ No ☐

7. **Are you active, on the go for at least an hour every day** Yes ☐ No ☐

8. **Do you drink at least one and a half litres of fluid a day, not counting strong coffee, alcohol or energy drinks and keep your alcohol levels within the recommended limit?** Yes ☐ No ☐

Score
1 for every yes, 0 for every no

If you **scored 6** or more, you are doing very well to eliminate any energy drains. If you still feel lacking in energy it could well be that your life is out of balance so try *idea 134.*

If you **scored 5 or less**, remember that dropping any single one of these good habits can wreak havoc with your energy levels. You should have some clues now as to how you can change things. You may be sabotaging yourself on several fronts but start with *idea 129.*

134. You're the boss of you

Taking responsibility for your own life may be the toughest thing you do in your quest for inner peace. But the sooner you realise that you're your own knight in shining armour the better.

The President of the United States is the highest office in that country for the same reason that you hold the highest office in your life; the buck stops with you.

The life you lead is the result of decisions that you have made and are constantly making. This is not to say that the outside world doesn't have any influence – of course it does – but ultimately you're running the show. You must not cave in to feeling powerless to make changes in your own life. While you may only have limited control over what you do, you can exercise full control over what you feel and how you react to those limitations.

Here's a typical example: your boss decides to give you a report to do last thing on a Friday night and wants it first thing on Monday morning. It is probably not a practical response for you to jack in your job (though if you have to miss your wedding or a relative's funeral to do it and your boss doesn't cut you some slack, you may do well to start looking at the jobs ads). However, how you deal with a) the feelings this invokes in you and b) the actual task ahead can be vital to your sense of inner peace.

A bad way to respond would be to stomp off home with the work, be in a bad mood all weekend and do it angrily and reluctantly, regularly sighing loudly and bemoaning your fate, while snapping at any poor family member silly enough to pass within a few feet of you.

A better way would be to accept that you've decided to do the work. And you have, because you didn't resign at the point that you were told about it. So you had the power to leave but you didn't. So, having made a decision to do something, do it well. Put on your favourite music, fix yourself something tasty to snack on while you work and maybe even get your partner to work in the same room so you can have a sense of camaraderie. Take regular breaks but, instead of breaking your flow by going to the TV room, go for a short walk instead or have a boogie round the room.

Society is organised in a very complex way and one of the side effects of this organisation is to make you feel very small and insignificant. If we want to buy a house, most of us have to get a mortgage. To get a mortgage you need a job – a very well-paying job if the house is to be in a nice area. To get the partner you want, you have to be attractive to him or her – be it in looks or behaviour. You have to continue to attract if you want to retain your partner. Let's not even start on the demands of the children. In short, it can very quickly seem as if everyone has got a vested interest in your life – except you. You can feel trapped by all of these social restrictions you put on yourself.

> ## Here's an idea for you...
>
> Do you know what your income and expenditure is? List all your income in one column and all your outgoings in the next and then create a budget that ensures you're not exceeding your income. It's not boring… well OK, it is a bit boring, but boring is better than the serious distress of insolvency.

443

Defining idea...

'Man is condemned to be free; because once thrown into the world, he is responsible for everything he does.'
JEAN-PAUL SARTRE, *being his ever-cheery but highly-perceptive self. Think not of it as being 'condemned' but more 'blessed'.*

The real revolution happens when you realise that this is your own construct. You have made this. You have decided you want this house or that job. Your choice of partner is determined by you. The way you raise your kids is partly determined by you. As such, if you're feeling unhappy and conflicted by any aspect of your life, YOU can change it. Feel that power coursing through your veins – doesn't it feel fantastic? Now get back out there and go 'Grrrrr!' at the world.

135. Be selfish

Being selfish isn't the most terrible thing you can be. In fact, if you're a bit of a doormat it may be the best thing you can do for yourself.

Good boys and girls aren't selfish. Good boys and girls have stress-induced heart attacks before the age of 40 or run off and abandon all the responsibilities they've kept up for years once they hit middle age. Be bad.

Imagine that there's a fisherman who sells his catch off the dock. A pretty girl walks by and asks the fisherman if he'll make a present of a fish to her. The fisherman, being a red-blooded straight male, agrees and gives her two for good measure. While he's busy chatting up the girl, a seagull swoops down and nicks two more of his fish before he can stop it. An old man comes by, criticises the state of the fish and asks for a discount of 50%. As the day is getting on now and the fisherman has yet to sell a fish, he agrees to a 50% sale. The man only buys one small fish. The fisherman doesn't have much of his catch left by now but just as he gets ready to holler out his wares, a man with a knife runs up to the dock, threatens the fisherman and steals the rest of his catch. The fisherman is left with nothing but the pathetic 50% sale of a small fish.

Did you like my metaphor there? Tortured, wasn't it? Well, there's a serious point behind it. While we'd like to believe in the abundance of the universe, the fact is that we are temporal creatures, bound to this space–time continuum, and time

Here's an idea for you...

Borrow a film that only you want to watch. Hog the TV and DVD player and watch that film that only you want to watch. If your partner or family protest, stick your fingers in your ears and go 'la-la-la-I'm not listening-lala- la' until they get fed up and leave.

is a finite commodity in our world. Your quest for inner peace will be seriously derailed if you let time bandits steal away your catch. Whether you overindulge in socialising (the pretty girl), extra unexpected chores (the seagull), family commitments (the old man) or work (the thief), you leave nothing but a tiny pathetic sliver of time for yourself – most of which you'll spend sleeping.

So what can you do about it? Get selfish. This is almost impossible for some as we've been brought up to believe that only very horrible people put themselves before others. Now I'm not suggesting that you leave for a golfing holiday just as your wife goes into labour or that you choose a spa break over a relative's funeral but I do believe that if you don't factor in some time for yourself, you will
explode like a pressure cooker. And nobody wants to clear up that sort of mess.

Women are usually the worst for this one as those evil little pod people, sorry, I mean 'children', can make you feel very selfish if their needs don't come first. Naturally when sprogs are babies, you shouldn't leave them with a dirty nappy and no food while you go get your nails done. I hear that sort of thing is frowned upon. But you should definitely come to an arrangement with the gentleman who provided 23 of those chromosomes that make up your little bundle of joy so that you can both enjoy at least one evening a month away from the demands of the petite dictator. And if you can rope a willing relative into looking after Junior so you can both escape together, so much the better.

Adopt a similar policy with regards to housework. Paid work is harder to get selfish about (unless you're the boss and can delegate things) but you can certainly ensure an equitable division of labour at home. But don't be rigid about it. If you love ironing but hate hoovering and your partner loves hoovering but hates ironing, you have the makings of a beautiful partnership. If you both hate doing everything, spend Junior's college fund on a cleaner. It's not selfish, it's sensible.

> ### Defining idea...
>
> 'I am a greedy, selfish bastard. I want the fact that I existed to mean something.'
> HARRY CHAPIN, *the musician and humanitarian philanthropist.*

136. Cure yourself of the disease to please

Make 'just say no' your new mantra.

A huge amount of stress is caused by the inability to say 'no'. Result? We end up running to other people's agendas.

This is traditionally seen as a female problem. But I'm not so sure. On Saturday night I had dinner with a male friend who told me that for the first time in his ten-year marriage, he'd managed to get his wife to agree to going on holiday on their own without inviting at least two other families. Extreme? Yes. But I know many men whose entire domestic life is run to their partner's agenda and who feel that somehow they're being a bad dad or husband if they say no to the relentless socialising, child-centred activities and DIY set up for them by their driven other halves. I also know men who don't want to stay at work until 8.30 most nights, or go to the pub for an hour on the way home, but can't say no to the pervading culture of their workplace.

Now and then, all of us have to do things that don't benefit us much in order to feel that we're pulling our weight. But if it's a daily occurrence then we're going to get run down and ill. Worse, we're going to get seriously fed up.

Try this quiz. Answer True or False to each of these questions:

I can't relax until I finish all the things I have to do   T/F

If I wasn't doing favours for other people most days, I wouldn't think
much of myself   T/F

I seldom say no to a work colleague or family member who asks a favour
of me   T/F

I often find myself changing my own plans or working day to fit in with
other people's wants   T/F

I rarely, if ever, feel comfortable with what I've accomplished   T/F

I often feel I'm so exhausted that I don't have time for my own interests   T/F

I feel guilty relaxing   T/F

I find myself saying 'yes' to others when inside a voice is saying 'no, no, no'   T/F

I honestly believe that if I stop doing things for others they'd think less of me   T/F

I find it hard to ask other people to do things for me   T/F

> **Here's an idea for you...**
>
> If you just can't say no, try an intermediate stage. Next time some asks you to do something, say: 'I'm not sure, let me get back to you.' The breather is often enough to stiffen your resolve.

Add up the number of Ts you scored. If your score is between 7 and 10, you think it more important to please others than please yourself. If it's between 4 and 6, you should be careful. You're on the slippery slope to terminal niceness. If your score is 3 or less, you're good at saying no and keep your own needs in balance with others.

Aim for a score of under 3. Here are some ways to get there.

1. List your top 10 'no's', the things you want to eliminate from your life. Start each sentence 'I will no longer…'

2. Think of situations where you need to say no to improve your life. Imagine yourself in these situations saying no. Practise the exercise in front of a mirror if necessary. (This is brilliant. I tried it myself and the experience of actually saying no out loud, albeit in private, makes it much easier in real-life situations.)

> **Defining idea...**
>
> 'I cannot give you the formula for success, but I can give you the formula for failure, which is: Try to please everybody.'
> HERBERT BAYARD SWAPE, *journalist*

3. Whenever you're asked to do anything, ask yourself: 'Do I really want to do this?' rather than 'Should I do this?' If the answer is no, then let someone else pick up the baton.

137. Take the stress out of your love life

Too stressed to talk? Remember, divorce is pretty stressful too.

Stress proof your relationship and everything else will fall into place – eventually.

There is absolutely no point in reading on until you put this idea to improve your relationship into action: it is the *sine qua non* of relationships. Once a week minimum, you and your partner have a 'date' where you focus completely on each other and nothing else. It may only be for a few hours. It doesn't have to involve a lot of money. You don't even have to go out – although I strongly recommend it. (Couples who spend too much time sloping around the same small space tend to lose that loving feeling.) Seeing your love in a new environment helps keep love alive, even if it's only your local park. But whatever you do, you must spend at least a couple of hours a week talking to each other or you are taking a mighty big gamble with your love.

If you want something – ask for it
Second guessing what your partner thinks or feels is such a waste of time. You're nearly always wrong, and your assumptions lead to fights. You might assume your partner can see that you spending five hours a night on housework is unfair. On the other hand you might assume your partner can see

Here's an idea for you...

Get into bed. Whichever one is feeling emotionally stronger should 'spoon' around the other. Hold your hands entwined resting on the recipient's heart. Regularise your breathing so you exhale and inhale at the same time. Lie there and breathe in unison.

that sex once a month isn't going to win you any prizes in a 'red-hot couple of the year' competition. (The two may well be related, by the way.) However, you could well be assuming wrong. Do the work yourself first. Work out what you want to make you happy. Then let your partner know. It might end up a compromise, but you've at least got a chance of getting it this way.

Keep surprising each other

No, not with the news of your affair with Geoff in accounts. To recreate the passion of your first romance, you have to see each other through new eyes. To do that you have to be passionate, engaged in your life, interested in the world. If you're not fascinated by your life, you can hardly expect anyone else to be. And remember the power of spontaneity. Plan to be spontaneous. Take it in turns to surprise each other, even if it's only with a curry – although the occasional weekend in Paris would be better.

Constantly plan and dream

A relationship that doesn't move forward will die. You have to dream big. Whether it's planning your next holiday, your fantasy house, another child, a downsize to the country. Not all these plans have to come to fruition, but you have to build common dreams and turn some of them into goals that you're working towards as a team.

Have sex

Call me old-fashioned, but I think this is important. Lots of couples don't of course, but I would say that unless you're both absolutely happy with this (are you sure? See first item on this list), then you're sitting on a potentially huge stressor.

Defining idea…

'My wife and I were happy for twenty years. Then we met.'
RODNEY DANGERFIELD, *American comedian*

Give your lover what they need to feel loved

This can melt away stress in a relationship. Find out what your partner needs to feel loved – meals out, compliments, sex, praise in front of your friends, jammy dodgers on demand. Ask. Then give it. Often. There is absolutely no use in you saying you love your partner, or showing them that you love them *in your way*, if they don't feel loved at the end of it. When your home life is stressed, ask your partner 'Do you feel loved?' And if the answer's no, do something about it.

138. Stop acting on impulse

Focus, concentration, sticking to what you've started. That will cut your stress levels instantly.

Yes, yes, yes. But how?

Some days I run around like a frantic hen. Charging to work, rushing home early to spend time with the kids, doing chores, doing research, phoning my mother. I react to events and whatever crisis looms next. I don't do anything properly. I don't do some things at all.

When I get to bed I remember the stuff that I didn't get round to and feel disappointed and frustrated with myself. When that happens it's time to go back to basics and use this idea. It helps you finish what you start and makes you feel on top of your life. Besides helping you become more focused, it also helps you curb your impulse to wander off and do other stuff rather than the one task that you have set yourself. It will show up the numerous times you have just got started on a project when it suddenly seems terribly important to water the plants, call your mum or make a nice cup of tea. But now you will be prepared and will observe your impulses as just that – impulses. And you will stay put with a wise 'Oh there I go, looking for ways to waste time again.'

Besides training you to focus and resist the impulse to waste time, this idea will achieve two further objectives: (1) It will build your self-esteem by fostering your sense of yourself as a person who follows through on their word. (2) It will clear your life of a ton of annoying little irritations that have been stopping you mentally from moving on.

> **Here's an idea for you...**
>
> Making a promise to yourself every night and keeping it the next day is the route to mental toughness. Every time you keep a promise to yourself, stick some loose change in a jar. It's a good visual record of your growing focus and strength – and, of course, you get to spend the cash at the end of it.

Step 1   Before you go to bed tonight, think of something you want to achieve tomorrow. Keep it really small and simple. It doesn't matter what it is, but you have to do it. Make it something restful – you're going to read a chapter of a favourite novel. Make it useful – you're going to clean the cutlery drawer. Make it worthy – you're going to take a multivitamin. Take this promise extremely seriously. Promise yourself you'll do it – and follow through. If you don't, no excuses. You've failed. But you're aiming too high. Make your next promise easier to achieve.

Step 2   Make a promise to yourself every evening for a week. And follow through.

Step 3   OK, now you're going to make a list of some tasks that you need to undertake but have been putting off. You will need seven, one for every day of the week. Some ideas: starting on your tax return; making a dental appointment; cancelling the gym membership you never use; sorting out your wardrobe; cleaning out the inside of the car; tackling just one pile from the many piles on your desk; grooming the dog; making a start on the garage.

Defining idea...

'He who every morning plans the transactions of the day and follows out that plan, carries a thread that will guide him through the maze of the most busy life. But where no plan is laid, where the disposal of time is surrendered merely to the chance of incidence, chaos will soon reign.'
VICTOR HUGO

Step 4 Write these down and keep them by your bed. Each night for the next week, pick one and promise yourself you'll do it tomorrow.

Step 5 Write another list. This time put on it things that are worrying you and driving you mad. Suggestions: discover if your pension plan will pay out enough for you to live on; write a letter to that friend you're upset with; paint the kitchen. Put on the list everything that is driving you nuts. Then pick one and break it down into manageable steps. Promise yourself to do the first of these steps tomorrow, and every day from now on, make a promise to take another step forward. Don't let impulse drive you off course.

This is an exercise in mental toughness. Making promises to yourself that you never keep brings you down and, over time, breaks your heart. But by breaking difficult tasks down into manageable chunks and building the strength of character to follow through and get them out the way, you take a huge step forward in reducing stress in your life.

Warning: don't make more than two or three promises a day. Keep it simple.

139. Tame your to-do list

The problem with to-do lists is that it takes seconds to scribble yet another entry – and a whole lot longer to get round to doing it.

The essential thing to remember is that you actually need to schedule the time to do your to-do list or else it's just another source of stress.

What revolutionised the to-do list for me was the idea of work days, buffer days and free days. In my experience, everything you ever need to do falls into one of these three categories. *Work days* – self-explanatory. *Free days* – fun days and these should be a complete break from work. These are for rest and recreation, and if you don't think there is time for this, remember recreation is just that – the time to recreate, and what you're recreating is yourself. If you don't have at least one of these a week you're going to end up stressed out and useless. *Buffer days* – these are so-called because they act as a buffer against stress. These are the days you get on top of all those little things that need to get done – filing receipts, updating your CV. These are never as important as other things – until your tax return is due tomorrow or you lose your job. Buffer days are those times when you truly stress proof your life in advance.

Step 1 Prepare the master list. You need a notebook in which you write down everything that needs doing – now or in the future, important or unimportant. I know a fashion editor who has her special book of lists, a beautiful leather one

Here's an idea for you...

When you complete an item on your to-do list, instead of putting a line through it, mark it through with a colourful highlighter pen. This raises your spirits and makes you feel you've achieved more. The more colour on the page, the more you've got through.

in which she writes lists for everything – presents, places she wants to visit, books that she wants to read – as well as all the humdrum stuff. I like her book. It turns the to-do list into a creative act. If the idea appeals to you, I urge you to purchase one.

Step 2   OK, now you have your list, divide it into two. You can do this with two different coloured marker pens. One half will be stuff you have to do (insuring the car, buying your son a birthday present, finishing a work project), the other half will be the wish list, stuff you'd like to do in an ideal world (sorting out your photos, clearing out the cupboard you haven't looked into since 1987).

Step 3   Now get your calendar. You can use your diary, but a calendar works better. I like a big one with a month on a page. Mark out work days, buffer days and free days. Decide on the top five things on your 'must-do' list – some of these will be work, some will be buffer. Schedule these in on your calendar at the next appropriate session. I recommend colour coding. You could use three different colours of pen for the different kinds of days – but I use three different coloured mini post-it notes, work, buffer and free, putting a task down on a separate post-it note and sticking it on the appropriate day. The reason for the multi-coloured stuff is that you can see at a glance when your life is getting out of balance. It gives you an immediate visual reference of where you're spending your time.

Step 4 Look at your wish list. Pick three things on it. These will probably fall into buffer or free days. If you look forward to it with unalloyed pleasure, it's for a free day. If there is any element of duty whatsoever, it's a buffer. Scribble these on appropriate colour-coded post-it notes and bang

Defining idea...

'My happiness is not the means to any end. It is the end.'
AYN RAND, *author*

them on the calendar. Every evening rip off the post-it notes for the next day and transfer them to your diary, sling 'em in the bin when you've completed them (which is very satisfying). And if you don't get something completed, take it home and find another slot for it on your calendar. If you don't use post-it notes, just scribble the items for the next day in your diary each evening, or transfer them to your PDA.

What have you achieved besides a multicoloured calendar bristling with post-it notes? A lot. You have prioritised your time and you've allocated all the urgent things a time slot. You've also prioritised some of the non-urgent ones, thus achieving the mythical work–life balance.

140. Perfect moments

The ability to create perfect moments is possibly the most valuable life skill you'll ever learn.

It's the only guarantee that tomorrow will be less stressed than today.

We humans are rubbish at predicting what will make us happy. We work our butts off to get the 'right' job. We scrimp and save for the big house and flash car. We think surely parenthood will make us really, really happy – and it does for a few years, until our adorable toddlers grow into worrisome teens. Human happiness is the holy grail, but no one yet has found a formula for it.

Or have they? In the last few years, neuroscientists have moved their attention from what's going wrong in the brains of depressed people, to exploring what's going right in the brains of happy people. And for the most part, it's quite simple.

Happy people don't get so busy stressing about building a 'perfect' tomorrow that they forget to enjoy this 'perfect' today.

It turns out that the surest, indeed, the *only* predictor of how happy you are going to be in the future is how good you are at being happy today. If you want to know if you are going to be stressed out tomorrow, ask yourself what are you doing to diminish your stress today? And if the answer's nothing, don't hold your breath. You won't be that calm and serene person you long to be any time soon.

Here's an idea for you...

Invest in an old-fashioned teasmade. Waking up to a cup of tea in bed can get the day off to a good start for little effort on your part.

We can plan the perfect wedding, perfect party, perfect marriage, perfect career. But we have absolutely no idea if when we get 'there', a perfect 'anything' is going to be delivered. The only thing we can do is guarantee that today at least we will have a perfect moment – a moment of no stress where we pursue pure joy.

What is a perfect moment for you? I can't tell. For me it is whatever helps trigger me to remember that unknown, unquantifiable, profoundly peaceful part of myself. Let's call it 'the spirit'. We could call it 'Joe' but it lacks that certain mystical something that I'm aiming for. Anyway. When I'm having a perfect moment, I'm absolutely happy, absolutely content. That doesn't mean everything is alright in my life, but it does mean that for this one moment, I've got enough to feel joyful.

Some people slip in to a perfect moment as easily as putting on an old coat. But me, I'm a pragmatist. I think if you want to have a perfect moment, you have to plan for it early before your day is hijacked. So I try to start each day with a perfect moment. All debris, mess and clutter is banished from my bedroom the night before. When I wake just about the first thing I see is a bunch of fresh cut flowers – big squashy pink peonies are a favourite. Before my eyes are quite open, I reach out and grab a book of poetry from my side table and I read for

Defining idea...

'Happiness not in another place, but this place...not for another hour, but this hour.'
WALT WHITMAN

five minutes. I choose poetry because it reminds me that life is a lot bigger than me and infinitely more interesting.

But your perfect moment might be snatched late at night, listening to jazz by candlelight when the family are asleep. Or it could be a glass of chilled wine as the sun slips beyond the horizon. You might best be able to access a perfect moment by running round your park or through practising yoga. Listening to music while you exercise often heightens the sensations of being in tune with your body and tips you into joy. Preparing, cooking, eating food can give perfect moments. Gardening is a good one. Sex is reliable. We all know the sensation of feeling 'bigger' than ourselves. All you have to do is give yourself the space to feel it more often – ideally, at least once a day.

But ultimately, only you know your own triggers. Write down a week's worth and plan for them. Schedule them in your diary. It obviously doesn't have to be the same activity every day and sometimes despite your best intentions, it all goes belly up. (I only get to read poetry when I'm not woken by the kids clamouring for cartoons and cereal.)

But planning for perfect moments means they are more likely to happen. Even if you don't believe now that striving for perfect moments will destress you, try it. At least you will be able to say 'Today, there were five minutes where I stopped and enjoyed life.' Enjoying life today is the only certainty you have of happiness and your best chance of being less stressed tomorrow.

141. Energy black spots transformed

Reframe your world. In even the most energy-draining situations, we can find a potential source of pep.

Some bits of the day just make us feel bad. Here's how to turn them around.

You hate getting up

Research has shown that pressing the snooze button doesn't actually make you less tired. An extra ten minutes – even an extra hour – doesn't refresh you. By getting up when you wake up, you reclaim time – and that is energising. Incapable of getting up? Instead of pressing the snooze button, try stretching. Think of a cat. Many animals have a good stretch before they rise to get their muscles stretched and warmed up and get oxygen into their blood stream. It will work for you too.

You hate your commute

See your commute as a chance to really get moving. There is nearly always some way you can make your commute to work more active. Walk to work. Or get off a stop early and walk a little of the way to work. Or walk up the escalator. Or walk up some of the stairs to your office. This will underline to your psyche that you are an active person, pursuing your vision of your future, energetically and dynamically. Play your own music on the way to work, if you don't already do so.

Here's an idea for you...

Eschew the lie-in. research shows that catching up on sleep at the weekend knocks out your body clock and will lead to you being even more tired in the following week. As far as possible, go to bed and rise at the same time each day – it makes you less tired in the long run.

You hate the way your working day disappears and you feel you've achieved nothing

Use your lunch hour productively. Too many of us, even if we take a break from our desk, don't differentiate our lunch hour from the rest of the day when we're a wage slave. This hour is *your* hour. Make it a habit to do two things for yourself every lunch hour that will boost your energy – one you don't want to do, but will make your life easier, and one you do want to do, that will cheer you up.

Make a phone call you're dreading, pay a bill, draft your CV – these are dull, but getting them off your list will make you feel better. Plan your next holiday, eat some chocolate, go for a walk – these are energising, and just for you. Reclaiming your lunch hour will mean every day has something positive in it.

You hate waiting

All those moments hanging around waiting at the check out, waiting for the train, or for the kettle to boil, or for the lift, can be put to use. Run over your goals and plans for the day. Think of the next challenge (whether that's a difficult phone call, exercising or facing someone you're not keen on). Run through the scene in your mind, imagining it going as well as possible and how you'll feel afterwards. 'Dead time' is usually filled with fantasies – often negative fantasies of all that could go wrong. Instead, start having positive fantasies that boost your confidence and energy. Or do some pelvic floor exercises – a toned pelvic floor means better orgasms for both sexes.

You hate Barbie

Kids sap our energy by demanding attention, usually when we don't want to give it. The single best piece of advice is to give them that attention wholeheartedly. Becoming engaged in what children are interested in can be remarkably relaxing to the adult brain. Instead of begging for a couple of minutes to yourself to read the paper, help your child dress Barbie, complete their jigsaw or win at their computer game when they want you to do it. You'll find that two minutes of your attention will energise you and mean they are satisfied enough to leave you alone. The point is that if you have children you do have to spend time looking after them. So, personally, finding a way to make it relaxing and energising even when I'm overworked and stressed out really helps. When you're bathing the children, feeding them or dressing them, try to sink into their world, their level of interest, rather than having your mind racing with what's next on your agenda.

> *Defining idea...*
>
> 'Regret is an appalling waste of energy. You can't build on it; it's only good for wallowing in.'
> KATHERINE MANSFIELD, *writer*

You hate hangovers

Nights out with friends are relaxing and essential, but have you noticed how rubbish you often feel the next day? A meal out, lots of booze, smoky atmospheres – no wonder. Suggest you see your friends in a different environment – a movie, a walk, a sauna or a night in a sushi bar (go easy on the sake) should make you feel better the next day rather than worse. If your friends like the pub and that's it, reduce your alcohol intake to one drink every second round.

465

142. Leave the office on time

Reduce interruptions. Reclaim your evenings.

Take control. Don't let your working day be hijacked by others. The secret is to have your goals clear in your mind.

Think weekly, then daily

Don't be a slave to a daily 'to-do' list. See the big picture. On Monday morning lose the sinking 'I've got so much to do' sensation. Instead, think 'What are my goals for this week?' Decide what you want to have done by Friday and then break each goal into smaller tasks that have to be undertaken to achieve all you want by Friday. Slot these tasks in throughout your week. This helps you prioritise so that the tricky and difficult things, or tasks that depend on other people's input, don't sink to the back of your consciousness. It also means you are giving attention to all that you have to do and not spending too much time on one task at the beginning of the week.

Concentrate on three or four items on your 'to-do' list at once. You won't be overwhelmed.

Work with your energy cycles

Some of us operate better in the morning, some in the late afternoon. If your job demands creativity, block out your most creative periods so that you can concentrate on your projects. Don't allow them to be impinged upon by meetings and phone calls that could be done anytime.

Make the phone call you're dreading Right now. That call that saps your energy all day. Just do it.

Have meetings in the morning People are frisky. They want to whizz through stuff and get on with their day. Morning meetings go much faster than those scheduled in the afternoon.

> *Here's an idea for you...*
>
> Create a 'virtual you' if you're getting stressed out in the office by the demands of others. When you're an administrative lynchpin, set up a shared file where people can go to find the information or resources they'd usually get from you.

Check emails three times a day First thing in the morning, just after lunch and just before you leave are ideal times. Keeping to this discipline means that you don't use email as a distraction.

Limit phone calls Talk to other people when it suits you, not them. In my working life I receive around twenty phone calls a day. Answer machines don't help me personally – the call-back list is another chore. This is how I turned it around. The most time-effective way of using the phone is to limit your calls as you do your emails – to three times a day. Make a list of calls you have to make that day. Call first thing. If someone isn't there, leave a message and unless you have to talk to them urgently, ask them to call you back at your next 'phone period'. Just before lunch is good. That means neither of you will linger over the call. Your other 'phone time' should be around 4.30 p.m. for the same reason. Of course, you can't limit phone calls completely to these times but most of us have some control over incoming calls. I don't have a secretary any more to screen calls, but I very politely say 'Sorry, I'm in the middle of something.' I tell the caller when I'll be free and most people offer to call me back then, saving me the hassle of calling them. No one minds that if their call isn't urgent. The

Defining idea...

'Take a note of the balls you're juggling. As you keep your work, health, family, friends and spirit in the air, remember that work is a rubber ball and will bounce back if you drop it. All the rest are made of glass; drop one of them and it will be irrevocably scuffed, tarnished or even smashed.'
JON BRIGGS, *voice-over supremo*

point of all of this is to keep phone calls shorter by putting them in the context of a busy working day. Social chat is important and nice but most of us spend too much time on it. Time restrictions stop us rambling on. And this goes for personal calls too. Check your watch as soon a friend calls. Give yourself five minutes maximum. Or better still save personal calls as a treat for a hardworking morning.

143. Speed parenting – better than stressed parenting

Children pick up adult stress like a dry sponge soaks up water. When you're happy, they're happy. And when you're stressed? Yep, you got it. That's when you need focused parental skills.

Calm parents usually means calm kids, but when you're frazzled, they reflect it and have a horrible tendency to get bad tempered, argumentative, clingy and sick.

That's because stress is contagious. You get stressed, your kids get tetchy – at best. At worst, they get ill. Most parents know the rule of 'reverse serendipity' that guarantees it's on the days when your car gets broken into and your job depends on you delivering a fabulous (and as yet unprepared) presentation that your youngest will throw a wobbly and hide under his bed refusing to go to school because he's dying.

It's not mere coincidence. Research shows that even when they're tiny, children pick up on their stressed parents' frowns, tense jaws, averted eyes and other physical signs of stress. In turn, they cry or become withdrawn.

Here's an idea for you...

Next time you talk to a child get on their level, eye to eye. They respond better. Kneel when they're toddlers. Stand on a stool when they're teenagers.

Up to the age of about ten, children think their parents' stress is their fault. After that, they're less egocentric and recognise that outside factors cause it, but still, they can feel it's their responsibility to sort out the problem for mum or dad. Parents often applaud this 'caretaker role' that children take on because they see it as a sign that their children are growing up responsible and caring. But since your twelve year old can't possibly stop your boss firing you or your mother's less than endearing habit of reeling around Sainsbury's drunk at 3 p.m., his efforts to lighten your load, although laudable, will only be a partial success. Children discover that their efforts aren't making you happy and that can transfer into adult feelings of guilt and low self-esteem.

Short-term answer

Explain that you're stressed out, tell them why, but also show them that you're working out a way to handle it. Your competence in the face of a stressful day is an invaluable lesson for later life. Saying 'I'm stressed, here's what I'm doing about it', and giving them a timescale of when they can expect you to be back to normal goes a long way to reassuring them.

And on those days when it's all going pear-shaped, your kids are being unbearable and not letting you get on with what you have to do, then the best advice is to give them what they want – your time. This piece of advice was taught to me by a grandmother and I've been stunned at how well it works. Pleading for an hour of peace won't work, but ten minutes of concentrating on them – a quick game, a chat, a cuddle and a story – calms them down and they tend to wander off and let you alone.

Defining idea...

'There is no way to be a perfect parent, but thousands of ways of being a great one.'
ANON.

Long-term solution

Besides demonstrating your competence in handling stress, the other side of stress proofing your kids is to make them feel secure. The more secure your child is, the better he'll be able to handle stress – even the stress that's caused by you. And the better he'll be at handling stress for the rest of his life.

More than all the myriad advice I've had on childcare from child behavioural experts, the most useful was from a taxi-driver who told me that since his three children were born he'd always made a point during the working week of spending ten minutes a day with each one of them. Ten minutes a day sounds meagre but it's enough – if you actually do it. It's better to be realistic and consistent than to aim for an hour and achieve it only once a week. Even worse is to keep interrupting your time together to take a call from the office. Chat, wash their dolly's hair, read a story (hint: older children still like being read to) – but treat that ten minutes as sacred.

144. Me, myself and I

Don't compare or compete with anyone but yourself. You're not a carbon copy of anyone — not even your identical twin, if you have one.

Each person on the planet is unique and we should celebrate that uniqueness by not constantly trying to measure up to somebody else.

The worst people for comparing themselves to others are overachievers. Instead of enjoying the successes and blessings they have had, they're too busy looking at the next target and this mindless dash to some imaginary finishing line that never comes. Will they be happy being the next Richard Branson? Hell, no! They don't want to be the 'next' anybody – they want to be the original, the one that people quote in business or reference books; the epitome of success.

The problem with being that sort of a person is that when life throws you a curve ball, you can be hit a lot harder than you'd expect. Redundancies happen, the business doesn't do as well as you thought it would, your loved one leaves and your supposedly 'perfect' marriage falls apart. Any manner of unexpected and unwelcome changes can happen. If you've spent your life living up to someone else's idea of success, it can be a terrible blow when that is taken away from you.

I know someone who always brings up the subject of salaries whenever we meet. She seems to want to confirm, every time we meet, that she is earning more than any of our other friends. Now I know from where this stems; she had a very unhappy childhood whereby she was the poorest kid in school and she was often mocked for having a modest home and never having the latest things. Instead of rising above the psychological wounds of her childhood, she is attempting to repair them by achieving material success and then by comparing herself to her peer group to satisfy herself that she is not the 'poor kid' any more. For those in our circle who don't know her very well, her questions are starting to grate and they now avoid her because it feels like she's lording it over them. This is very sad as it is the exact opposite to her desired outcome – acceptance.

We all have benchmarks by which we measure success. It may be money, it may be how handsome and charming our lovers are or by how good we look. Since all of these things have no intrinsic value in themselves, we only learn of their value through comparison. I once had the unenviable task of choosing between

Here's an idea for you...

Channel your future self. This is an exercise you can do simply for fun. Relax your body and close your eyes for a minute, imagine that you're about 65 years old and about to retire (if you are that age then take it another 20 years forward). Then write down some questions about your life that you'd like answered by your future self. A typical question might be 'Did I live abroad at all?' and then try to see your future self answering that question for you. You don't have to put much store by it but it does open you up to the way you would like things to pan out.

Defining idea...

'Envy consists in seeing things never in themselves, but only in their relations. If you desire glory, you may envy Napoleon, but Napoleon envied Caesar, Caesar envied Alexander, and Alexander, I daresay, envied Hercules, who never existed.'
BERTRAND RUSSELL, *philosopher and Nobel Laureate*

two men. Both were gorgeous, both rich and both very clever. In the end I chose neither. Why? Because when I thought about them, I thought about the fact that they were rich and handsome rather than that I really loved them. I intuitively knew that those value judgements would go out the window when I met the right guy. I'd no longer be thinking whether my guy would impress my friends but whether I enjoyed his company and whether he made me laugh.

In the same way, you should measure your success not by whether it meets the criteria of others or society but by whether you're happy with it. Happiness for you could be a small doughnut shop in a busy part of town while for the guy down the road it may be a baked goods empire, providing doughnuts to supermarkets across the world. You be the judge.

145. Guilt be gone

Guilt can be one of the most useless emotions out there and the sooner you can excise it from your life, the better.

Guilt exists for one purpose only, to flag up when we've done something wrong that we should feel bad about. It is our moral centre kicking us in the backside for perceived wrong-doing. It is our conscience pricking us to make amends. It exists to ensure we're nicer people who don't treat others in a way that would be considered cruel or hurtful. However, there is another type of guilt that has nothing to do with morality or right and wrong. It's a false guilt that is the result of your inability to forgive yourself for not doing what's expected of you. Do not succumb to that second sort of guilt.

Do you often do things out of a need to avoid feeling guilty? Make phone calls, maintain friendships with people you don't really like, sign up to make charity donations you can't really afford, agree to do things for the Parent Teacher Association because you don't want to seen as not pulling your weight? Such a widespread misuse of guilt has to be halted. We need to appreciate the true reasons for guilt and, as long as you're not a felon, you really don't need to feel half as much guilt as you probably do.

The best way out of having guilt as your motivating factor in doing things is to learn the liberating effect of just saying 'no'. Most children go through a phase,

Here's an idea for you...

Excise the word 'sorry' from your phone conversations for a week. You won't be able to do it because it is actually impossible. Try it and you'll see. Imagine what a conversation without 'sorry' sounds like: 'I couldn't come to your wedding. I hope you had a good time.' Saying that will sound to your ears as if you're calling the mother of the bride a crack ho. The conditioning is very, very strong and you'll be hard pressed not to say the 's' word but try anyway and may the force be with you.

at around the age of two, where they will start yelling 'NO!' in response to just about everything. That's why they call it 'the terrible twos' but psychologists reckon we all go through this phase as this is the first time we start to see ourselves as separate individuals and so we experiment with asserting an independent will. If you are to effectively get rid of guilt, you'll have to revert to this stage for a bit. You also need to experiment to find out what is your true will and what has simply been imposed upon you through an attempt to avoid guilt.

The next time someone asks you to do something, say 'let me check and get back to you'. That way you're buying time to consider whether you do actually want to do it. We often respond to things hurriedly, in a fluster, and then have to cancel afterwards – causing us more guilt for having let someone down. Even if you don't cancel it, having to do something because you couldn't think of a reason/excuse on the spot to say 'no' will only leave you feeling resentful and 'put upon' later. So buy yourself that time to respond.

Before you start to feel too guilty about anything, ask yourself whether you could have helped what happened. If you could have, well, it's too late now, it's in the past. All you can do is offer a heartfelt apology and find a way to make amends. Wringing your hands about it won't transport you back to that time when you could have done things differently. So it's now time to move forward.

We are often a lot more compassionate toward the guilty feelings of others than those of our own. If a friend feels guilty for letting down a member of her family, we comfort her and tell her to stop beating herself up about it. No such nice words of solace for our own selves. The next time you feel unduly bad about something, think about what you'd say if a friend was in that position. Would you hate her for not being able to do x, y or z? Of course not! So give yourself the same break.

Defining idea...

'Guilt: the gift that keeps on giving.'
ERMA BOMBECK, *American humorist and columnist*

146. The perfection trap

Your need to 'get it perfect' isn't about perfection. It's about staying in control. And staying in control is not a virtue if it's making you miserable.

I have a friend who ran her first marathon. And she did run the whole way, never once slowing down to a walk. She felt fabulous for about six hours afterwards – she deserved to. Then before she'd even had her evening meal, the self-doubt began – she should have run faster, pushed herself more, achieved a better time. All she'd wanted beforehand was to complete the race but now that she had, she couldn't stop beating herself up for not doing it 'better'.

When she told me this story, I sat dumbstruck by her perfectionism. She looks better than me, earns more than me, achieves more than me, but the price for her success is a small voice inside telling her endlessly that she's just not good enough. Does it have to be that way? I think perfectionists can achieve just as much if they let that voice go for good. They tend to think not. They know their perfectionism is neurotic but they cling to it because they think they are lazy and that without the voice they would just give up and slope around the house in old tracksuits not brushing their teeth.

This is unlikely. However, only you can learn to ignore the little voice. What I do know is that if you don't ignore it, you'll never be free of stress. Often that little voice belongs to someone we know, often someone who brought us up, who has no idea of the complexity of our world. In their world, with one role to fulfil it was easy to do it perfectly. In the world we live in, chocka with choice, where we can fulfil so many roles, there's no way we can do all of it perfectly. And even if you did, you still wouldn't be happy. Give it up!

> **Here's an idea for you...**
>
> Restrict your 'to-do' list to seven items only. Less a 'to-do' list than an 'I absolutely have to do' list. Chinese medics say that any more and you get stressed out by the sheer volume and fed up when you don't complete them.

- Ration your perfectionist behaviour. You probably won't ever lose it completely. However, you can limit it. One woman I know whose energy levels had plummeted finally made the connection between her habit of staying up late reading and answering emails and her inability to get to sleep (duh!). So now she allows herself two nights a week to check emails late. Go through your own life working out where you can cut down or cut out perfectionist habits.

- Lose your fear of the person who made you this way. Even if you were always the sort of kid who liked to colour code your books, no one becomes a perfectionist unaided. Someone somewhere had high expectations of you. Accept something pretty basic: if you haven't earned their unconditional approval by now, you probably never will. Let it go. And if you can't, get therapy.

Defining idea...

'The question should be, is it worth trying to do, not can it be done.'
ALLARD LOWENSTEIN, *political activist*

- Walk barefoot in the park. Remember Jane Fonda begging Robert Redford to stop being such a stuffed shirt and to walk barefoot in Central Park. You could try the same – just to see if you like it. You probably won't – but it might teach you something valuable: that nobody cares but you. Whatever your version of mad devil-may-care spontaneity – asking friends to dinner and ordering a takeaway curry, or letting your roots show, or putting on a few kilos, or refusing to take the kids swimming on Sunday morning because you simply can't be fagged – go on: *do it*. The kids will not implode with disappointment. The world will not fall apart. Slip up and nothing happens.

No one cares if you're perfect but you (and the person who made you this way, see above, but we've dealt with them already).

147. Blitz your home in a weekend

Decluttering. Space clearing. Majorly destressing.

Get rid of your clutter and you're free to redefine yourself. Life becomes a lot simpler.

Everything I own fits pretty neatly into the average living room – and that includes my car. I started decluttering about ten years ago, and I haven't stopped since. It's addictive, it's life affirming. Nothing makes you feel so serene and in control of your life as chucking out stuff you don't need.

Smug? You bet. Life wasn't always this way. For all of my twenties and most of my thirties I had all the furniture, plants, ornaments, designer clothes and bad taste costume jewellery you'd expect of someone who reached her majority in the 80s. Then in the early 90s I thought I'd write about this new gimmick I'd heard rumours about – feng shui (remember that!). And that's how I ended up inviting space clearer Karen Kingston into my less than fragrant home. She told me to clear out the wardrobe, clean out the junk under my bed and get rid of my books – 'let new knowledge in'. Then the magic started to happen.

Life picked up a pace. In the three years following my meeting with Karen, I moved out of the home I'd lived in for years, travelled extensively and reorganised my working life so I earned enough from working half the hours.

Here's an idea for you...

Try the 'one in, one out' rule. For instance, if you buy a new pair of shoes, then you must get rid of an existing pair. An added bonus is that this system protects you against impulse purchases of stuff you're not really fussed about as you have to focus your mind on what you'll chuck out when you get home.

My job is to research and write about what is called self-help or 'mind, body, spirit'. I've done it all from meditation to colonic irrigation. But nothing transformed my life like decluttering or to give it its esoteric name, space clearing.

Chuck it out, lose the guilt

How does it work? Most of us live among piles of ancient magazines, defunct utensils, clothes that neither fit nor suit us. The Chinese believe that all these unlovely, unwanted things lying about haphazardly block the flow of energy – the chi – in our homes. My theory is that by losing them, we lose a ton of guilt – guilt that we'll never fit into those hellishly expensive designer jeans again, guilt that we spent all that money on skis when we only go skiing once a decade, guilt that we never cook those fabulous dinners in those two dozen cookbooks. You get my point. Just about everything in your home probably engenders some sort of guilt. Cut your belongings by 90% and you do the same to your guilt.

The big clear up

'Useful or beautiful, useful or beautiful' – that's the mantra. If any single object doesn't fulfil one of these criteria, bin it. Cultivate ruthlessness. If you haven't worn it, used it or thought about it in a year, do you really need it?

Have three bin bags to hand as you work. One for stuff to chuck out, one for stuff to give to charity, one for things you want to clean or mend. Visit the charity shop as soon as you can – make it a priority. Give yourself two weeks to tackle the 'mend or clean' bag.

Something neither useful nor beautiful, but that you don't like to get rid of for sentimental reasons? Put it away for a year. Time out of sight makes it easier to get rid of.

Do this little but often. Try a couple of one-hour sessions per week. I operate the 40–20 rule: 40 minutes graft followed by 20 minutes sitting around feeling virtuous. You get better at decluttering. Soon it's second nature. Do two to three sessions a month.

Find a home for everything you own. You're allowed one drawer that acts as a glory hole for all the odd items.

> *Defining* idea...
>
> 'If more of us valued food and cheer and song above hoarded gold, it would be a merrier world.'
> J. R. R. TOLKIEN

148. Live the lottery life

Winning the lottery may seem like a pipe dream but leading the life you'd have if you won may not be.

The first principle in making anything come about is to know what you want. Most of us think we know what we'd do if we came into a lot of money but really we don't have a clue beyond 'pay off my mortgage' and 'go on holiday'. Fine, but then what? Think properly about what you'd do if money were no object. I once spoke to a London cabbie about this and I really agreed with what he said. 'I don't understand people who go back to their normal work place when they've won a lot of money,' he said. 'It shows a lack of imagination. I mean, if I had a lot of money, I'd be in the Med, painting on a beach.' The man was a philosopher and he'd thought long and hard about what would make him happy. He knew because he'd already been for a short holiday to play out his millionaire lifestyle and so he knew what his ultimate goal was.

Wealth is not about money. Wealth is about how much you love life and lead it to the full. I noticed, during a time that I had very little money, that a free trip to the park was as exciting for my niece and nephew as the expensive outings I used to give them when I had money. It wasn't the pricey shows they were craving, it was my time and attention. So don't concentrate on the money when you think about what your perfect 'lottery life' would be like.

What you need to figure out is what you'd do after the initial excitement had worn down. Would you return to your usual job? If so, you're very lucky as that means you do actually enjoy doing your job so much that you'd do it even if you didn't have to. Would you set up your own business? Or would you not work and live off the interest? If so, where would you live? How would you spend your day? Write out an itinerary of your perfect day, post-winning the lottery. Do you live by a beach; would you go for an early morning beach run? Who would you meet for lunch? At which restaurant?

> **Here's an idea for you...**
>
> Save up and visit a spa. A pampering visit to a place that smells nice and is geared toward your relaxation and enjoyment makes you feel like a million pounds sterling. If a spa isn't your scene then perhaps a round of golf somewhere? The point is that if you save up you can sometimes enjoy the same pleasures as the very rich and that will make you realise that the experience and not the bank balance is what really matters.

Daydreaming about a perfect life where money's no object is an enjoyable way to learn about yourself and what it is that you want out of life. You may surprise yourself. You may think you're a bit of a homebody but then you discover that you'd travel continuously if you could, in which case adventure is more important to you. Compare your choices with that of your spouse and see if you both agree. It can lead to some interesting discussions. In the case of one couple I know, it was such an exciting prospect that they sold their urban flat and moved to Cornwall to start living in the way they said they wanted to when thinking about their lottery lives. This idea can change your life, if you really put your heart and soul into it. You see, money isn't always what's holding you back, fear of taking a risk often is. Go wild and become one of life's millionaires.

149. Run away, run away

Or to give it the grown-up name, retreat.

Some time alone with your own thoughts is deeply relaxing.

This idea is about obliterating the low-grade noise pollution that is now the background for most of our lives. Stop for a moment and think just how much noise is generated in your home now compared to the home you grew up in. Televisions in every room. Telephones wherever you go. Music playing where it never played before (in the workplace, on the end of the phone while you wait).

This constant barrage of noise is stressful. Here is a three-step plan to give yourself a break.

Step 1: switch off the TV

TV will eat up your life. Some 9 year olds are watching up to four hours a day and these children perform less well on all measures of intelligence and achievement. TV does exactly the same thing to adults. It is such a very passive form of entertainment – it's been proven that just lying on the couch doing nothing burns off more calories than watching TV, presumably because without TV at least you're generating some thoughts in your head. Reclaim hours of your time by limiting TV to one or two favourite programmes a week. The rest of the time, switch it off. Listen to voice radio or music if you must have some noise.

Step 2: be silent

This is difficult to manage if you live with other people. But take a day off work and experiment with no noise. No TV, no radio, no phone – switch them off. Silence is golden, honest. Not talking gives you the chance to listen to what your inner voice is trying to say to you.

> **Here's an idea for you...**
>
> Listen to some Bach, Chopin or Beethoven prior to falling asleep. It's been shown that people who listen to classical music in bed fall asleep more easily and sleep better than people who watch TV or listen to other sorts of music.

Step 3: retreat

The best way of doing this is to go on a dedicated retreat – all sorts of institutions, religious or otherwise, run them. You can retreat and do yoga or dance or write or paint – or do absolutely nothing.

Of course, you don't have to leave home for that. It's much easier if you can escape but it's not impossible to put aside the hassles of everyday life and retreat in your own home. Clear away any clutter. Put away laptops, phones, diaries, PDAs – all work paraphernalia should be banished. Make your house as calm, restful and serene as possible.

Seven steps to retreating

1. Set aside at least 24 hours, preferably longer. Warn everyone you know that you don't want to be disturbed.

2. If you have family, do the best you can to escape. One way of doing it is to come back on your own a day early from a break, or leave a day after everyone else.

487

Defining idea...

'Silence propagates itself and the longer talk has been suspended, the more difficult it is to find anything to say.'
SAMUEL JOHNSON

3. Get in all the food you'll need. Plan ahead. Make it especially tasty and nutritious. You don't want to have to venture out for supplies.

4. Switch off the phone. Don't open your mail.

5. Don't speak.

6. This is your opportunity to go inwards and not only relax fully but work out what you really want to do with your life. For that reason keep the TV and radio off. Listen to music if you like but make it classical and not too emotional. Limit reading to an hour a day.

7. Write in a journal, paint or draw, invent recipes. Do anything creative.

Better yet, be very still. Lie on the couch with a blanket and your thoughts. Breathe. Stay silent for as long as you can.

Index

Page references in **bold** refer to
Here's an idea for you boxes

accountants, 294–6
accounting, 192–3, 320, 334
    annual stocktake of finances,
      366–8
    profit and loss sheets, 270–2,
      276–8
    see also banks
action, 11, **52**
    delivering on an idea, 118–19
    'depth activities', 390
    finances and, 377
    rehearsal and, 70–2
active listening, 146–8
advising, 164–6
Amazon, 305
ambition *see* aspiration
analysis checking, **180**
anger control, 97–9
appearance, personal, 82–4, **83**,
    144–5, 414
appraisals, 140–2, **238**
aromatherapy, 410–12
aspiration, **10,** 47, **151, 370**, 484–6
    building the dream, 396–7
    proactive behaviour and, 51–3
assertiveness *see* self-assertiveness
assessment centres, 234–6

bankruptcy, 314, 342–4
banks, **262**, 263, 268
    influencing, 264–6

loan and overdraft facility,
    282–4, 334–5
multiple accounts, 317, **396**
savings and, **358**
see also accounting
body language, **37**, 71–2, 94–6,
    216–18, 245
bonuses, 189
borrowing, 314
    clearing debt, **349**–50
    consolidated debt
    statements, 349
    consolidation loans, 342, 343,
      372–4, **373**
    credit card debt, 342, 343,
      346–7, 361
    credit management, 345–7
    interest rates and, 348–9
    loan and overdraft facility,
      282–4, 334–5
    severe debt, 351–3
    see also budgeting; finances;
      investors
brand value, 6–8
budgeting, **343**, 344, **482**
    business planning, 273–5
    practicalities of, 360–2, 369–71
    savings and, 357–9
    strategically, 191–3
    see also borrowing
bullies, 434–6
business angels, 285–7
business development
    organisations, 312–13

business plans, 270–2, 278, **286**,
    300–2

career planning, xvi–xvii
    adopting CEO mentality, 143–5
    appraisal interviews and,
      140–2
    attention to risk and return,
      115–17
    being on the organisation's
      wavelength, 173–5
    changing employers, 211–13
    creating a job, 123–5, **125**
    discretion and, **138**
    personal development plan,
      149–51
    pragmatic approach to, 106–8
    proactive approach to, 51–3
    see also self-employment
cash flow, 278, 309, 311, 316–18
Cazenove, 375
CEOs *see* Chief Executive Officers
    (CEOs)
change and innovation
    communication and
      persuasion, 76–8, 181, 211–13
    drivers of, 279–80
    reinventing businesses, 319–21
    resistance to, 222–4
    see also creativity
Chief Executive Officers (CEOs),
    130
    as role models, 143–5
    golden handshakes, 188–9

clichés, 33
colleagues, 46
commission and discounting, **156**
communication, **46**, 126
    achieving changes, 76–8, 181, 211–13
    with banks, 264–6
    factual information and, 85–7, **86**
    giving approval, 58–60
    giving incentives, 73–5
    group discussion rules, 235–6
    language and, 61–3, 71–2
    listening and, 79–81, 88–90, 101–2
    mind reading, 64–6, **65**, 67–9
    paying compliments, 49–50
    politeness, 97–9
    presentations, **34**, 161–3, 180, **232**
    producer/customer contact, 186
    rehearsing before acting, 70–2, **71**
    through appearance, 82–4
    see also negotiation
company policy, 115–17
    see also employers
company status, 288–90
competition, 303–5
computer programming, 35
concentration, **411**, 454–6
conceptual changes, 21–3, 28, 30–2
confidence *see* self-esteem
conflict management, **135**, 137–9, 222–4
    resolution, 89, 97–9, **98**
consolidated debt statements, **349**
consolidation loans, 342, 343, 372–4, **373**

consultants, 179–80
costs, 310
Courage CVs, **13**
creativity
    action and, 11, **52**
    challenges and, 9–10
    conceptual changes, 21–3, 28
    change of routine and, 30–2
    generic ideas and, 33–5
    new jobs and, 123–5
    role-play, 36–8
    sense of experience, 325–7
    speed of throughput and, 18–20
    see also change and innovation
credit card debt, 342, 343, 346–7, 361
credit crunch, 348–50
credit management, 345–7
crisis management, 401–3
Curricula Vitae (CVs), **13**, 205–7, 208–10
customer contact
    importance of, 185–7
    problem solving, 112–14
    questionnaires, 328–30
    terms, **317**
    testimonials, **186**
customers, identifying, 267–9

data gathering, 87
deadlines, **28**
Debord, Guy, 32
debt *see* borrowing
debt collectors, 352–3
decision-making, 319–20
    counting the consequences, 39–41

and follow-through, 118–20
    prioritising and, 131–3
    sharing, 171–2
    see also long-term thinking
delegation, 132, **159**, 391
design, 327
development plan, 149–51
diet, 399, 400, 422–4, **426**
differentiation, 280, 325–7
drivers of change, 279–80
drunkenness, 32

emotional intelligence (EQ), 4–5
    dealing with difficult people, 222–4
    perception, 21–3, 28
    mind reading, 64–6, **65**
employees *see* recruitment; sales force
employers
    changing, mid-career, 211–13
    loyalty of, 106–8
    staff contracts, 291–2, **292**
    see also company policy
employment seeking, 198–9
    company attitude to risk/return, 219–21
    CVs, **13**, 205–10
    proactively, 202–4, 246–8
    role-play and assessment centres, 234–6
    see also interviews; self-employment
enabling, 164–6, **172**, 183
energy levels, 425–30, 440–1, 463–5, 482
engagement *see* motivation
entrepreneurship, 279–81
    see also self-employment

Esser, Klaus, 188, 189
exercise, 390, 399
experience, creating sense of, 325–7

facilitators, 179–80
factual information, 85–7, **86**, 320
    financial literacy, **376**
family life
    children, 465, 469–71
    house blitzing, 481–3
    mothers and work, 203
    stress and intimacy, 451–3
    see also lifestyle
farmer sales people, 157
Ferguson, Penny, 147, **165**
finance departments, 186–7
finances
    attitudes to, 340–1, 348–50,
        378–80
    bankruptcy, 314, 342–4
    coaches, 342
    emergency funds, 397
    for the self-employed, 260,
        261–6, 268, 270–2, 273–5,
        274, 276–8, 282–4, 285–7,
        294–6, **304**, 309–11,
        314–15, 316–18, 334–6
    mortgages, **370**
    net worth, **367**
    optimum management, 375–7
    stocktake, 366–8, 376–7
    see also borrowing; budgeting
firing people, 176–8, **183**, 244–5
    and redundancy, 335, 336
Fleming, Alexander, 19
'fluidity' of labour, 107

Forster, Mark, *Get Everything Done*,
    392–4
funding see finances

gender-based behaviour, 38
Glouberman, Dr. Dina, 420
Gnesson, Simone, 342
graduate job candidates, 231–3
group discussion, 235–6
Grove, Andy, 18
guilt, 475–7, 482
    and martyrdom, 50

happiness
    maintaining, 45–7, 204, 460–2
    the right work for, xii–xvii,
        51–3, 106–8
headhunters, 177–8
heirarchy of needs, 299
Hewlett Packard, 120
honesty, **108**
Human Resources (HR), **177**
hunter sales people, 156–7
'hygiene factors', 299

In Search of Excellence, 7, **8**
Incomplete Manifesto for Growth, 30
induction programmes, 299
influence see communication
Innocent Juices, 326
innovation see change and
    innovation
insecurity, overcoming, 395–7
    dealing with bullies, 434–6
insurance, public liability, **259**
Intel, 18
interest rates, 348–9
internal politics, 108

internet
    as a distraction, 406
    as marketing route, 322
    information sources, 86, 267–8
    online personality tests, **25**
    personality creations, 38
interruptions, 404–6, 467–8
interviews, 208–10
    acknowledging own
        strengths/weaknesses,
        228–30, 237–9
    assessing company attitude
        to risk/return, 219–20, 221
    before a panel, 243–5
    body language, 216–18, 245
    questions and responses,
        208–9, 222–4, 225–7,
        231–3, 240–2, 246–8,
        249–51
    see also employment seeking
investors, 188, 261–3
    shareholders, 115–17, 188
    venture capitalists and
        business angels, 190, 285–7
    see also borrowing
invoicing, **304**

James, Anne Scott, 232
job purpose statement, 142
job seeking see employment
    seeking

knowledge, 298

language, 61–3, 71–2
leadership qualities, 167–9
    enabling others, 164–6, **172**,
        183

team management, 170–2
legal issues, 291–3
Leonard, Thomas, 48, 402
life assurance, 259
lifestyle, 384–5
    assessing and improving,
        386–8, 422–4, 460–2, 484–6
    attitude to work routine,
        413–5, 466–8
    creating order, 416–18, 478–80
    crisis management, 401–3
    dealing with interruptions,
        404–6
    diet, 399, 400, 422–4, **426**
    energizing, 425–30, 440–1,
        463–5
    exercise, 390
    happiness, xii–xvii, 45–7, 51–3,
        106–8, 204, 460–2
    leisure time, 389–91, 398–400,
        407–9, 410–12, 431–3, **485**
    meditation, **429**
    overcoming insecurity, 395–7,
        434–6
    overcoming procrastination,
        392–4
    retreats, 487–9
    sleep, 27–9
    taking responsibility, 17,
        442–4, 445–50, 475–7
    see also family life; self-
        esteem; stress
limited companies, 288–9, **292**
limited liability partnerships, 289
listening, 79–81, 88–90, 101–2,
    146–8, **236**
lists and spreadsheets
    for building self-esteem, **49**, 52

for improving
    communication, **62, 68, 80**
    gratitude journal, **387**
    joy list', 204
    on choice of job, **247**, 248
    on leadership, **168, 169**
    priority, **132**, 455–6
    profit and loss sheets, 270–2,
        276–8
    to-do lists, 42–4, 390–1,
        92–4, 457–9
loans see borrowing; investors
long-term thinking, 158–60,
    179,191–3
    see also decision-making
lunch breaks, 46

management summaries, 110
managers
    crisis management, 401–3
    customer contact, 185–7
    excellent employees, 76–8, 77
    extending senior contacts,
        110, 111, 112–14, 120–2, 152–4
    firing people, 176–8, **183**,
        244–5, 335, 336
    handling the budget, 191–3
    interview hurdles, 243–5
    leadership qualities, 164–9,
        167–9, **172**, 183, **184**
    personality types, 135–9
    sales force and, 155–7
    self-promotion, 109–11
    team strategy, 170–4, 179–81,
        183–5, 222–4
Mannesman, 188
marketing, 301–2, **307**
    differentiation, 280, 325–7

identifying customers, 267–9
    product, price, place and
        promotion, 319
    routes, 322–4
    sales projections and, **271**, 276
martyrdom, 50
    guilt and, 475–7, 482
Maslow, Abraham, 199
Mau, Bruce, 30
measures of profitability, 311
meditation, **429**
men's appearance, 83–4, 144–5
mindset, entrepreneurial, 280–1
mission statements, 175
mistakes, 19, 114, 122
mortgages, **370**
motivation, 10–11, 73–5, 164–6,
    172, 183, **298**, 299, **332**

NatWest Bank, 259
negative behaviour, **183**, 222–4
negative thinking, 10–11
    open and closed questions,
        80–1
negotiation, 100–2
    on salary, 6–8, 128–30, 189, 190
    see also communication
network-marketing, **323**, 323–3
networking, 8, 91–3
    fact-finding, 86–7
    marketing, **323**, 323–3
    recruitment and, 297–8
    within the company, **110**,
        111, 120–2, **121**
net worth, **367**
New World of Work, 132–3, 168,
    279–80, 321, 326
newsletters, 111

night-walking, 30–1
non-verbal communication (NVC)
    see body language

Office of Fair Trading (OFT), 373
online personality tests, **25**
opinion seeking, 171
overdraft facility, **283**

panel interviews, 243–5
partnerships, 289
pay system, 363–5
payback, 17
pensions, 259, **364**
perception, 21–3, 28
    mind reading, 64–6, **65**
perfectionism, 478–80
personal development plan, 149–51
personality, 26
    conceptual changes, 21–3, 28,
        30–2
    CV description, 210
    manager types, 135–9
    player mentality, 56–7, 114
    perception, 21–3, 28, 64–6, **65**
    perfectionism, 478–80
    role play, 36–8
    tests, **25**
    see also communication; self-
assertiveness; self-awareness;
self-esteem
Peters, Tom, 7
pilot schemes, 269
planning see preparation and
    planning
player mentality, 56–7, 114
Plcs, 290
portfolio careers, 53

positive thinking, 10–11, **77, 124,**
    407–9
'power of 10' solution, 39–41
pragmatic approach, 106–8
preparation and planning
    before negotiating, 100–1,
        140–2, **141**, 355–6
    conflict resolution, 89, **98**
    for interviews, **217, 226, 229,**
        235
    Plan B, 395–7
    rehearsing before acting,
        70–2, **121**
    strategic thinking, 158–60, 179
presentations, **34,** 161–3, 180, **232**
Price, Deborah L., *Money Magic*, 386
price/earnings ratio, 117, 220
pricing, 310
prioritising
    martyrdom and, 50
    'power of 10' solution, 39–41
    problem solving and, 27–9
    to-do lists, 42–4, **132**, 390–1,
        392–4, 455–9
    see also time management
proactive behaviour, 51–3
processes and systems, 320
procrastination, **40, 119**, 392–4
productivity, 42–4
profit and loss accounting, 192–3,
    270–2, 276–8
profitability, **192,** 309–11
promotion, 109–11, **129**, 143–5
property purchase/lease, 291, 308

questionnaires, customer, 328–30
questions, **165**
    interview, 208–9, 222–4,

225–7, 231–3, 240–2, 249–51,
    246–8
    open and closed, 80–1

raising funds, 261–3
reading, 431–3
record-keeping, 92–3, **265**, 295–6
recruitment, 297–9, 304, 307, 320,
    327
redundancy, 335, 336
research companies, 87
research reports, 268
responsibility
    in the workplace, **124**, 140–2
    lifestyle and, 17, 442–4,
        445–50, 475–7
    restoration days, 398–400
retreats, 487–9
risk taking, 188–90, 314–15
    risk and return, 115–17, 219–21
role models, 60
role-play, 36–8, 234–6
routine change, 30–2

salaries, true expenditure, 274–5
salary negotiations, 128–30, 189,
    354–6
    at interview, 249–51
    company pay system, 363–5
    flexibility, **355**
    personal brand value and, 6–8
    share options, 190
sales force, 155–7
saving see budgeting
Schwabb, Charles, 42
self-assertiveness, **107**, 127, 266
    getting to the right person,
        101, 134–6

making suggestions, 109–11, 123–5, **189**
'selfishness', 50, 445–50, 475–7
see also personality; self-awareness; self-esteem

self-awareness, 17, 51–3, 228–30, 237–9, 411
self-delusion, 15–17
see also personality; self-assertiveness; self-esteem
self-employment, 256–7
assessing progress, 331–3
business plans, 270–2, 278, **286**, 300–2
choosing company status, 288–90
choosing the right people, 297–9, 307
competition, 303–5
customers, finding and keeping, 267–9, 328–30
financial factors, 258–60, 261–3, **262**, 263–6, 268, 270–2, 273–5, **274**, 276–8, 282–4, 285–7, 294–6, 309–11, 314–15, 316–18, 334–6
legal issues, 291–3
maximising potential, 306–8, 312–13, 322–4, 325–7
property purchase/lease, 291, 308
see also career planning; employment seeking; entrepreneurship
self-esteem, 47
achieving desired changes, 76–8

giving/receiving approval, 58–60, **435**
maximising, 48–50
motherhood and, 203
self-containment and, 472–4
see also life-style, personality; self-assertiveness; self-awareness
self-promotion, 109–11
selfishness see self-assertiveness
selling off assets, 335–6
share grants and options, 190
shareholders, 115–17, 188
Shiatsu facial massage, 429–30
simplicity, 327
skills, 298, 307, **314**
sleep, 27–9, **464**
sole traders, 289–90
solicitors, 291–3
specialising, 24–6
spreadsheets see lists and spreadsheets
staff see recruitment
Starbucks, 326
start-ups, 159
strategic thinking, 158–60, 179
company budget and, 191–3
strengths, personal
and weaknesses, 228–30, 237–9
focusing on, 12–14, 24–6
stress
assessing burn out, 419–21
facing up to causes of, 15–17, 45
parenting and, 469–71
relieving, **59, 390, 399, 467**
unemployment and, 202–4
see also life-style
Sun Tzu, 303

suppliers, 317–18
support teams, 144
SWOT analysis, 113–14, **180**, 180–1

team strategy, 170–4, 179–81
handling difficult people, 222–4
taking over a team, 183–5
testimonials, **186**
thinking partnerships, **165**
time management
dealing with interruptions, 404–6, 467–8
decisiveness/assertiveness, 131–3, 445–7
see also prioritising
to-do lists, 42–4, **132**, 390–1, 455–6
managing, 457–9
trainability, 298
training in profitability, 311

unemployment see employment seeking

value, 280
venture capitalists (VCs), 190, 285–7
volunteering, 111

websites, 292, 322
White, Judith, 410–11
women's appearance, 145
work routine, attitude to, 413–15, 466–8
workplace, 46, **46**